PARALEGAL CAREER STARTER

PARALEGAL

career starter

3rd edition

New York

Library of Congress Cataloging-in-Publication Data:
  Paralegal career starter / by LearningExpress—3rd ed.
    p. cm.
  Rev. ed. of: Paralegal career starter / Jo Lynn Southard with Lauren B. Starkey.
  2nd ed. c2002.
  ISBN 10: 1-57685-571-6
  ISBN 13: 978-1-57685-571-3
  1. Legal assistants—Vocational guidance—United States. I. Southard, Jo Lynn.
  Paralegal career starter. II. LearningExpress (Organization)
  KF320.L4S68 2006
  340.023'73—dc22

                                                                2006022522

Printed in the United States of America

9 8 7 6 5 4 3 2 1

Third Edition

ISBN 10: 1-57685-571-6
ISBN 13: 978-1-57685-571-3

For information on LearningExpress, other LearningExpress products, or bulk sales,
please write to us at:
    LearningExpress
    55 Broadway
    8th Floor
    New York, NY 10006

Or visit us at:
    www.learnatest.com

Contents

Introduction

Why Enter the Paralegal Field?

PARALEGALS, ALSO known as legal assistants, interview and communicate with clients, locate and depose witnesses, compose letters and pleadings, assist with depositions and hearings, and conduct will executions and real estate closings. Indeed, paralegals do any kind of legal work that is not the actual practice of law. This book gives you the information you need to join the ranks of this exciting and ever-growing career.

Paralegals have the opportunity to be involved in some of the most interesting and rewarding work in the legal field, including research, writing, and interviewing clients and witnesses. The paralegal profession is growing faster than other professions because it is an exciting and important occupation, and you can prepare for it with a reasonable and manageable commitment of resources.

The first thing to know is that a paralegal and a legal assistant are exactly the same thing. Sometimes, situations such as local court rules that allow a "legal assistant" to sit at the counsel table in a courtroom determine which term is used. "Paralegal" seems to be growing in popularity and is the term generally used in this book.

But what *is* a paralegal? Basically, as mentioned, paralegals do many of the same things lawyers do, except they do not present arguments to a court nor give legal advice. Throughout this book, you'll find details on the kinds of work that paralegals do as a matter of course. If the law interests you, and you enjoy attending to detailed work, but you don't particularly care if you get to argue in court, you might prefer being a paralegal to being an attorney. It certainly doesn't usually take as long to get your training.

This guide contains an extensive discussion of how you go about getting paralegal training. There are hundreds of different paralegal training programs in the United States, representing a variety of perspectives on the profession. You'll find out how to distill all this information to find the right program for you. To get you started on—and probably complete—your search for a paralegal program, this book includes a state-by-state list of hundreds of paralegal programs, as well as information that will help you find and apply for financial aid to help pay for your schooling.

To help you find your first job after you complete your training, there's information on job-search strategies, resume preparation, writing cover letters, handling job interviews, and networking as a means of job hunting, as well as tips for making the most of your first job as a paralegal. Think of this book as a road map: If you follow it, you'll end up in an interesting and rewarding profession that is growing every year and shows no signs of slowing down. Here's a preview of some of the things you'll see and do along the way:

STEP 1: INVESTIGATE WHAT PARALEGALS DO

Paralegals work under the direct supervision of an attorney. One way of looking at the role of the paralegal is that paralegals do the legal background work. This means paralegals do a lot of research, both book research in a library or, more often these days, online, as well as client and witness interviews. A good lawyer knows that preparation is the key to success, and many lawyers rely on paralegals to perform a lot of that preparation. Paralegals also keep track of client files, making sure that they are complete and that things are done on time. They often write the first draft of a memo or brief; in many instances, paralegals send out correspondence under their own names.

Typically, paralegals who work for solo practitioners or in small offices are generalists, who may perform their duties under the rubric of criminal law one day, real estate law another, and torts the next day. On the other hand, paralegals who work for the government or in very large law firms specialize in particular areas of the law. Paralegals who work in the legal department of a corporation specialize in the area of the law appropriate to the company, for example, insurance law or employment and corporation law. See Chapter 1 for more discussion of the duties and specializations of paralegals.

STEP 2: DECIDE ON YOUR TRAINING

At a minimum, you will need a high school diploma or General Educational Development (GED) diploma to attend a paralegal program; in some cases, you'll need a bachelor's degree. There are more than 1,000 paralegal training programs in the United States, ranging in length from a few months to four years. Some programs provide a general paralegal education, and some allow you to specialize in various ways. You'll have to decide, based on a variety of factors, what kind of paralegal education you want. Chapter 2 helps you analyze your talents, background, and interests to make this decision.

That chapter also gives you information about the various programs and what you can expect from them. It includes sample curricula from paralegal programs and information about accreditation that you can use to help you determine which program is right for you.

STEP 3: FIND AND PAY FOR YOUR TRAINING

Appendix A offers a list of hundreds of paralegal programs; chances are, you can find one that meets your needs. There are also pointers for finding other schools in your area.

Chapter 3 provides information on financing your education, including loans, scholarships, and grants. You'll find out what forms you need, where to get them, how to fill them out, and where to send them, as well as get some tips for surviving this arduous process.

STEP 4: ATTEND A PARALEGAL PROGRAM AND GET THE MOST OUT OF YOUR CLASSES

Once you begin attending a program, you want to make sure you get the most you can out of it. Chapter 2 offers pointers on succeeding in your classes.

You'll also find note-taking abbreviations that will not only help you in school, but also help you communicate with attorneys once you begin working.

STEP 5: CONDUCT A JOB SEARCH

While you're still in school, you should begin thinking about job hunting. In Chapter 2, you'll learn how an internship can lead to your first job, and in Chapter 4, you'll find information on using other resources of your school to help you find your first job and to help you succeed on it.

Chapter 4 also includes some other effective methods for finding a good job once you finish your training, including networking. In Chapter 5, you'll learn how to write effective and attention-getting resumes and cover letters, and nail the scariest part of job hunting—the interview. Job hunting is rarely painless, but the hints in that chapter will ease your anxiety and allow you to come through the whole process intact and with a good job.

STEP 6: SUCCEED IN YOUR NEW PROFESSION

Chapter 6 gives you information that you can use to make any paralegal job—especially your first one—go smoothly and successfully. It includes hazards to watch for in the legal workplace and how you can avoid them— or recover from them. This chapter also shows you how to fit into your new job and get along with your boss and coworkers. And you will learn the importance of having a mentor and how to go about finding one, as well as other ways that you can promote yourself.

This book will tell you everything you need to know about becoming a paralegal and will direct you to other resources as well. Whether you are just getting ready to graduate from high school or from college with a bachelor's degree or whether you are in the workplace and want a change of career or are returning to work outside the home, the information in this book can help get you where you want to be. Good luck!

PARALEGAL CAREER STARTER

CHAPTER one

BECOMING A PARALEGAL

WHAT PARALEGALS do depends on who they work for and where they are in their professional development. Generally, they research the law, prepare documents, conduct investigations, keep track of the status of clients' cases, and interview clients and witnesses; that is, they do almost anything a lawyer does, except actually give legal advice or represent clients in court. In this chapter, we'll look at some of the different places paralegals work and the things they do.

THE PARALEGAL profession is one of the fastest-growing careers around, and it appears that it will continue to grow as more and more lawyers learn about the value of paralegals. From *Law & Order* to *Boston Legal*, television has given us one version of what a lawyer does. The media has never told us much, however, about what paralegals do. It's probably just as well; TV lawyers are probably very different from the lawyers you know. For one thing, TV lawyers seem to work independently; but real lawyers depend on support from clerical staff and paralegals. *Para* is Greek and means "alongside." So a paralegal is one who works alongside a legal professional, or lawyer. *Real* lawyers, not TV lawyers.

Here are some definitions of *paralegal*. According to *The Occupational Outlook Handbook, 2006–2007 Edition*, published by the U.S. Bureau of Labor Statistics, "Paralegals—also called legal assistants—are continuing to assume a growing range of tasks in the Nation's legal offices and perform many of the same tasks as lawyers. Nevertheless, they are still explicitly prohibited from carrying out duties that are considered to be the practice of law, such as setting legal fees, giving legal advice, and presenting cases in court. . . . Employment for paralegals and legal assistants is projected to grow much faster than average for all occupations through 2014." The National Federation of Paralegal Associations (NFPA) defines a paralegal as "a person qualified through education, training, or work experience to perform substantive legal work that requires knowledge of legal concepts and is customarily, but not exclusively, performed by a lawyer. This person may be retained or employed by a lawyer, law office, governmental agency, or other entity or may be authorized by administrative, statutory, or court authority to perform this work."

The National Association of Legal Assistants (NALA) offers this definition: "Legal assistants, also known as paralegals, are a distinguishable group of persons who assist attorneys in the delivery of legal services. Through formal education, training, and experience, legal assistants have knowledge and expertise regarding the legal system and substantive and procedural law which qualify them to do work of a legal nature under the supervision of an attorney."

Finally, the definition of paralegal adopted by the American Bar Association (ABA) in 1997 is: "a person, qualified by education, training, or work experience who is employed or retained by a lawyer, law office, corporation, governmental agency, or other entity and who performs specifically delegated substantive legal work for which a lawyer is responsible."

WHY BECOME A PARALEGAL?

There are several reasons to become a paralegal. Read on to find out more about the many benefits of this growing profession.

Job Satisfaction

According to a survey conducted by the NFPA, paralegals find that contact with attorneys and a sense of responsibility are the most satisfying parts of their work. Of course, job satisfaction among paralegals can vary greatly. Once you have received paralegal training, you have a certain flexibility in the kind of work you do. That's even more true when you have a few years of experience. So if you do end up in a job that you find is not satisfying, it is fairly easy to change positions. Of course, the market for paralegals varies across the country, but if you have a certain amount of drive, you can find or create a fulfilling position.

A potential area for dissatisfaction is the duties you, as a paralegal, are expected to undertake. The profession is still new enough that not all lawyers really understand what a paralegal is, especially as compared to a legal secretary. Many others, in small firms and solo practices, feel that economics keep them from hiring both a legal secretary and a paralegal. As a result, paralegals are often asked to undertake tasks that are clerical in nature. For the most part, a paralegal who works in an environment where everyone—including the attorneys—pitches in as needed probably doesn't mind performing the occasional clerical duty. On the other hand, a lawyer who understands and is respectful of your position will realize that although paralegals and legal secretaries both do important and difficult work, the two jobs are not the same. Most people, for example, wouldn't expect someone lacking legal training to conduct research or draft a pleading. Nor should they expect someone trained as a legal assistant to do clerical work. It can be a good idea to ask for a written job description when you apply for a job.

A paralegal may also become dissatisfied with the job when the workload increases too much. In recent years, some law firms, in an effort to reduce costs, have increased the amount of work a paralegal is responsible for. At the same time, the nature of that work is changing. Although being given increased trust and responsibility in the workplace is gratifying, some paralegals complain they are doing the work that first-year lawyers would do, without the commensurate pay.

Professional Growth

As you gain experience as a paralegal, opportunities for advancement will present themselves. If the firm or company you work for is fairly large, you will have a chance to advance in-house into supervisory and management positions. However, if you work for a smaller firm or company, you may need to make a lateral transfer to a bigger employer to move on to a managerial position. Certainly, even if you work for a very small employer, you will be given more responsibility and be expected to perform your duties with less supervision as time goes on. Hopefully, you will also receive the appropriate pay increases.

One way to demonstrate that you have continued to grow in your profession and, therefore, deserve to advance in your career is by receiving certification. Certification is voluntary, and currently, few paralegals receive certification, but it may become more important as the field grows.

A Word about Certification

Except in California and North Carolina, paralegal certification is voluntary. Other states are considering requiring certification for paralegals; in most cases, the state would offer an exam, similar to the bar exam for lawyers, that a paralegal would have to pass to work in the state.

Several paralegal associations offer national certification for paralegals. It is important to note that this certification is not the same thing as the certificate you may receive from your paralegal training program (see Chapter 2). Since 1976, NALA administers the Certified Legal Assistant (CLA) exam. Recently, NALA added the designation Certified Paralegal (CP) for those who prefer it. The exam is part of an effort to recognize national minimum standards of competence for paralegals. According to NALA, as of June 1, 2005, 25,000 paralegals had participated in the program, and there were more than 12,000 CLA/CPs working in the United States. By comparison, *The Occupational Outlook Handbook*, compiled by the U.S. Bureau of Labor Statistics (BLS), estimates that, in 2004, there were 224,000 paralegals working in the United States. So fewer than one-tenth of paralegals have a CLA/CP designation.

To sit for the CLA/CP exam, a paralegal must demonstrate graduation from a paralegal program that is approved by the ABA, or an associate degree program, a post-graduate program, a bachelor's degree program, or a legal assistant program of at least 60 semester hours. Alternatively, a paralegal may have a bachelor's degree in any field plus one year of experience as a paralegal, or a high school diploma and seven years of experience and 20 hours of continuing legal education credit in the two years prior to the test.

The two-day CLA/CP exam is based on federal law and procedure. The topics include communications, ethics, legal research, judgment, and analytical ability, followed by five substantive law examinations. The first section of Part 2 tests the American legal system, and is followed by tests in four of the following specialties, selected by the test takers:

Administrative Law	Family Law
Bankruptcy	Criminal Law and Procedure
Business	Litigation
Organizations/Corporations	Probate and Estate Planning
Contracts	Real Estate

In 1994, the membership of the NFPA voted to offer certification. NFPA now offers the Paralegal Advanced Competency Exam (PACE). The PACE is a four-hour computer-generated exam that has two tiers. The first tier tests critical thinking, legal knowledge, and ethical issues and may also include questions specific to the law in a particular state. The second tier tests knowledge of specific practice areas. To maintain a PACE certification, a paralegal must participate in ongoing continuing legal education programs.

The newest certification is offered by the American Alliance of Paralegals, Inc. (AAPI) and is called the American Alliance Certification Program (AACP). To receive an AACP, a paralegal does not need to take an exam, but must demonstrate graduation from an accredited program and must have no fewer than five years of paralegal experience.

Although, with a few exceptions, certification is voluntary, more and more states are considering requiring it. Or, it may be required simply because more paralegals become certified, and it is necessary be certified to compete for jobs. At any rate, it is a good idea to keep the notion of certification in the back of your mind as you prepare for the career. Remember that to some extent, attorneys exert influence over the paralegal profession, and the majority of them had to pass grueling bar exams to practice. They may decide that certification of paralegals is a good idea, too.

Salary and Benefits

According to the BLS, the average paralegal salary in 2002 was $37,950. However, the earnings of paralegals can vary a great deal, depending on the level of education and experience of the paralegal, the geographic location, and size and type of the employer. Throughout the country, paralegal salaries range from less than $24,000 to more than $61,000. As a rule, if you are in a large urban area and work for a large firm, you will make more than paralegals in smaller cities at smaller firms. The average salary of paralegals employed by the federal government is about $5,000 more than that earned by legal assistants in the private sector, but there are opportunities to make more in the private sector.

Paralegal benefits vary as well. Most paralegals receive vacation, sick leave, life insurance, and medical benefits. Less than half of paralegals have access to a pension plan. In addition, many paralegals receive bonuses.

A current issue in the paralegal profession is overtime. Most paralegals are nonexempt employees; that is, they must be paid overtime for working more than 40 hours a week. Some paralegals would prefer to be exempt employees and be paid a straight salary; they believe that nonexempt employees, because they are paid an hourly wage, are seen as less professional.

In 2004, the Department of Labor instituted new rules governing exempt and nonexempt workers; under the new rules, anyone making less than $23,660 annually is entitled to overtime pay for any hours worked over 40. When the department called for public comment on the new rules, the NFPA declined to take a position, noting that their membership was evenly divided on the issue.

Another issue that has arisen in recent years and may affect paralegals' salaries is outsourcing. With outsourcing, a lawyer or firm may hire a free-lance paralegal for a specific job or task, perhaps decreasing the number of paralegals needed on staff. However, outsourcing, especially outsourcing to workers in foreign countries, may create other problems, including a lower quality of work done by the freelance paralegal, conflicts of interest, and attorney/client privilege. The NFPA's position on the issue is that, at the least, legal clients should always be told if some of the work on their cases is being outsourced.

WHAT DO PARALEGALS DO?

The paralegal profession was born in the 1960s, during former President Lyndon Johnson's "War on Poverty," as a way of providing basic legal assistance to the poor. Although unable to give legal advice, a paralegal could help clients fill out forms, prepare them for court appearances, maintain contact with them, and help attorneys prepare their cases. A few attorneys, assisted by paralegals, could provide services to many more people than the lawyers would be able to handle alone. Originally, paralegals worked in public agencies charged with providing legal services to the poor. Over time, corporations and private attorneys began to see the benefit of employing paralegals in their practices as well; now, about seven out of ten paralegals work in large, private law firms. Initially, paralegals were trained on the job; in the 1970s, paralegal training programs began to appear. There are now over 1,000 distinct training programs, many of which are listed in Appendix A.

Although the term *paralegal* is generally preferred over *legal assistant*, tradition and even court rules dictate which term is used in different areas. Paralegals are also distinct from legal secretaries, although many legal secretaries become paralegals. Of course, the size of a legal office can affect this distinction; also, the advent of computers means that almost everyone— even attorneys—does some clerical work. As the Iowa Bar Association puts it, "In general, the legal assistants are performing a number of activities involving client contact, and their activities for the most part are different from, and more demanding than, those normally associated with secretarial or stenographic work."

Typical Duties

Paralegals do a variety of tasks, just as lawyers do. As a paralegal, some of your duties could include:

▶ Research: Library, online, public records, medical, scientific
▶ Investigation: Interview clients, witnesses, experts; on-site analysis
▶ Writing: Draft memos, briefs, correspondence, interrogatories, pleadings, contracts
▶ Administration: Index documents, digest documents, organize pleadings, organize trial exhibits, monitor tax and corporate filings
▶ Docket control: Prepare discovery requests and responses; schedule depositions; notify clients, witnesses, and attorneys of trial dates; file motions and pleadings

As you look at this list, it becomes apparent that there are a few basic skills you need if you want to be a paralegal. A good legal assistant is bright, personable, literate, organized, and even more organized. Lawyers depend on paralegals to do much of the background work for any given client. This includes getting information from the client, researching the particular area of the law involved, preparing memos that keep the attorney informed of the progress in the case, maintaining the client's file, and making sure that all deadlines are met. Falling short in one of these areas is one of the worst things an attorney can do; if it's up to you to keep the lawyer on track, it becomes your nightmare, too. In addition, computer skills are now essential to paralegal work.

Morning Appointments		Afternoon Appointments		Things To Do Today	
7:00		12:00		✓	Research motion to
7:30	NALA Breakfast	1:00			quash
8:00		1:30	Eddie Evidence—	✓	Prepare quitclaim
8:30			testimony prep		deed
9:00	Meet w/ Paula	2:00		✓	Notify Cathy Client of
	Partner	2:30	Deposition of Jerry		trial date
9:30			Justice at Barrister,	✓	File pleadings re: Tess
10:00	Initial interview with		Counselor, &		Torts
	Rex Retainer (2nd		Solicitor	✓	Update partner
	OUI)	3:00			billings
10:30		3:30			
11:00		4:00	Continuing Legal		
11:30	Arraignment—Miles		Education Seminar		
	Misdemeanor—	4:30			
	Court B	5:00			
		5:30			
		6:00			

The particulars of any paralegal job will depend on your employer and the firm's clients. Because paralegals work under the supervision of an attorney, it is up to your boss to determine which tasks you will be assigned in any given case. As in any profession, different attorneys have different ways of working. You might find that you have a great deal of autonomy to handle a case, or your boss may prefer a team approach. A mere glance at this "daily planner" wouldn't tell you whether it came off a lawyer's desk or a paralegal's.

What a paralegal cannot do that an attorney does is practice law. Believe it or not, this is a fine line, and it's not always easy to see when it's been crossed. It is imperative that, as a paralegal, every time you communicate with a court, client, witness, or opposing counsel, you make sure you make it clear that you are a paralegal and not an attorney. And never tell someone what to do about a legal matter. For example, paralegals frequently help clients fill out forms, such as tax, corporate, or bankruptcy forms. However, a paralegal cannot advise a client, for example, on what type of bankruptcy to file or what type of corporation to create. Such advice crosses the line into practicing law. See the NALA Code of Ethics and Professional Responsibility on pages 31–33 for more information.

No matter what kind of office you work in, there are a few things you can count on if you decide to become a paralegal. First, the work will be interesting. When people come to a lawyer, it is because something has happened—or is going to happen—in their lives that they want help dealing with. For example, the first thing most of us would do if we were arrested is hire an attorney. And it's probably going to be interesting to hear the story behind a person's arrest—and, no doubt, an explanation of why he or she is innocent! Less obvious things can be quite interesting, too—for example, why your client wants to cut someone out of a will or how one company is attempting a hostile takeover of another.

Second, the work will be varied. Even when you specialize in a particular area of the law, your clients will have an assortment of legal issues. In corporate law, for example, you may deal with companies that produce anything from apple cider to zoo enclosures. Third, the work will be satisfying. While it is true that a lawyer can't solve every problem just exactly the way a client wants it solved, in most cases people seem to feel that the attorney helped them through a troubling time. Also, from your perspective, most of the tasks you work on have an end, a solution. Sometimes when you begin researching a legal problem, you feel as if it's brand new and no one ever faced it before. Then you usually find that the law has dealt with it and there is an answer. It can be very gratifying when you are the one who finds that answer.

Finally, as the paralegal profession continues to grow, you will be presented with more and more opportunities for growth within your career. Whether you take on more responsibility within a job or take the plunge and leave your job for a new paralegal position in another area of the law, you will be in charge of your own professional destiny. As the demand for paralegals grows throughout the country, it can even provide you with the opportunity to move to a new area—and almost be guaranteed you'll be able to find a job.

SPECIALIZATION

What area of the law you work in may depend largely on the specialty of the employer. In a small general practice firm, the area of the law pretty much depends on the problems of the clients who come through the door. Was your client arrested? Then you'll be researching criminal law. Does your client want a divorce? Then you'll bone up on family law. A will? Estate planning and probate. The possibilities are almost endless. For many people, that's part of what makes the law interesting; others prefer to become specialists in one or two of these areas.

Common specialty areas include:

administrative law	criminal law and procedure
family law	intellectual property
civil litigation	estate planning
bankruptcy	probate
corporate and business law	real estate law

Others, such as environmental law, will continue to grow but are currently less common specialties. There are many other areas that are very specialized and limited to a rather small numbers of law firms, such as Native American law or education law. Following is information about a few of the most common areas of specialization.

Administrative Law

Administrative law refers to the law that is generated by governmental administrative agencies. Although these agencies may fall under the legislative branch of the federal, state, or local government, most of them are under the rubric of the executive (the president, governor, or mayor) branch. The agencies may be in federal or state government and vary from state to state, but they include the Social Security Administration, the Internal Revenue Service, and, in states, areas such as education and worker's compensation. In addition, more and more cities have human rights boards that deal with discrimination issues within the city. Specializing in this area may allow paralegals to represent clients in adversarial settings before administrative law judges, because in many cases, petitioners may be represented by anyone they choose; it need not be a lawyer.

Family Law

In family law, you will be dealing with divorce, child custody and support, and adoption. This can be a very rewarding area of the law, but it can also be quite stressful. A lot of people who specialize in this area have very strong political beliefs (about the rights of women or of children) that impel them to work in family law, where they feel they can make a difference. For many firms, especially small firms, family law is the real bread-and-butter of the business. As a paralegal, you will draft divorce and child custody petitions, gather financial and asset information, and spend a lot of time with clients.

Civil Litigation

Litigation involves lawsuits and the possibility of court battles, although most lawsuits are settled before reaching trial. *Civil* refers to the areas of the law that are not criminal—that is, disagreements between parties that do not involve the police power of the state. By definition, this area deals with disputes, one side trying to prove it is right and the other side is wrong. To be successful in this area, you need to be flexible; you may be on a side you don't personally believe in, but you must represent your client zealously. You also need to be organized and detail oriented. Clients can lose cases because their attorneys failed, for example, to file a response on time. This also opens the offending lawyer up to a malpractice suit. As a litigation paralegal, you will be responsible for, among other things, keeping track of dates and deadlines. You will also conduct investigations and witness interviews. It can be very interesting and varied work. On the other hand, some cases drag on for years!

Bankruptcy

Bankruptcy, a process that allows some debtors to discharge their debts, allowing them a fresh start, is a growing field. Controversial new bankruptcy rules went into effect in 2005. Some felt that the rules, supported by banks and credit card companies, would hurt debtors. The purpose of the new rules was to require people who could make some payments on their debts to do so, before the remainder of the debt was wiped out by bankruptcy. Just before the rules went into effect, most bankruptcy firms saw an increased number of clients, followed by a drop once the new rules were in place. Within a few months, however, numbers were nearly back to normal. In fact, 2005 saw a record number of bankruptcy filings, up 30% from 2004.

As a paralegal, you may work for an attorney who represents debtors, creditors, or trustees. Obviously, debtors are the ones who owe the money, and for them, you will gather together financial information, draft the bankruptcy petition, prepare the schedule of assets and liabilities, and file any periodic reports. If you work for the person to whom the money is owed—the creditor—you will draft and file the proof of claim. If you work for a trustee (who may or may not be a lawyer), you will notify all parties who might have claims, track any transfers or payments of assets, and review claims.

Unlike most areas of the law, bankruptcy can be handled by a paralegal from beginning to end, except for the decision to file and the decision about which chapter to file. There is very little "practicing of law" in bankruptcy.

Corporate and Business Law

Although many paralegals work for corporations, not all of them are practicing corporate law. Paralegals who work, for example, for an insurance company and deal with customer claims are working in insurance law. These paralegals are sometimes called corporate but are more appropriately labeled in-house legal department paralegals. On the other hand, corporate law deals with business transactions, incorporations, mergers and acquisitions, and ongoing corporate matters. These include drafting or amending articles of incorporation or bylaws; drafting shareholders' agreements and stock options; and preparing meeting agendas, notifying meeting participants, and taking meeting minutes.

Criminal Law and Procedure

Criminal law involves violations of the rules of society, such as rules not to drive drunk or assault someone. Criminal procedure involves constitutional law, in the form of the Fourth Amendment to the U.S. Constitution, which states, "The right of the people to be secure in their persons, houses, papers, and effects, against unreasonable searches and seizures, shall not be violated, and no warrants shall issue, but upon probable cause, supported by Oath or affirmation, and particularly describing the place to be searched, and the persons or things to be seized."

On occasion, the people and situations you deal with in criminal law and procedure are a bit unsavory, but it is always interesting work. And nothing is more important in our society than protecting individual constitutional rights.

Intellectual Property

The practice area of intellectual property involves protecting the creations, ideas, and inventions of people and businesses. This area of the law deals with trademarks, which protect manufacturers' rights to the identification of their products; patents, which protect inventors' rights to make and market their inventions; copyrights, which protect the products of authors and artists; and trade secrets law, which deals with a company's right to keep secret formulas, designs, and other information that gives them a competitive advantage. Intellectual property deals with the property that results from using one's intellect.

This is a very specialized area of the law; in fact, lawyers who work in this area are members of a distinct bar. The advent of computers and all the software that goes with them have made this a very hot and fast-growing field.

Estate Planning and Probate

Like bankruptcy, many paralegals are attracted to estate planning and probate because it is a field in which they can work quite independently. Estate planning involves helping clients utilize procedures—such as the creation of trusts—that allow them to bequeath their property without having to go through probate. Probate is the legal procedure by which a deceased person's property is located and distributed. If the decedent had a will, it is called a testate proceeding; if there is no will, it is an intestate proceeding, and state law will determine how the person's property is disbursed. Conservatorships and guardianships are also under the purview of the probate courts. A conservator is appointed to care for an adult who is deemed to be incompetent. A guardian does the same thing for a child.

Estate planning in particular requires knowledge of accounting procedures and investments, as well as the law of trusts and estates. For paralegals who have this knowledge, there is a great deal of autonomy in the field; there are even times when you can appear in court on behalf of a client.

Real Estate Law

Real estate law is another field that allows paralegals to work autonomously. This area involves representing buyers and sellers of residential or commercial property; lenders or borrowers of the financing for these sales; and landlords or tenants. To do this, paralegals deal with titles, the documents that give possession of property to a particular owner, and also with any rights that others may have to the property (through a lien or lease, for example). Titles must be thoroughly searched in order for a sale of real estate to commence.

Once the title is clear and the sale is going through, paralegals are often responsible for seeing that the closing of the sale goes smoothly. This involves drafting any documents needed, such as mortgages, deeds, or bills of sale; estimating what the closing will cost; and managing the documents for the title company. A great deal of this work can be done by a paralegal with only minimal supervision from an attorney.

Other Areas of the Law

If you decide to pursue training and a career as a paralegal, you will no doubt be struck by how the law seems to touch every aspect of our lives. Almost anything can conceivably be a specialty area of the law. In addition to the areas I've already discussed, here are others you may run across:

AIDS law
agriculture law
alternative dispute mediation (ADR—also known as mediation)
animal rights law
antitrust law
civil rights law
computer and Internet law
elder law
employment law
entertainment law
environmental law
human rights law
immigration law
labor law
legal malpractice law
medical malpractice law
Native American law
personal injury law

private (business) international law
sports law

Almost anything you are interested in, or an expert in, can be a specialty area of the law. Sometimes, being a specialist means that you will be highly sought after and, as a result, highly paid. Sometimes, you must content yourself with minimal income and the satisfaction that you are doing something that is interesting and important to you. The only thing restricting you is the market; how many people where you are need what you have to offer? For example, it might not make sense to be an agriculture law specialist if you live in Manhattan. You may not find a situation where you can practice your specialty exclusively, but maybe you can join a firm where you can at least do it some of the time. In other cases, if you are determined enough to specialize in a particular area, you may have to create the market.

WHERE DO PARALEGALS WORK?

Most paralegals work in private law firms. However, law firms may be composed of a few lawyers or several hundred. Paralegals also work for corporations, the government, nonprofit employers, and a variety of other places. Almost every agency of the federal government employs legal assistants; the majority of them are at the Departments of Justice, Treasury, Interior, and Health and Human Services. Many state and local government departments employ paralegals as well.

Where you work has a large impact on what kind of work you do. The specialty of the firm or agency will determine your specialty. In addition, different workplaces have different cultures. The local Legal Service Corporation office or environmental action group will no doubt offer a much more casual work atmosphere than a large firm or a court. It's wise to keep in mind some of the different kinds of work settings as you embark on your paralegal career.

The Large Firm

The relative size of a large law firm depends on the city in which it is located. In Chicago, for example, a 100-lawyer firm is probably considered medium-size, while in Springfield, Illinois, that same firm would be large indeed. Clifford Chance, LLP, with its main office in London, claims to be the world's largest law firm, with more than 3,230 lawyers (but those lawyers are divided among 28 offices in 19 countries). In most places, however, a firm with more than 100 lawyers is considered a large firm. In some large law firms, there will be even more paralegals than lawyers!

Large law firms are generally divided up into departments, such as litigation, probate and estate planning, corporate and business organizations, and international law. This specialization allows the paralegals who work for these firms to specialize as well. A large firm may also contain a structured paralegal "department." This doesn't affect the specialization of the work you would do, but rather provides a paralegal supervisor and, possibly, paralegal assistants. This structure usually also means that there will be an in-house training program and regular staff meetings. All of this can be very helpful, both in keeping you apprised of the latest developments in the firm and in the law, and in providing an intermediary between you and management. This structure also provides opportunity for advancement as a paralegal.

The attorneys in large firms will be either partners (although there may be senior and junior partners) or associates. Associates are usually hired right out of law school, although they may have clerked for a judge for a year or two before joining the firm. It used to be that most associates expected to become partners of the firm in about seven years. In the mid-1990s, there was a glut of lawyers on the market, and some were finding themselves unemployed after a few years, rather than gaining the key to the partner restroom. Since then, the demand for lawyers has increased, so advancement within firms is more assured. But the number of law students has also increased, meaning that competition for entry-level jobs is fierce.

Generally speaking, paralegal training is more practical than law school. Even as a newly hired paralegal, you may find you know more useful legal information than your recently graduated associate boss! As Audrey Casey, chair of the Paralegal Studies Department at Andover College in Portland, Maine, noted, "I've worked with attorneys who say, 'I know everything there is to know about a complaint, but how do you do one?'" On the other hand, at a large law firm, your new boss probably graduated from a prestigious law school and has now been hired by a large, important firm and is no doubt feeling pretty pleased with life. This creates a situation in which your boss may not want to hear that you know something he or she doesn't. This kind of situation can lead to clashes among the personnel of law firms, and when it's a large firm, there are more chances for disputes to arise.

The stereotype of large firms is that they tend to be stuffy. As with many generalizations, this is both true and not true. Traditionally, the largest firms have been considered the slowest to change: the slowest to hire women associates, for example, and the last to consider changing their workplace conditions to meet the needs of their employees. Large firms tend to be more hierarchical and structured; they are places where things are done a certain way because that's how they've always been done. Some people like that; some people prefer more flexibility.

Large firms offer many advantages as well. First of all, the salaries they pay paralegals are among the highest. They also may be more willing to hire new graduates, because there will be other paralegals at the firm who can train and mentor them. Large firms have more resources than smaller firms. Their in-house library will probably be fairly complete, and they will have access to a variety of the latest technology in research. The physical equipment in a large firm—computers and the like—is more apt to be state of the art than in smaller firms. All in all, a large firm can be a very rewarding work environment for a paralegal, particularly one who has recently graduated from school.

Sample Job Advertisements

Litigation Paralegals

A nationally recognized litigation practice has immediate openings for seasoned paralegals to join our successful team. To be chosen, a candidate must have three to five years experience in any of several areas: insurance defense, torts, environmental litigation, or class action. We prefer a four-year degree and certification. Candidates should demonstrate strong research and writing skills and computer prowess. Competitive salary and benefits. Flexibility for overtime and travel a must.

Benefits and Compensation Paralegal

Large law firm in city center has opening for a paralegal experienced in employee benefits and executive compensation matters. Position has both paralegal and administrative components, including drafting resolutions, preparing form documents, maintaining legal files, scheduling, and transcribing. Winning candidate must have strong computer skills. Salary $40,000+.

Entry Level

Recent paralegal graduate with four-year degree sought for corporate position. This position with a great international firm requires demonstration of excellence in UCC course work. A permanent employee will be expected to obtain certification within three years.

Logging Hours on the Job

Firms of any size generate their income via billable hours. These are the actual hours of work that can be billed to a client, and they include the time that the lawyers and paralegals spent working for that particular client. They don't include time for taking a break or learning how to unjam the copy machine. As a firm paralegal, you'll have to keep track of your time and be accountable for it. In 2005, according to the International Paralegal Management Association, billing for paralegals ranged from $87 to $215 per hour.

In any firm, no matter what the size, the length of your workday will vary. Although it doesn't usually affect paralegals as much as the new associates, when there is a looming court date, it's not unusual to find the lights burning in the law office long into the night. And you can bet it's usually not the senior partners who are losing any sleep!

The Small- to Medium-Sized Firm

When you work in a small- to medium-sized firm, you will have to take on a greater variety of duties than in a large firm. Although some smaller firms, and even solo practitioners, specialize, most are general practitioners. Even if they specialize, they often supplement that work with an extensive general practice. Your work on any given day depends a great deal on who walks through the door. Small firms do a lot of criminal law, usually for more minor offenses such as traffic violations. Family law is also a large component of a small practice. Real estate law and probate and estate planning are two more areas that come up often in small firms.

In addition to a variety in the areas of law practiced, there is also variety in the work assigned to people who work in smaller firms, including the attorneys, paralegals, and secretaries. When there is a lot of business, everyone has to be willing to pitch in to run the copy machine. When it's quieter, everyone can afford to stick to their own job descriptions more closely. As a result, a paralegal in this setting may easily become an important and trusted member of a team rather than just one among many paralegals in a large firm. The environment of smaller firms is usually more relaxed and more open to change than larger firms.

On the down side, smaller firms usually have fewer resources. This means that their law library may be quite small, and you may have to go to the local law school or courthouse to do your research. Increasingly, however, even the smallest firms subscribe to online research companies. It is also not unusual for paralegals to be expected to perform some clerical duties in a small firm. In frantic times, everyone should be willing to pitch in, but make sure that your duties are clearly defined when you are hired. Not all attorneys are really aware of the differences between paralegals and legal secretaries. Many of them can't afford to have all the clerical staff they would like. In addition, as computers become more and more a part of our daily life, many of us are doing more clerical work than before. Working in a small firm can be a great experience; just make sure that you and your employer have an understanding about your job duties.

If, as you finish your training and begin job hunting, you are still unsure whether or in what you want to specialize, working in a small- to medium-sized firm will give you the opportunity to dabble in many different areas of the law. Many paralegals and attorneys prefer to remain generalists throughout their careers; exposure to a variety of legal areas will help you decide if you want to specialize and in what.

Sample Job Advertisements

Corporate Transactional Paralegal

Enjoy the diversity of a small firm (25 attorneys). If you are a proactive, energetic professional with a desire to expand your areas of expertise, this is an opportunity to consider. At least two years of corporate/transactional experience required. Competitive salary; stable environment.

Entry- to Mid-Level Paralegal Position

Mid-size energy, environmental, and civil firm needs paralegal with excellent computer skills. Must have the ability to conduct research on a wide range of topics. Strong academic background, attention to detail, and good organizational skills essential. Position provides extensive contact with attorneys, discovery team participation, and high level of responsibility. Please mail or fax resume to Managing Paralegal.

Entry-Level Family Law Paralegal

Small, well-respected family law boutique in suburbs seeks an entry-level paralegal to join our close-knit team. Must be a multitasker and comfortable in a small office. Paralegal degree required; family law classwork a plus, but will train the right person. Fax resume to hiring partner.

A Few Words about Small- to Medium-Sized Firms

At one time, few small firms thought they could afford to hire paralegals; in recent years, though, small firms are learning that hiring paralegals is cost efficient. More than half of all paralegals employed by private firms are employed by firms that contain one to ten attorneys.

The ABA's Standing Committee on Paralegals points out to attorneys that hiring paralegals benefits legal practices. Paralegals may be able to spend more time with clients than an attorney can—which clients appreciate—and paralegal work is billed to the client at a lower rate than that of an attorney—which clients also appreciate. The committee notes that incorporating paralegals into a firm lowers costs and that the paralegal department may even become a profit center. Employment for paralegals in small- and medium-sized firms should continue to increase.

Corporations

When you work in the in-house legal department of a corporation, you will probably deal with some of the corporate law topics discussed earlier and also with the law of the specific industry you are in. On the corporate side, you may assist corporate attorneys with employee contracts and benefit plans, shareholder agreements, and stock option plans. You may send notices of meetings and take minutes at those meetings.

In addition, you will work in the area of the law that relates to your corporation. It is the responsibility of the legal department to stay on top of all the government regulations that relate to your business, such as antitrust, environmental, and equal employment opportunity, as well as any rules that relate more directly to your industry, such as banking or insurance regulations. Most in-house legal departments are too small to handle all of the legal issues that arise, so you'll be working with outside counsel in some cases.

When you work as a paralegal for a corporation, the company is your client. That's your only client, so you don't have to worry about billable hours. (Which doesn't mean you don't have to account for your working time!) And although unusual things can always happen if there is a lawsuit under way, most of the time you'll work regular 9–5 hours. This can be a very important perk if you have a family.

Of course, because you have only one client, you will have less variety than if you had several clients in a law firm. Some people find that it becomes boring after a while. On the other hand, it allows you to become an expert in a particular area of the law, such as banking or insurance or manufacturing. If you feel after a few years that you are ready to move on, you will be in a position to present yourself as an expert, and that can only enhance your job possibilities.

A rather new trend in small corporations is to have a legal department that consists only of a paralegal, although it's rarely called the legal department. Most often, the legal assistant will work in human resources or as an assistant to one of the higher-ranking officers. One of the main reasons companies do this is that much of what legal departments do doesn't require an attorney. Taking the minutes at a board meeting, for example, does not involve the practice of law. And when a lawyer is needed, it may be cheaper for the company to hire outside counsel to do the final version of the work. So the paralegal can, for example, draft an employment agreement that fits the needs of the business, and an outside attorney can verify the legal points. Paralegals in these kinds of positions are also responsible for recognizing when outside counsel is needed.

The title of such jobs may not always be *paralegal* or *legal assistant*. It may be something like "special assistant to the president" or "human resources specialist." You need to look closely at the job description to realize that the job requires someone with paralegal training.

Sample Job Advertisements

In-House Paralegal

Life insurance company, a dynamic, diversified financial services organization. Due to our growth, we are seeking a paralegal for our legal and executive departments. You will be responsible for a variety of legal research and writing activities and will provide an equal amount of support to our legal and executive departments. Specific responsibilities include preparing insurance/regulatory findings, monitoring market compliance, litigation support, and supporting complaint investigations. You have a BA or BS and a minimum of five years of paralegal experience, with excellent legal research and writing skills. Also, you possess interpersonal skills and experience with spreadsheets, personal computers, and word processing software. You also have a strong interest in continuous learning and self-development. We offer a friendly, professional environment with competitive compensation and benefits. Send your resume and a writing sample.

Computer/Litigation Paralegal

Corporation has an immediate opening for a computer wiz/litigation paralegal with the following software skills: LegalFiles, CompuLaw, Abacus, PCLaw, AmicusAttorney, Westlaw, Excel. Candidate must be systems oriented. Duties: Tracking/reporting expenses, inputting invoices, legal research, discovery, and organization and maintenance of litigation/arbitration files. Exceptional communication skills and flexibility needed; must be a team player. Excellent salary and benefits.

Commercial Loan Closer

Freedom from the office! Travel to three networked banks to do commercial loan closings. Employer needs detail-oriented professional to report directly to bank president. This position requires you to have a car for travel. Employer pays mileage and parking. Terrific position for team-oriented person interested in banking! Good benefits plus FREE checking and other bank perks.

Government

If you go to work for the government, the kinds of duties and responsibilities you have will depend on what department or agency you work for. Some possibilities include the Department of Justice, the Department of the Interior, the Environmental Protection Agency, the Internal Revenue Service, and the Immigration Service. Many of these agencies have state corollaries, although the names may be different. In addition to all of the departments and agencies, there are the court systems, both federal and state. There, you could work in the offices of the district attorney or public defender. In the courts themselves, there are positions such as court administrator, which involves managing the court's docket and personnel and perhaps conducting research for the judge. Other government positions that may not use the term *paralegal* or *legal assistant* in the title include export compliance specialist, a person who investigates commodities and data being exported outside the United States, and patent examiner, a person who assists in determining if certain inventions are eligible for patent.

Working for the government provides great job security and other benefits. In the legal field, the pay usually starts out higher than in the private sector but caps at a lower level. Getting a government job involves a lot of red tape; whether federal, state, or local, government jobs usually have strict evaluation and hiring guidelines. You have to follow the procedures exactly; there's usually no way for an employer to "give you a break" if you don't.

Sample Job Advertisements

Legal Assistant (Court), GS-986-5

Salary Range: $28,382 to 36,899. Executive Office for Immigration Review, Office of the Chief Immigration Judge, Florence, AZ. Duties: Examines, prepares, and processes charging documents. Reviews incoming files and determines need for assembly and preparation of a variety of legal documents. Develops and updates records of proceedings. Develops and maintains electronic files according to established guidelines. Conducts searches for case information applying legal regulations, specialized techniques, and procedures. Personally takes care of many matters and questions including answering substantive questions concerning pending and closed matters and cases, as well as functions and general procedures of the office. Some travel may be required. Qualifications: Applicants must have at least one year of specialized experience related to the position. A qualified (40 wpm) typist is required.

State University Paralegal

Job Summary: Assists attorneys with trial and pretrial matters. Job duties: Organizes, enters, and cross-references documents in a computerized database. Obtains, assembles, and organizes documents pertinent to litigation. Prepares discovery requests and responses. Assists in the preparation of statements and declarations of witnesses. Assists general counsel in organizing and carrying out special projects as assigned. Performs other related duties as assigned or requested. Job qualifications: Must have specialized paralegal training and one year of experience. May combine experience and education as substitute for minimum education or experience. Prefer a bachelor's degree, certificate from an ABA-approved program, and two years of experience. Skills: Must have the ability to assemble and coordinate manuscripts, compose letters, gather data, input data, communicate with others to gather information, maintain filing systems, prioritize different projects, research information, schedule appointments, write memorandums for own signature, and coordinate work of others.

City Attorney's Office/Internal Litigation Unit Paralegals

This is paraprofessional legal work of moderate difficulty assisting attorneys in case preparation and processing. An employee of this class is responsible for performing paraprofessional legal tasks routinely handled by attorneys and assisting in the coordination of case activities. Some positions may require working part time or evenings (until 9 P.M.) or require the ability to communicate in Spanish. Minimum qualifications: More than one year of experience in a private or governmental law firm performing primarily litigation-related case management and legal research under the direction of an attorney; an associate degree or a certificate of completion from an accredited college or technical school as a legal assistant or paralegal; or an equivalent combination of education, experience, and training that provides the desired knowledge, skills, and abilities.

Nonprofit Organizations

Nonprofit organizations that hire paralegals may be advocacy groups, such as poverty law organizations that provide legal services to disadvantaged persons, or activist groups, such as environmental, women's, or civil rights groups. Often, the same group will participate in both activities. For the most part, people who work for these organizations do so because they believe in the cause; the pay usually isn't all that good. The nonmonetary rewards of these jobs are significant, however. Nonprofits, although they are serious about the work they do, can rarely be described as stuffy. Usually, the office environment is quite casual, and the staff is open to new ideas.

Advocacy nonprofit organizations include groups such as the Legal Services Corporation (LSC), a private corporation that was established by Congress in 1974 to provide equal access to the law for impoverished Americans. It seems that Congress threatens to eliminate funding for LSC every year, but so far, it's still around. LSC offices are usually strapped for money, as is true of most nonprofits. They occasionally hire paralegals, but they are perhaps better sources for volunteer internships. If you do decide to work for a nonprofit, you may find the work stressful at times, but when you are working for a cause you believe in, it's very rewarding.

As with corporate jobs, sometimes nonprofits won't be looking for a paralegal, but your training will nonetheless qualify you for the position they are trying to fill. If you are committed to working for a nonprofit group, keep your eyes open for all sorts of job titles.

Sample Job Advertisements

Immigration Paralegal

A national public interest law firm dedicated to protecting and promoting the rights of low-income immigrants through impact litigation, policy analysis, training, technical assistance, and the publication of training materials is looking for a paralegal to add to our staff of 11.

Qualifications: Prefer four-year college degree or paralegal training. At least two years of responsible paralegal experience in which independent judgment was utilized and client interaction was emphasized. Thorough knowledge of legal procedures. Familiarity with immigration law and a second language are a plus. Salary: $31,704 to $40,515.

Community Organizer

A community organization whose goals are to empower parents with the necessary skills to help their children succeed in school, to bring the community and delinquent youth together, and to help citizens take action to improve their neighborhoods needs a community organizer. Job duties include conducting constituent interviews, research, recruiting volunteers, developing volunteer leaders, implementing issue campaigns, writing, media relations, and fund-raising. Hours: 45 to 50 hours per week (most evenings; occasional weekends); flextime.

Qualifications: Four-year college degree, excellent written and oral communications skills, commitment to grassroots organizing and citizen empowerment; bilingual (Spanish) and computer skills are helpful. Salary: $31,000 to $34,000 (depending on experience); health insurance and two weeks vacation.

Junior Attorney

Nonprofit organization in Washington, D.C. seeking an experienced legal assistant or junior attorney to review, draft, organize, edit, and proofread proposed legislation and related documents; research legal and regulatory issues; and respond to inquiries from clients and attorneys. This is not an attorney position, but job is being vacated by an attorney who gained excellent experience during tenure.

Requirements: Bachelor's degree and paralegal certificate, or JD. One year of experience with criminal law preferred. Strong writing and editing skills and familiarity with desktop computing and computer-based legal research.

Other Workplaces

Contract Paralegals

Contract, or freelance, paralegals are hired by attorneys or companies to work on a case-by-case basis. It is quite rare for a newly graduated paralegal to attempt such a career, but it may be something you'll want to consider after you have several years of experience. The benefits of self-employment include the freedom to structure your own time and to choose the projects you want to work on. The disadvantages include uncertainty about your income and the necessity of paying your own business expenses. In addition, you must be able to market yourself.

Temporary Paralegals

Some paralegals prefer to work through temporary agencies. Some are placed by companies such as Kelly and Manpower that place a variety of workers in a variety of jobs. In a few larger cities, legal temporary agencies are sprouting up. These agencies place attorneys, paralegals, and legal secretaries in temporary positions. Many people enjoy temporary work; it gives you more control over your own time than full-time employment, with a bit more security than freelancing. If, as you finish your paralegal training, you're still unsure about the kind of paralegal work you'd like to specialize in, temporary placements give you an opportunity to try out a variety of positions. But it is less secure than full-time employment. You may have periods in which the agency has no assignment for you, and at times, you may have to take positions that you aren't interested in.

Independent Paralegals

Independent paralegals work directly with clients; their work is not directly supervised by an attorney. Independent paralegals help consumers, for example, fill out forms for bankruptcy, estate planning, and taxes. However, they still cannot give legal advice. So your clients need to know before they come to you which bankruptcy chapter they should file under, for example, or whether they should set up a trust. Once these matters have been determined by the client in conjunction with a lawyer, however, the client can save money by hiring a paralegal rather than a lawyer to fill out the forms.

To be a successful independent paralegal, you should have several years of experience. You will find, even as you attend your paralegal training, that all your friends suddenly have legal questions they want to ask you. Sometimes, it can be difficult to distinguish between giving friendly advice and practicing law. You'll find your stock answer to certain questions becomes "You should check with an attorney practicing in that area." In every state in the United States, it's illegal to practice law without a license, and you must be completely certain about what you can and cannot do.

Litigation Support

In recent years, litigation support companies have sprung up all over the country. These companies, as the name suggests, support attorneys during litigation. They may specialize in certain areas of the law—criminal, contract, or adoption, for example—or may specialize in certain activities needed to prepare for trial—such as finding and interviewing witnesses or experts, or preparing graphics for use during trial. Employment with these companies will be similar to working for a law firm, with the same variations depending on the size of the company and the ways in which it specializes.

ENTERING THE FIELD

How Do I Find My First Job?

As you may have gleaned from the aforementioned job descriptions, most employers prefer to hire paralegals with some formal training. On the other hand, many employers, particularly large employers, want to train their own paralegals. Most often, this in-house training is in addition to your paralegal education; occasionally, these employers want to hire someone with a bachelor's degree (but no paralegal training), or they promote a legal secretary from within the organization. Sometimes, people with a background that is particularly desirable to a law firm or company, such as nursing or tax preparation, will be hired and trained in-house as legal assistants. But most people enter the profession after receiving formal paralegal training.

Many paralegal training programs offer or require an internship for their students. This is an excellent entree into the profession. Many lawyers were hired by their firm after interning there, and the same is true for paralegals. After all, firms don't take on an intern unless they have some work that needs to be done, and the internship period allows them to see if they like you and you like them before either of you contemplate making the arrangement permanent. And even if your internship doesn't result in a job offer, or if you decide to decline the offer, an internship provides valuable experience that will help get you your first job.

Most paralegals who don't get their first job through an internship will hear about openings through their paralegal school's placement program. It's very important to find out as much as you can about a placement office before you decide whether to attend a particular school.

Will There Be Jobs When I Start Looking?

In the early 1980s, the Department of Labor said that paralegalism was the fastest-growing profession in the country and that by the year 2000 there would be 100,000 paralegals. Their estimates were off a bit. Six years short of 2000, there were already 111,000 paralegals in the United States, and by 2004, there were about 224,000. According to the U.S. Bureau of Labor Statistics, employment of paralegals should continue to grow much faster than average through the year 2014. Most of these jobs will be newly created positions, as companies and law firms continue to learn about the benefits of adding paralegals to their staffs. Of course, as more and more paralegal jobs open up, more people will enter the job market as paralegals, and the competition for available jobs will continue. This is one reason the training discussed in the next chapter is vital; if you want to become a paralegal, you will want the best possible training to be competitive.

The paralegal profession is affected by economic factors such as recessions, just as other occupations are. But paralegals can usually ride out any economic impact by being creative. In a recession, for example, people might put off spending money on estate planning, but more people will be filing bankruptcy. Also, it is unlikely that Congress or anybody else is considering the possibility of making fewer laws in the future; as long as they keep churning out laws, we will all need legal professionals to help us deal with them.

Where Will Paralegals Be Working?

Most paralegals will work in private law firms in the future, just as they currently do. Private companies, such as banks, real estate firms, insurance companies, and other corporate legal departments, will hire more paralegals in the future as well.

Government agencies and departments on the federal, state, and local levels will also hire more paralegals in the future. Nonprofit organizations will probably continue to hire more paralegals as well, especially if the tide continues to move entitlement programs away from the government into the private sector. And as long as Legal Services Corporation manages to be refunded every year, it will continue to hire more paralegals in an effort to help keep costs down.

What Makes a Good Paralegal?

The next chapter on training discusses some of the traits of a successful paralegal in the context of looking at different kinds of training.
Note that, in addition to having good training, paralegals need to be
able to communicate well, both orally and in writing. They are
expected to attack problems in a logical and methodical way. They
must be organized and flexible in their approach to their work assignments. Paralegals have to be able to work well as part of a team and also
on their own.

As a paralegal, you will often have to deal with the public. Even in large
firms, it is often the paralegal who does the initial interview with a potential
client. Working with the public takes courtesy and patience, but in a legal
setting, it can sometimes take even more. For many of your clients, seeking
out a lawyer is not a happy experience. Perhaps they have been arrested or
sued; maybe they are getting divorced, or have been injured, or must file
bankruptcy. As a paralegal, you may be the first person clients talk to when
they decide to seek help. Like a bartender or cab driver, you must not only
perform your professional duties, but also be a little bit of a therapist.

Finally, it is imperative that a paralegal always behaves in an ethical manner. There are a variety of sources of ethical standard for paralegals. First,
every state defines the unauthorized practice of law, which is exactly what
you don't want to do. In addition, many state legislatures or state bar associations have addressed the role of paralegals in the legal profession, and
professional organizations such as NALA address ethical issues. It is up to
every working paralegal to keep abreast of all the ethical concerns of the
profession.

National Association of Legal Assistants
Code of Ethics and Professional
Responsibility

Canon 1

A legal assistant must not perform any of the duties that attorneys only may perform nor
take any actions that attorneys may not take.

Canon 2

A legal assistant may perform any task which is properly delegated and supervised by an attorney, as long as the attorney is ultimately responsible to the client, maintains a direct relationship with the client, and assumes professional responsibility for the work product.

Canon 3

A legal assistant must not: (a) engage in, encourage, or contribute to any act which could constitute the unauthorized practice of law; and (b) establish attorney-client relationships, set fees, give legal opinions or advice or represent a client before a court or agency unless so authorized by that court or agency; and (c) engage in conduct or take any action which would assist or involve the attorney in a violation of professional ethics or give the appearance of professional impropriety.

Canon 4

A legal assistant must use discretion and professional judgment commensurate with knowledge and experience but must not render independent legal judgment in place of an attorney. The services of an attorney are essential in the public interest whenever such legal judgment is required.

Canon 5

A legal assistant must disclose his or her status as a legal assistant at the outset of any professional relationship with a client, attorney, a court or administrative agency or personnel thereof, or a member of the general public. A legal assistant must act prudently in determining the extent to which a client may be assisted without the presence of an attorney.

Canon 6

A legal assistant must strive to maintain integrity and a high degree of competency through education and training with respect to professional responsibility, local rules and practice, and through continuing education in substantive areas of law to better assist the legal profession in fulfilling its duty to provide legal service.

Canon 7

A legal assistant must protect the confidences of a client and must not violate any rule or statute now in effect or hereafter enacted controlling.

Canon 8

A legal assistant must do all other things incidental, necessary, or expedient for the attainment of the ethics and responsibilities as defined by statute or rule of court.

Canon 9

A legal assistant's conduct is guided by bar associations' codes of professional responsibility and rules of professional conduct.

Copyright © 1997 NALA

The Unlicensed or Unauthorized Practice of Law

What constitutes the practice of law, or the unauthorized practice of law, is determined by each state's judicial branch. Therefore, the definition varies from state to state. It is vital that as a paralegal you are constantly aware of the practice of law in your state and take care that you don't practice law.

The definition of *practice of law* is continually evolving. The practice of law is often defined in the negative. Someone (a paralegal, a real estate broker, a banker, a notary public, etc.) may undertake an activity that someone else perceives as the practice of law and, therefore, something that should be done by lawyers only. Then, a complaint is made against that person, and eventually, a court determines whether the activity is or is not the practice of law. And so, one more activity is added to one side of the list or the other.

By way of example, here is the definition of Unauthorized Practice of Law according to Texas statutes: "A person commits an offense if, with the intent to obtain an economic benefit for himself or herself, the person: (1) contracts with any person to represent that person with regard to personal causes of action for property damages or personal injury; (2) advises any person as to the person's rights and the advisability of making claims for personal injuries or property damages; (3) advises any person as to whether or not to accept an offered sum of money in settlement of claims for personal injuries or property damages; (4) enters into a contract with another person to represent that person in personal injury or property damage matters on a contingent fee basis with an attempted assignment of a portion of the person's cause of action; or (5) enters into any contract with at third person which purports to grant the exclusive right to select and retain legal counsel to represent the individual in any legal proceeding. This section does not apply to a person currently licensed to practice law in this state, another state, or a foreign country and in good standing with the State Bar of Texas and the state bar or licensing authority of any and all other states and foreign countries where licensed."

Violation of this Texas law is considered a third-degree felony. In some states, a board or committee appointed by the state supreme court can offer advisory opinions as to whether certain activities constitute the practice of law. In any given situation, in any state, it is necessary for a paralegal to be current on all laws, court decisions, and advisory opinions on the unauthorized practice of law. This issue is very important to the future of the paralegal profession and will continue to be high on the agenda of paralegal associations, bar associations, and paralegal educators.

THE INSIDE TRACK

Who: Amanda Leff

What: Former Legal Assistant, Sullivan & Cromwell

           Currently a graduate student in English at New York University

Where: New York City

INSIDER'S STORY

As an English major about to graduate from Yale, I felt that there weren't a lot of fields open to people like me. I didn't want to be a teacher, and after four years of college, I knew that I wanted to jump right into the work world. Becoming a paralegal seemed like a good option—with overtime, you can make as much as $50,000 your first year—enough to live in Manhattan. I was also toying with the idea of going to law school, so paralegal work would offer me a chance to test out the profession.

I found out about becoming a paralegal through undergraduate career services at college. Because I started my job search while I was still in school, I relied on on-campus recruiting: I submitted resumes through my college career services office to the law firms recruiting on campus, and had on-campus interviews; only after passing the first-round interviews did I interview at the firms themselves. I also asked around and found a few people working at big New York City firms that were not recruiting on campus. I contacted these people, asked them about their firms, and had them pass my resume on to human resources. I also talked to a few attorneys about being a paralegal and working at a corporate law firm. Although I didn't personally know any paralegals, I found that networking with lawyers gave me a pretty good idea of what the job would entail, which was especially helpful for my interviews.

From my brief stint as a paralegal, I learned a valuable lesson, and I strongly suggest that anyone considering law as a profession work for a year or two as a paralegal first—you will find out whether or not you're cut out for the profession. Many people go to law school these days simply for lack of anything better to do, and I think that's a big mistake; law—corporate law, in particular—often requires an aggressive, type-A personality. To be successful, you have to be willing to spend years working very long hours, having virtually no personal life, and doing pretty mundane work—and this is essentially what you'll do as a paralegal, too. Being a paralegal quickly convinced me that the legal profession was not for me. If you don't like being a legal assistant, it is likely that you won't like being a corporate lawyer.

On required skills: Everyone writes on their resume or cover letter that they have good "interpersonal skills," but you'll really, really need them to be a paralegal. You have to deal with a wide range of personalities—administrators, other paralegals, and the sometimes "dreaded" lawyers. Big law firms enforce a very strict hierarchy—the paralegals are the indentured servants of the associates, who are in turn the indentured servants of the partners. If you can't manage and smooth out difficult relationships, you'll have a hard time making it as a paralegal. It is also essential for a paralegal to have very good language skills: A lot of what you'll be doing is editing and proofreading briefs and other documents. Another major duty of a paralegal is research—in the library, on the Internet, and using services like LexisNexis and WestLaw.

Ultimately, the most important characteristic that a paralegal should possess is a tendency to be obsessive compulsive. You will be managing huge quantities of documents, files, and information. You need to be fanatical about labeling things, color-coding things, and creating "systems" to organize things. You might be working on a case involving hundreds of thousands of pieces of paper, and you will be responsible for numbering every single sheet, making sure nothing gets lost, and being able to find the tiniest, most insignificant bit of information at a moment's notice. If you are a big-picture person and can't be bothered with details, being a paralegal is not a good career fit for you.

Where you work as a paralegal is also important. Being a paralegal at a big law firm is totally different from being a paralegal at a small law firm. When you work at a big firm, you get all the perks that a big corporation can offer: You can expense cars and taxis home late at night, you get free dinners, corporate discounts on health clubs and theater tickets, and so on. You also get to work on some very high-profile cases. However, you also get fewer responsibilities—big firms have armies of associates and they like their associates to write all of their own briefs. At a smaller firm, you would get to actually write legal documents, rather than just edit them. Small firms can also be a lot cozier. In an intimate working environment, you can really develop good professional relationships. On the other hand, if you don't like a particular person or situation at a small firm, it can make your daily routine difficult.

Another good reason to try your hand at paralegal work is that if you didn't get accepted at the law school of your choice, being a paralegal for a year or two can improve your odds of getting in. And rumor has it that a firm will usually offer you a job after you graduate law school if you have worked there as a paralegal throughout law school.

For me, finding out what you don't want to do is as valuable as figuring out what you *do* want to do. I realized that the legal profession wasn't for me, and I switched careers. I'm now pursuing a PhD in English literature.

CHAPTER two

ALL ABOUT TRAINING PROGRAMS

THIRTY YEARS ago, there was really only one way to receive paralegal training: on the job. Some paralegals began as legal secretaries and gradually took on more and more responsibility; others had bachelor's degrees and actually were hired as paralegal trainees. Now, if you want to become a paralegal, you need to undertake specialized paralegal training, which is discussed in this chapter.

AS DISCUSSED in the first chapter, the paralegal profession was born in the 1960s, during the "War on Poverty," so it's not surprising that the first paralegal school didn't appear until the late 1960s; by 1971, there were still fewer than a dozen paralegal training schools. Today, there are close to 1,000 paralegal training programs; every state in the United States has at least one school, and in most cases, residents have a variety of schools to choose from. With the explosive growth of the paralegal profession since 1960, the choices for training have also grown. If you're interested in becoming a paralegal, the first thing you need to decide is whether you need training and what kind you should get.

Should You Enroll in a Training Program?

Most people interested in becoming paralegals will need some kind of formal training. If you have a bachelor's degree, it is possible for you to get a job as a paralegal without any further training; this will depend a great deal on the market in your area. If most of your job rivals have some kind of specialized training, you will find it difficult to compete with, for example, only a liberal arts degree. Certainly, your situation—because of classes you took or assistantships you held while in college, or even work outside of college—may make you very competitive; see Chapter 5 for resume tips for someone like you.

The National Federation of Paralegal Associations (NFPA) estimates that 85% of legal assistants receive some type of specialized paralegal training. In addition, even if you find an opportunity for on-the-job training, that can be a lonely and limiting way to receive your training. As Audrey Casey, a former paralegal, noted, "I wish I'd had that opportunity [specialized training] because it's much more isolated and difficult, doing it on your own." So in most cases, your first step toward becoming a paralegal should be choosing the institution you want to attend to receive your training.

According to a 2004 survey conducted by NALA

33% of paralegals have an associate degree

44% have a bachelor's degree

5% have a graduate degree, master's, or JD

6% have a PhD

TYPES OF TRAINING PROGRAMS

There is such a variety of training programs available in the paralegal field that it is tempting to lay down some hard-and-fast rules you can use to help you make your choice. Unfortunately, that method ignores the fact that there are many kinds of training programs partly because the market for paralegals varies greatly from place to place. For example, it would be easy to tell you that you should only consider training programs accredited by the American Bar Association (ABA). But that ignores an important consideration: competition within the market. In some areas, there may not be ABA-approved programs, but it doesn't mean the schools are not dedicated to training competent paralegals. In fact, according to the BLS, only 260 of approximately 1,000 training programs are ABA-accredited. The key is finding out the norm in the market in which you plan to work.

So, just how *do* you go about deciding which program is right for you? First, let's talk about the kinds of programs you will likely have to choose from.

Certificate Programs

Among all the choices of programs, there is the greatest variety within certificate programs. Many times, these programs are offered by proprietary colleges—that is, they are private, for-profit institutions. Some of these schools are called, or used to be called, business schools. In most cases, the length of these certificate programs range from three to 24 months. These programs may require only a high school diploma for admission; however, many certificate programs are intended for students who already have an associate or bachelor's degree. In some cases, students who have significant exposure to the law, such as working as a clerk or secretary in a law office, may attend a certificate program even without a degree.

Another type of certificate program is the post-bachelor's certificate, offered at a four-year college or university. These certificates are offered by the continuing education or extension divisions. The courses may or may not bestow college credits and are intended for someone who has completed a bachelor's degree and needs only paralegal-specific training. Many of these programs can be completed in a year or less.

Here is an example of the curriculum of a certificate program. This one is from Rice University in Houston and is intended for students who have completed a bachelor's degree. This is a five-month, part-time program. In this program, all students complete a Fundamentals/Core Skills course and three substantive topic courses. The total cost of the program, excluding books, is $4,995. Books cost approximately $500.

Five-Month Paralegal Certificate Program Curriculum:

Fundamentals/Core Skills:

Introduction to the Legal Field
Participants will learn about paralegal career opportunities and the types of tasks a paralegal may perform.

Legal Terminology
By following an actual legal matter through the legal process, participants will be introduced to relevant legal terms. The case presented will be tracked through both the civil and criminal court procedures.

Legal Analysis
To understand the process and structure of proper legal analysis, participants will develop the skills to analyze both case law and statutory authority.

Legal Memorandum Form
After learning the analytical process, participants will analyze provided cases and statutes to prepare internal and external memoranda.

State-Specific Instruction
Local and state trial and appellate courts specific to Texas jurisdiction will be discussed. Participants will also be provided with information related to researching the law within Texas.

Federal Court Structure
Participants will be instructed in the basic differences between state and federal jurisdiction, as well as the jurisdictions for the various federal courts in Texas.

Stages of Litigation
Participants will learn the three stages of the litigation process and the functions a paralegal may perform during each stage.

Government Structure

Because each branch of government uses various forms of law, participants will learn the structure of government and the laws that apply to each branch.

Ethical Considerations

Because a violation of an ethical rule may affect the supervising attorney as well as the paralegal, it is critical that participants be familiar with the rules of ethics and learn to maintain a high ethical standard.

Court Rules

Court rules are the procedural requirements for trials. Students are taught the most relied-upon court rules as well as the skills necessary to find any rule for specific procedural questions.

Discovery Preparation

Participants will be taught form utilization and will create sets of interrogatories, requests for admissions, and requests for production and inspection of documents. Participants will be provided with templates, just as they would within a law-firm environment.

Discovery Coordination

The discovery process is one of the most important aspects of a paralegal's involvement in the litigation process. Participants will learn the rules relevant to discovery.

Pleading Preparation

Pleadings are documents filed with the court asking the court to take a specific action. Participants will study pleadings and will prepare a complaint (with a summons) and an answer.

Utilization of Legal Forms

In a law-firm environment, a paralegal would rarely prepare a document from scratch, but would rely on previously existing forms and templates. In this class, participants will learn to manipulate templates and utilize formbooks to become more effective and efficient paralegals.

Preparing for Depositions

A deposition is the oral questioning of a witness under oath, usually outside a courtroom. Participants will learn the considerations for deposition setup.

Deposition Digesting

Students will be provided with a deposition transcript and will learn to summarize that document, an important paralegal skill.

The Arbitration Process

Arbitration is the pretrial process that encourages parties to avoid trial. Participants will learn how the arbitration system works.

Application of Hearsay Rule and Rule "Elementization"

The Hearsay Rule will be discussed, and participants will utilize the developed skill of rule "elementization" to properly analyze and apply rules to facts.

Index Research

The foundation of all legal research is the ability to use indexes. Participants will learn to efficiently utilize fundamental research tools.

Interviewing Clients

Specific techniques to be considered when interviewing a client will be discussed.

Law Office Investigation

Participants will learn techniques of in-office and out-of-office investigations, including interviewing witnesses.

Legal Research Skills

By using hands-on, interactive training devices, participants will learn proper law library utilization, how to locate primary authority, how to use secondary sources, how to update research sources, and how to utilize specific legal materials, including *American Law Reports*, *American Jurisprudence 2d*, *Corpus Juris Secundum*, *West Digests*, *Words & Phrases*, *Am. Jur. Proof of Facts*, formbooks, treatise research, legal periodicals, *Shepard's*, and state and federal statutory research. Participants will also be trained in the use of the two most important legal research systems, the Key Number System and the Total Client Service Library.

Online Legal Research Skills

Due to a special relationship between the Rice Paralegal Certificate Program and LexisNexis, enrolled participants will be trained in and have access to LexisNexis Online Legal Research for approximately one year.

Bluebook Citation Form

A citation is an address to a legal document. Bluebook is the most widely accepted form of citation. Participants will be thoroughly trained in citation form.

Informal Advocacy

Advocacy is the process of acting on behalf of another's interests. Being able to obtain information through informal techniques is an invaluable skill for a paralegal.

Authority Identification

Authority is anything a court can use to reach its decision. Participants will learn to identify the various types of authority, including primary, secondary, mandatory, persuasive, and non-authority.

Strategies for Employment

Multiple strategies for seeking employment will be discussed, including traditional and nontraditional methods.

Substantive Course Topics include:

  Criminal law

  Tort law

  Contract law

  Real estate law

  Probate

  Corporate law

  Texas civil procedure

  Bankruptcy

  Immigration

  Environmental law

To contact Rice University Paralegal Certificate Program, go to www.scs.rice.edu/scs/Paralegal_Certificate_Program.asp?SnID=1316048930.

Associate Degree Programs

The associate degree is received after a student completes a two-year program at a community college, proprietary college, or a few four-year colleges and universities. One-quarter to one-half of the classes are law courses, and the remainder are general education classes in English, math, science, and the humanities, among others. Most students will have the opportunity to choose as many as two classes per semester; most of the curriculum is predetermined, however. The City College of San Francisco offers a two-year program in paralegal studies; upon completion, graduates receive the associate in arts degree, with an Award of Achievement in Legal Assistant/Paralegal. Here is the curriculum.

The tuition for California residents is $26 per semester unit; for out-of-state residents, add $144 per semester unit.

Course	Units
First Semester	
Introduction to Legal Assisting	3
Introduction to Legal Writing	3
Commercial Law	3
Additional graduation requirements	
Second Semester	
Civil Litigation	3
Commercial Law	3
Legal Research and Writing	3
Applied Psychology	3
Additional graduation requirements	
Third Semester	
Tort Law and Claims Investigation	3
Wills, Trust, and Probate Administration	3
Law Office Management and Procedures	3
Additional graduation requirements	
Fourth Semester	
Family Law	3
Civil and Criminal Evidence	3
Investigation, Discovery, and Trial Preparation	3

Course	Units
Additional graduation requirements	
Total Units	**39**

Possible electives include:
Business and Corporate Law
Environmental Law
Legal Aspects of Employee Benefits and Executive
   Compensation
Debtors' Rights and Creditors' Remedies
Intellectual Property
Immigration Law
Medical Law
Communications Law
Civil Litigation

To contact the City College of San Francisco Paralegal Studies Program, go to www.ccsf.edu/Departments/Business/Paralegal-Legal_Studies_Program.

Bachelor's Degree Programs

Bachelor's degrees are conferred by four-year colleges and universities. A student is expected to complete approximately 120 semester hours of work; approximately 18 to 45 of those hours will be in paralegal studies, depending on whether the program is a major or a minor in paralegal studies. A bachelor's program usually combines general education, business, and legal courses. If you are just finishing high school, a four-year liberal arts program allows you time to mature and provides skills that are necessary for the workplace. However, for some people, four years is simply too great an investment in time and money. If that describes you, it might still benefit you to get some information on any four-year programs in your area. In the long run, the more education you acquire, the greater your chance for career advancement will be.

Recently, the National Federation of Paralegal Associations (NFPA) adopted a policy urging future paralegals to obtain bachelor's degrees to become a paralegal. NFPA continues to recognize the viability of associate degree programs, but has stated a preference for the four-year degree. So, even if you start out with an associate degree, you may someday decide to go on to get your bachelor's. Often, the credits you received during your associate program may be transferred to a bachelor's. Here is an example of a bachelor's curriculum, from the paralegal studies program at the University of Louisville. Tuition is $231 per hour for residents and $629 for nonresidents. In addition to completing all of the core requirements of the university, paralegal studies students take:

Required Courses:

Legal Systems and the Paralegal

Legal Research and Writing

Advanced Legal Research and Writing

Professional Ethics for Paralegals

Other Paralegal Courses (students choose five):

Family Law

Torts for Paralegals

Litigation

Criminal Litigation

Bankruptcy Law for Paralegals

Worker's Compensation/Social Security Law for Paralegals

Business Associations and Transactions

Wills, Estates, and Trusts

Consumer Law

Real Estate Law for Paralegals

Insurance Law for Paralegals

Contracts

Uniform Commercial Code

Environmental Law

Healthcare Law

Practical Skills Internship:

An internship consisting of 140 hours of supervised practical experience in a legal setting is required of all students without prior paralegal work experience.

To contact the University of Louisville Paralegal Studies Department, go to www.Louisville.edu/a-s/polisci/paralegal.

Master's Degree Programs

Master's degree programs are not the same as post-bachelor's certificate programs. Both, of course, require a bachelor's degree for admission. A master's program, however, may also require completion of a graduate school admissions test, such as the GRE (Graduate Record Examination) or even the LSAT (Law School Admission Test). Upon completion of the program, you will be granted a master of arts or science degree (different universities use different designations). Master's programs usually take a minimum of two years to complete and frequently require completion of a thesis or similar project for graduation. If you can afford the time and money to obtain your master's degree, it may enhance your employability. Because the phenomenal growth of the legal assistant field translates into more training programs that are graduating more paralegals, setting yourself apart from other paralegals may help you in your future employment. On the other hand, in some markets, you may be considered overeducated when employers have the option of hiring paralegals with an associate degree.

One caveat about master's degree programs: Some of these programs are intended to provide top-notch training to paralegals. On the other hand, they may be intended to give legal training to people who are already successful in another profession—in other words, people who are not intending to seek a career as a paralegal but feel their current position would be enhanced with legal training. Programs are usually quite clear about which type of student they were created for. The curriculum of a master's program is similar to an undergraduate curriculum, except that the core courses (in English, science, math, and the humanities) are not included, just the legal courses.

Here is the curriculum from Montclair State University in Upper Montclair, New Jersey, where students may obtain a master of arts in legal studies, specializing in general legal studies, dispute resolution, or governance, compliance and regulation or legal management, information and technology. Students must complete 36 credit hours of graduate-level courses and may be required to complete a master's thesis on an approval topic. Tuition in the graduate school at Montclair State University is $409 per credit for residents and $603 for nonresidents.

Required Courses:
Ethical and Professional Issues in the Legal Environment
Research Methods and Analysis
U.S. Legal System

Students select 24 credits in accord with their areas of concentration or interest. Each student's program is designed in consultation with the graduate director. All students are required to write a master's thesis on an approved topic or to take a comprehensive examination.

Statutory and Regulatory Analysis
Comparative Legal Systems
Evidence
Terrorism: Legal and Regulatory Perspectives
International Criminal Law
Private Civil Responsibility: Contracts and Torts
Juvenile Law
Introduction to Jurisprudence
Computer Crimes
Administrative Law
Entertainment Law
Trademark Law
Criminal Trial Preparation
Advanced Computer Applications in the Legal Environment
Cyberlaw
Intellectual Property: Copyright, Licensing, and Advertising
Law Office Management and Technology
Negotiation Theory and Practice
Mediation Theory and Practice
Arbitration and Other Alternative Adjudicative Processes
Conflict Management and Peer Mediation in Schools
Family Mediation
Dispute Resolution in the Workplace
Law Office Financial Management
Cross-Cultural Conflict Resolution
Advanced Conflict Resolution in Education

Administrative Law

Legal Information Management

Seminar in Law and Literature

Human Rights

International Law and Transnational Legal Issues

Legal Aspects of Human Resource Management

Private Sector Compliance with Public Regulations

Field Experience in Legal Studies

Cooperative Education in Legal Studies

Independent Study in Legal Studies

Environmental Law and Policy

Selected Topics in Legal Studies

Advanced Patent, Trademark, and Copyright Law

Advanced Civil Litigation

To contact Montclair State University Legal Studies Department, go to chss.montclair.edu/legalstudies/programs/graduate/lsmamain.html.

Distance Education

Distance education—which used to be called *correspondence school*—is also an option for paralegal training. There is a certain amount of variety among these programs. Most rely very heavily on the computer, providing interactive lessons and online classrooms. Others allow you to read texts and take exams at your own pace; these may also be supplemented with videotapes. You need to be very organized and dedicated to succeed in distance education, and some people shy away from it for those same reasons. For some, knowing that they are required to attend classes and complete assignments at a certain time is more effective. On the other hand, as the Kaplan College notes, "The skills you learn to be successful as a distance education student are the exact skills you need to be an effective paralegal. Organization, self-reliance, motivation, the desire to learn, the will to succeed, and the ability to solve problems and make decisions are all a part of the distance education and paralegal processes. Success as a self-directed student demonstrates to your employer that you are goal-oriented and have the ability to work independently. Employer surveys taken over the last ten years have indicated overwhelming satisfaction with graduates of accredited paralegal distance education training programs."

By its very nature, distance learning provides a greater possibility for fraud than a school that is established in a particular place, but that is no reason to avoid distance learning; many schools are quite well respected. If home study seems like the best option for you, just be careful in choosing a program. Find out as much as you can about the faculty and how available they will be to answer your questions. Ask for the names of former students whom you can contact for information about their experiences with the school. Get complete information on the course of study, and compare it with the curricula of schools you know to be reputable. Make sure that the distance education school you choose is accredited by an organization such as the Distance Education and Training Council. The U.S. Department of Education can tell you about other accrediting agencies at www.ed.gov. Finally, check with the Chamber of Commerce, the Better Business Bureau, or the attorney general's office in the state where the school is headquartered to see if the school has had complaints lodged against it.

Here is the curriculum from the Blackstone Career Institute, a distance education school established in 1890. Blackstone provides a course that can be completed in eight months to two years and results in a certificate. Tuition is $880. Blackstone students receive 14 volumes that they must complete to receive a legal assistant/paralegal certificate. They are:

Volume I: Law—Its Origin, Nature, and Development and Contracts (220 pages)

- Nature of Law
- Sources of Law
- Classifications of Law
- Beginnings of Law
- Making of the Common Law
- Enlargement of the Common Law
- Maturity of the Law
- American Development of the Common Law
- History of Contracts
- Offer and Acceptance
- Reality of Consent
- Contracts Under Seal

- Consideration
- Statute of Frauds and Perjuries
- Capacity of Parties
- Legality of the Subject Matter
- Limits of Contractual Obligation
- Assignment of Contracts
- Joint and Several Contracts
- Interpretation and Construction of Contract
- Promises and Conditions
- Rules on Conditions
- Impossibility of Performance
- Breach of Contract
- The Discharge of Contracts

Volume II: Torts (234 pages)

- Fundamental Notions
- Trespass to the Person
- Battery
- Assault
- False Imprisonment
- Trespass to Property
- Excusable Trespasses
- Conversion
- Nature of Conversion
- Particular Instances of Conversion
- Legal Cause
- Negligence
- Contributory Negligence
- Two Species of Defamation
- The Plaintiff's Case in Defamation
- The Defendant's Response
- The Response Prima Facie Defense
- Judgment and Damages
- Malicious Prosecution
- Interference with Domestic Relations
- Interference with Contractual Relations
- Interference with Business or Employment

- Right of Privacy
- Acting at Peril—General Principles
- Liability for Animals
- Liability for Inanimate Forces
- Liability for Injuries from Lawful Use of One's Land
- Joint Tortfeasors

Volume III: Criminal Law (154 pages)

- The Subject Defined
- The Act
- The Intent
- Incapacity or Limitations to Criminal Capacity
- Circumstances Affecting Criminal Responsibility
- Justification
- Parties to Crime
- Incomplete Offenses
- Homicide
- Assault, Battery, Mayhem
- Rape
- False Imprisonment
- Kidnapping and Abduction
- Burglary and Arson
- Larceny
- Robbery
- Embezzlement
- False Pretenses
- Receiving Stolen Goods
- Malicious Mischief
- Forgery
- Counterfeiting
- Extortion
- Offenses Against Religion, Morals, and Decency
- Offenses Against the Public Peace
- Offenses Against Public Authority

Volume IV: Real Property—Part I (180 pages)

- Nature of Ownership
- Origin and Terminology

- Real and Personal Property
- The Feudal System
- Manors
- Sources of Title in This Country
- Tenures
- Seisin and Livery of Seisin
- Growth of Individual Rights
- Estates
- Fee Simple
- Determinable or Base Fee
- Estates Tail
- Rule in Shelley's Case
- Life Estates
- Restraints on Alienation
- Estates upon Condition
- Uses
- Equitable Conversion
- Remainders and Reversions
- Contingent Remainders
- Conditional Limitations
- Rule Against Perpetuities
- Application of Rule Against Perpetuities
- Rule Applied to Charities
- Rule Applied to Powers
- Co-Tenancy in General
- Tenancy in Common
- Joint Tenancy
- Coparcenary
- Estates Arising by Marriage
- Courtesy

Volume V: Real Property—Part II (184 pages)

- Dower
- Homestead Exemptions
- Rights Appurtenant to Land
- Fruits of the Soil
- Waste Boundaries

- Fences
- Natural Rights to Land and Air and Water
- Lateral and Subjacent Support
- Easements Licenses
- Profits
- Party Walls
- Rent
- Covenants Running with Land
- Forms of Conveyances
- Surrender and Release
- Delivery and Acceptance
- Other Essentials to Valid Conveyance
- Abstracts of Title Covenants of Title
- Recording Laws
- Torrens System of Land Registration
- Dedication
- Public Lands
- Powers
- Acquisition or Transfer of Title
- Forfeiture for Crime
- Sales on Execution
- Partition
- Adverse Possession
- Accretion, Alluvion, and Reliction

Volume VI: Pleadings in Civil Actions, Practice in Civil Actions, Criminal Procedures (206 pages)

- Necessity of Pleading and Importance of Subject
- History of Courts and Pleading
- Course of Action
- Common Law
- Causes of Action
- Proceedings in Other Courts and Effect of the Code on Forms of Action
- Parties to Actions and Joinder of Actions
- The Plaintiff's First Pleading
- General Rules of Pleading
- The Defenses to an Action
- Defendant's Pleadings and Rules Governing Them

- The Plaintiff's Second Pleading
- Closing of Issues and Judgment
- Beginning Suit
- Preliminary Motions
- Non-Jury Cases
- Jury Trials
- Opening Statements—Excluding Witnesses
- Depositions
- Examinations of Witnesses
- Charging the Jury
- Verdicts
- Entering Judgment
- Appeals
- Introduction to Criminal Procedure
- Jurisdiction and Venue
- Preliminary Proceedings
- Indictments
- Procedure Between Indictment and Trial
- The Trial
- Steps After the Trial

Volume VII: Wills and Trusts (190 pages)

- Introduction and Classification
- Descent
- Distribution
- Wills Defined
- Origin, History, and Nature of Wills
- Capacities of Testators and Beneficiaries
- Execution of Wills
- Revocation of Wills
- Republication and Revival
- Lapsed and Void Legacies and Devises
- Ademption
- Probate of Wills
- Administration of Estates
- Guardian and Ward
- History of Trusts
- Trusts Distinguished from Other Relationships

- Creation of Express Trusts
- Creation of Implied Trusts
- Private Trusts
- Public Trusts
- Trustee—Appointment, Qualifications, and Powers
- Trustee—Duties, Rights, Liabilities, and Removal
- Beneficiary—Rights and Liabilities
- Beneficiary—Remedies

Volume VIII: Partnerships and Corporations (222 pages)

- Legal Conception of Corporation
- Formation of Corporations
- Irregularly and Defectively Organized Corporations
- Promotion of Corporations
- Subscribers and Stock Subscriptions
- Corporation and State
- Corporate Powers
- Ultra Vires Transactions
- Corporate Crimes and Torts
- Directors
- Corporate Membership
- Rights of Stockholders
- Corporate Creditors
- Dissolution of Corporations
- Foreign Corporations
- Partnerships—Characteristics
- Creation of Partnership
- Name and Property of Partnership
- Partnership Liability
- Duties of Partners
- Remedies of Creditors
- Actions Between Partners
- Action Between Partners and Third Persons
- Termination of Partnership

Volume IX: Constitutional Law—Part I (104 pages)

- Constitutions, Their Nature, and Law
- American Constitutions and Constitutional Law

- Organization and Powers of U.S. Government
- Relations Between Union and the States
- Powers of President
- Powers of Congress

Volume X: Constitutional Law—Part II (118 pages)

- Constitution as a Bill of Rights
- Political Privileges and Their Protection
- Civil Rights and Their Guaranties
- Protection of Person Accused of a Crime
- Due Process of Law
- Equal Protections of Law
- Impairment of Obligation of Contracts
- The Constitution of the United States

Volume XI: *Finding, Reading, and Using the Law* by Anne M. Stevens (471 pages) and *Legal Research Study Guide* by Tracey Biscontini (98 pages)

- Sources of Law
- Finding the Law
- Computer Assisted Legal Research
- Legal Research
- Finding the Current Law
- Understanding the Results of Legal Research
- Using the Law: Legal Analysis
- Legal Writing

Volume XII: *Legal Research and Writing: A Study Guide to Accompany the Finding, Reading, and Using the Law Textbook* by Tracey Biscontini (72 pages)

- Writing Legal Correspondence
- Legal Research Memoranda
- Trial Court Legal Memos
- Writing Appellate Briefs

Volume XIII: *Paralegal Career Starter* by Jo Lynn Southard (206 pages) and *How to Find a Job as a Paralegal Study Guide* by Tracey Biscontini (72 pages)

- Choosing a Career as a Paralegal
- Finding Your First Job
- Job Search Skills; Resume and Cover Letter; Interviewing
- Succeeding on the Job

Volume XIV: Ethics for Paralegals (94 pages)

- Tasks of a Paralegal
- Attorney vs. Paralegal Responsibilities
- Certification and Licensing
- Freelance and Independent Paralegals
- Confidentiality, Ethical Walls, and Screening
- Integrity of the Paralegal Profession
- ABA Model Guidelines
- NALA Model Standards
- NALA Code of Ethics
- NFPA Code of Ethics

To contact Blackstone Career Institute, go to www.blackstonelaw.com.

A Well-Rounded Curriculum

The National Federation of Paralegal Associations (NFPA) states that legal assistant students "need to have exposure to the following theory/practice areas":

Litigation and Civil Procedure	Legal Research and Writing
Real Property Transactions	Business and Corporate Law
Wills and Trust and Estate Planning	Family Law
Torts	Contracts

NFPA also notes that other courses may be desirable depending on the market. For example, a program may consider offering:

Advanced Legal Research and Writing	Advanced Litigation and Civil Procedure
Bankruptcy and Debtor/Creditor Rights	Administrative Law
Pension and Profit Sharing	Law Office Economics and Management
Tax Law	Labor Relations and Employment Law
Intellectual Property	Criminal Law
Immigration Law	Social Security Law
Constitutional Law	Environmental Law
Elder Law	

(NFPA Suggested Curriculum for Paralegal Studies)

Ethics Courses

In addition to legal courses, it is very important that a program offer courses in paralegal ethics. Each state has rules that govern the unlicensed practice of law; essentially, only trained attorneys who have been admitted to the Bar of a particular state can give legal advice. This means that if you are not a member of the Bar, you may not counsel clients as to the law. This is not always as clear as it may seem. As a paralegal, you may, for example, help someone fill out a bankruptcy form. You may not, however, help them decide which kind of bankruptcy to file; that constitutes giving legal advice. And, of course, people are always trying to get free legal advice. So it is imperative that your legal assistant program teaches ethics; it is best if it offers a separate paralegal ethics course. Some schools, however, may choose to teach ethics throughout the curriculum, in conjunction with the other law classes.

A PERSONAL ASSESSMENT

As you can see, many variables come into play when comparing paralegal training programs; in addition to the type and length of the program, you must also take into account cost, location, and reputation of the school. So how do you begin to determine which program is right for you? Start by taking stock of yourself. You have to figure out what you need to get out of a paralegal training program in order to find the one that's right for you. Read on to determine the kind of program that is right for you. This assessment looks at four areas:

1. **Education.** How much education will you have completed prior to entering paralegal training? Are there areas of your education that are particularly strong or weak?
2. **Choosing a specialty.** Do you have work or educational experience that will make you particularly attractive to a certain kind of employer?
3. **Where to get your training.** Are you willing to move to a new city to receive paralegal training? Maybe you want to move; maybe you'll have to move.

4. **Your schedule; your demands.** How much are you willing/able to pay for your paralegal training? Do you need other special services, such as help with transportation or child care?

Let's look at these areas more closely.

Education

What level of education have you completed?

_____ High school or GED

_____ Associate degree

_____ Bachelor's degree

Degree you have:

High School or GED	Associate	Bachelor's

Programs you can attend:

Certificate _____	Certificate _____	Certificate _____
Associate _____	Bachelor's _____	Master's _____

Usual length of program:

Certificate	Associate	Bachelor's*	Master's
varies	two-year	four-year	two-year

*Bachelor's degrees in paralegal studies are relatively unusual, but that doesn't mean that you should discount the idea of getting a bachelor's degree. If the college you want to attend doesn't have a program, you may be able to design a bachelor's degree that will fit your needs. Many business and political science departments offer law courses; if the college is affiliated with a law school, undergraduates may be able to take some law courses. Talk to a counselor at the college or university you are interested in for more information.

	highly skilled	needs work	need to learn
a. Communication skills	_____	_____	_____
b. Research skills	_____	_____	_____
c. Organization skills	_____	_____	_____
d. Prioritizing skills	_____	_____	_____
e. Independent thinking	_____	_____	_____
f. Analytical skills	_____	_____	_____
g. Investigative skills	_____	_____	_____
h. Concentration skills	_____	_____	_____
i. Computer skills	_____	_____	_____

Analysis of Your Skills

Successful paralegals possess certain skills. You may have some of these skills now; if you don't, you'll need to seek out a paralegal training program that will teach you the skills you are lacking. For each skill, consider whether, at this time, it is one you already have, one that needs some work, or one that you need to learn. It will help you get the most out of your paralegal training if you are honest with yourself now.

All of these are skills that a good paralegal program will address and give you the opportunity to brush up on. Organization, prioritizing, independent thinking, and the ability to concentrate on several projects at the same time are vital to the success of a paralegal. Legal research skills will be taught in paralegal programs, but if you feel that your general research skills are lacking, you will want to make sure your program affords you the opportunity to improve them. Analytical and investigative tasks that paralegals undertake are specialized to the law—and you'll learn them in a good program. It will be easier for you, however, if you already have abilities in these areas. The point of this list is for you to look at the work you need to do in order to succeed as a paralegal and make sure that the program you choose gives you the opportunities to do that work.

Two of the most important components of an excellent paralegal program are training in communications and training in computers. It is absolutely vital that you are able to communicate effectively, both orally and in writing. And in even the smallest, most rural law offices, computers and computer research are integral parts of the practice of law.

Communication

You need to be able to communicate effectively to be successful in the law, and as a paralegal you may find yourself working for a lawyer who doesn't know how to write or speak well. There's not much you can do about your boss's speaking ability, but whether it's fair or not, your boss may depend on you to make sure that the documents that leave your office are well written. It may fall to you to not only edit your boss's work, but also, as a paralegal, write many of the documents, some of which will go out in your name.

It is difficult to be honest with yourself about your communication skills. Most of us think that we speak and write just fine. But the truth is, communication skills are not stressed a great deal, especially in high school and in certain college programs. In the professional world of the law, you must be able to do more than make yourself understood. You must be able to express yourself accurately, succinctly, and correctly. Look back over the grades you received in English and any other classes in which you had to write or speak. Think back over comments you received about your work. If you need to, ask a teacher or school counselor for an assessment of your communication skills. If you feel they are lacking, it is imperative that you choose a program that will help you in this area. And if you feel that your communication skills are pretty good, well, we can all use a little more practice, right?

Computer Skills

If you're not a computer geek, don't panic. Most paralegal programs require, or at least make available, computer training. Keep in mind that there are two skills you need to master. One is the ability to use a computer—keyboarding, really—and common business software; the other is the ability to perform legal research on a computer. Both of these are vitally important. If you run across a paralegal program that *doesn't* teach computer-assisted legal research, don't attend. It won't adequately prepare you for a career as a legal assistant.

The ideal paralegal training course will do the following:

1. offer you the opportunity to learn/improve your basic keyboarding skills
2. introduce you to commonly used computer software (legal-specific programs include Abacus Law, Amicus Attorney, and Tabs3)

3. offer you training in WestLaw and LexisNexis, computer legal research programs

WestLaw and LexisNexis are subscription services; there are other research services on the Web, such as VersusLaw and Loislaw. A good computer research class will introduce you to several of these services and allow you the opportunity to practice using them.

Much of the drama in television and movie depictions of lawyers occurs in the courtroom. In reality, most attorneys spend little time in the courtroom. One important rule of questioning a witness is to never ask a question that you don't already know the answer to. One way an attorney knows an answer is through questioning a witness before the trial, in a deposition. If the witness should say something different in court from what she or he says in a deposition, it can cast doubt on the witness's entire testimony. But you have to be able to find that discrepancy in the deposition.

Gayle Lund, a litigation paralegal in Los Angeles, does a great deal of computer work. On occasion, Gayle's work provides dramatic courtroom moments.

"One of the really interesting things that we do is take videos of depositions, and we match them with the stenographer's transcript, and we put them on CD-ROM. As the person is talking on the video, as the questions are being asked and they're answering, you see that in one-third of the screen. And then in another third of the screen you see the reporter's text, with the actual words typed. A highlighting bar highlights the words on the text as the person is talking. . . The lawyers take their laptops into the courtroom, and if they want to challenge somebody, they can, within a couple of seconds, do a search and find the portion of the text they're interested in and highlight it . . . and play it back. What the jury sees is the [video] clip on the screen of the person saying, 'Oh, no, I never did that.'"

Most weaknesses in your educational background can be overcome in a good paralegal training program. Be sure you check not only the classes offered in the paralegal program, but also the classes from which you can choose your electives. In addition, ask about the availability of tutoring in your weak areas.

CHOOSING A SPECIALTY

The question *Do you have work or educational experience that will make you particularly attractive to a certain kind of employer?* may seem a little premature to be talking about employment when you're just worried about where to go to school. But what you want to do as a paralegal has a great deal to do with where you decide to receive your training. And what you want to do as a paralegal depends a lot on your background. This doesn't mean that you shouldn't try to get a good general legal education. Indeed, a general legal education is what most paralegal training programs offer. It is important to be introduced to areas of the law that you are not familiar with. You might find them more interesting than you thought.

Nonetheless, your background may influence your career choices. Do you have any medical training or experience? You might be perfect for a law office that does a lot of medical malpractice. You could take a course in tort law to prepare. Penny, a career counselor with the Affiliates (a nationwide legal placement service) in Houston, Texas, says, "That's a market that doesn't seem to have a lot of competition in it. Registered nurses who have litigation experience—not necessarily practicing nurses, but people who do litigation and have an RN degree—we have a lot of those positions open that we can't fill." Do you have experience or training in social work or education? Perhaps you will be drawn to family law, and you will want to be sure that such a course is available. You might plan to do something completely different from what you end up doing. It is to your benefit to find a paralegal program that offers you as many options as possible for a well-rounded education, while at the same time offering training in the area(s) you are most interested in.

Don't despair if the school or schools you are most interested in lack a particular course you are interested in, such as employment law or administrative law. It may be possible to receive training in your particular area in another way. One of the best alternatives is an internship. In this case, you want to make sure that your program will not only help you get an internship, but also offer contacts in several different areas of the law. If you were interested in employment or administrative law, for example, you could intern in a human resources office or with a government administrative agency. If an internship simply can't be worked out, you may still be able to receive your specialized training. Perhaps you can take a relevant course at another college, and maybe your program will agree to transfer the credit. As noted earlier, sometimes law schools let undergraduates take certain law courses; if not, you might be able to audit.

If all of your attempts to find training in a particular specialty seem to fail, go have a chat with the placement counselors in the programs you are interested in. Ask them if they have ever placed someone in your field, what contacts they have, and how much work they are willing to do on your behalf. If their answers satisfy you, consider attending the school, even if it lacks the course you want. Remember, your personal background already gives you an advantage in the field. And it is always possible you will discover you like another area of the law better.

If you are interested in (or have a background in):	Look for courses such as:
The Arts	Contracts
	Copyrights
	Entertainment Law
	Sports Law
Civil Rights	Administrative Law
	Civil Rights Law
	Constitutional Law
	Elder Law
	Employment Discrimination Law
Corporations	Antitrust Law
	Business Law or Corporate Law
	Contracts
	Employment Law
	Intellectual Property
	Labor Law
Criminology	Criminal Law
	Criminal Procedure
	Evidence and Trial Practice

Environmental Issues	Administrative Law
	Environmental Law
	Property
Financial Matters	Bankruptcy
	Taxation
	Trusts and Estates
	Wills and Probate
Litigation	Civil Procedure
	Contracts
	Evidence and Trial Practice Torts
Medicine	Administrative Law
	Insurance Law
	Torts
Real Estate	Contracts
	Landlord/Tenant Law
	Property
	Real Estate Law
Social Issues	Administrative Law
	Family Law
	Poverty Law

WHERE TO GET YOUR TRAINING

Many people leave their hometowns when they go off to college or graduate school; people are more apt to attend a two-year college close to home.
This doesn't mean you can't move across the country to attend a community
college. It is worth your while to consider this issue seriously. It is highly
desirable to attend a program that is located in the geographical area in
which you want to work. For example, as mentioned earlier, some paralegal
programs are not accredited by the ABA. So that's not a very important consideration for employers here. If you wanted to work here, it would be
unnecessary for you to go out of your way to attend an ABA-accredited

school. On the other hand, if you want to work in a market where most of the legal assistants graduated from ABA-accredited schools, it would be worth your while to attend one yourself.

Another advantage to attending school in the market in which you want to work is that you learn the laws of that area. If you attend law school and join the Bar in Iowa, that doesn't help you much if you want to know California or Georgia law. Laws can vary a great deal from state to state, and it is to your benefit to learn the local law. Finally, attending paralegal school in the state in which you want to work allows you to make contacts for future job hunting. Chapter 5 discusses this kind of networking more, but having friends from school when you're out in the job market can be a big help. Not to mention that the placement office is best at placing in its own area.

If you can't attend a program in the place where you want to work, you're not out of luck. If you know where you are going to end up, research that area to find out what kind of training most paralegals receive, and duplicate it as best you can. If you're not sure where you are going to end up, it's up to you to make the most of the education you do receive. Are you unable to attend an ABA-accredited school? Try to attend one that at least meets ABA standards. Also, rely on your internships and the faculty of the school you attend. Most of these people will be lawyers who just may have attended law school with, or in some other way, know an attorney in the town where you end up. Well-trained paralegals, with good references from their internships and professors, are always in demand.

YOUR SCHEDULE, YOUR DEMANDS

The final point on your personal inventory is resources. The question of how to pay for your training is addressed in Chapter 3. This is about more than simply the cost of a program, although you should factor in the cost when comparing schools and making a decision. But other resources are important, too. Let's say you could attend a paralegal program in your hometown or one in a town 30 miles away. In addition to all the other comparisons, transportation now becomes an issue. No matter which school you attend, child care may be an issue for you. You need to not only get information about any help the schools can give you in these areas, but also have serious talks with your family and friends about any help they're willing to give. Although this book has referred to two-year or four-year programs, that is not entirely accurate. Those periods apply to students who are able to attend full time.

Another possibility you might want to consider is attending school part time. Indeed, your resources might dictate that you consider this option.

Part-Time Attendance

By attending classes part time, you can spread the cost of the program over a greater period of time. Schools usually charge students based on the credit hours they are taking in a given period. If full-time students take 12 hours and you are taking six, it will cost you half as much for that period. Of course, it will take you longer, and ultimately, you will both pay the same amount; you can just take longer doing it. As a part-time student, you will also have more flexibility in your scheduling. This can be a great help, for example, with child care. Finally, a part-time schedule allows you to work, even full time, while you go to school.

Make a list of any time management concerns you have and how you will deal with them. For example, if your spouse or partner can take care of the children only if you take classes in the evening, you will have to find a program that offers evening classes. On the other hand, maybe you will need to take classes only while your children are in school; night school won't work for you. If you've decided that you need to keep working while you attend class, you'll need to find a program that will allow you to attend part time and that offers flexible scheduling of classes. Every time you think of one of these "obstacles," jot it down. Then consider how you can solve the problem. If you need to, brainstorm with a friend or relative, or simply call a school in the area (it doesn't even have to be a paralegal school) and ask an admissions counselor what other students in your situation have done.

Here are some things to consider regarding your schedule and demands:

▶ **Children.** Are you solely responsible for child care? Who can help you with child care? Family? Friends? Professionals? Who can help you with emergency child care? Is child care available through your paralegal school? Because of the age of your children, are you restricted to attending classes only at certain times of the day (such as when they are in school)?

▶ **Transportation.** Can you walk to school? Can you take public transportation? Can you join or form a car pool? Is your car reliable? What will you do in an emergency?

▶ **Finances.** Have you considered nontuition expenses? Textbooks and supplies? New clothes for your internship? Food expenses?

▶ **Employment.** Will you be working while you attend paralegal training? Full time? Part time? What constraints does your job put on your schooling? Scheduling classes? Scheduling study time? Are your work hours flexible? How will an internship affect your current employment? Will you be forced to quit your job? Can you schedule your job around your internship?

▶ **Support.** Is your family supportive of your decision to become a paralegal? Will family members help you when you need it? Are your friends supportive of your decision to become a paralegal? Can you count on them for support?

MAKING THE FINAL DECISION

By now, with the help of your personal inventories and the list of schools in Appendix A, you should have narrowed down the number of schools that you are considering. You may be lucky enough to find the final decision quite easy; if not, here are some things to keep in mind while evaluating the programs on your finalist list. You can get most of this information from the program catalogue, which the school will be happy to send you. You may have to call an admissions counselor to get answers to some of your questions. Don't be shy about asking for information. Remember, you are the consumer; the schools are interested in selling their program to you.

Is the School Accredited?

As noted earlier, it may not be necessary to attend an ABA-accredited program. ABA accreditation is voluntary, and the process can be quite expensive.

For these reasons, many fine programs choose not to seek ABA accreditation. There are more than 1,000 paralegal programs in the United States; 260 of these are currently accredited by the ABA. However, many schools model their programs on the ABA guidelines. These guidelines are useful in distinguishing one school from another. The best schools will follow the ABA guidelines fairly closely. To be considered for ABA accreditation, a legal assistant program must be a postsecondary school program that

▶ is part of an accredited educational institution
▶ offers at least 60 semester hours (or the equivalent) of classroom work (Courses must include general education classes and at least 18 semester hours of law courses.)
▶ is advised by a committee composed of attorneys and legal assistants from the public and private sectors
▶ has qualified instructors who are committed to paralegal education
▶ has student services available, including counseling and placement
▶ has an adequate legal library available
▶ has appropriate facilities and equipment

These ideals are expressed in very general language. Many of the standards were already mentioned; for example, appropriate facilities *must* include computer terminals. Here are a few of the other points on the list.

Make sure that even if the program isn't accredited by the ABA, the school is accredited. There are a variety of accrediting agencies, depending on the kind of school in question. Examples include the Accrediting Council for Independent Colleges and Schools (ACICS), New England Schools and Colleges (NESC), and Distance Education and Training Council (DETC). In addition, in some states, the program itself may be accredited or approved by the state bar association.

Are the Faculty Qualified?

The faculty should consist of people who are committed to paralegal education and who are up to date on changes in the legal assistant field. This may mean practicing attorneys, but it really isn't necessary for everyone on the faculty to be a practicing attorney. Practicing legal assistants, and former attorneys and para-legals who are dedicated to paralegal education, are perfectly fine instructors.

What Resources Does the School Offer?

Try to get a feel for the student services that are available. These should include, at a minimum, counseling and placement. In a small school, the teaching staff may take most of the responsibility for these tasks. Just make sure that the staff seems as committed to those parts of their job as they are to teaching. A faculty made up of only practicing attorneys and paralegals might be hard to find when you need one-on-one attention. Make sure they are at least expected to have regular office hours. Finally, make sure that the program you are interested in has access to a decent law library, such as one at a law school or courthouse.

Certification

As previously mentioned, there are currently three certifications available to qualified paralegals. They are the Certified Legal Assistant (CLA), adminis-tered by the National Association of Legal Assistants (NALA), the Paralegal Advanced Competency Exam (PACE), administered by the National Federation of Paralegal Associations, Inc. (NFPA), and the American Alliance Certification Program (AACP), administered by the American Alliance of Paralegals (AAPI). Please note that these are not the same kinds of certificates as those you receive when you complete one of the certificate programs mentioned under Types of Training. Nonetheless, while choosing a program, you may want to keep in mind the requirements you will have to meet if you one day are interested in becoming certified.

The CLA is a credentialing program that was established by NALA in 1976. To sit for the CLA, a paralegal must meet one of the following requirements:

1. Graduation from a paralegal training program that is accredited by the American Bar Association; or

a program that is authorized to award an associate degree; or a post-bachelor's certificate program in legal assistant studies; or

A bachelor's degree program in paralegal studies; or a legal assistant program that consists of a minimum of 60 semester hours (or the equivalent), of which at least 15 semester hours are substantive legal courses

2. A bachelor's degree in any field *and* one year of experience as a legal assistant (Successful completion of at least 15 semester hours of substantive legal courses will be considered equivalent to one year's experience as a legal assistant.)

3. A high school diploma or GED *and* seven years experience as a legal assistant under the supervision of a member of the Bar, *plus* a minimum of 20 hours of continuing legal education credit, completed within a two-year period prior to the examination date.

Specifics of the examination are discussed in Chapter 1.

To sit for the PACE, a paralegal must have:

1. An associate's degree in paralegal studies from an accredited school and/or ABA-approved paralegal education program, *and* six years of paralegal experience; or

2. A bachelor's degree in any course of study from an accredited school *and* three years of paralegal experience; or

3. A bachelor's degree and completion of a paralegal program with an accredited school, with the paralegal program embedded in the bachelor's program and two years of paralegal experience; or

4. Four years of paralegal experience on or before December 31, 2000.

Details of this examination are discussed in Chapter 1.

It is not necessary to take an examination to receive AACP. Any paralegal with five years of substantive paralegal experience, who also has a bachelor's or advanced degree in any field; or an associate degree in paralegal studies from an ABA-approved school or one that is an institutional member of the American Association for Paralegal Education; or a certificate from an ABA-approved paralegal program or program that is an institutional member of the AAfPE is eligible to apply for AACP certification.

Although it is possible to take the CLA test as soon as you graduate from a paralegal program, most legal assistants wait until they have a few years of experience before obtaining a certification. It's not a bad idea to keep the standards in mind, though.

Note: When you are job hunting, keep in mind the difference between having a certificate (because you graduated from a paralegal program) and having certification (CLA, PACE, or AACP). Employers may be confused about this, and when they advertise for a certified paralegal, they may actually mean a legal assistant with a certificate.

MAKING THE MOST OF YOUR TRAINING PROGRAM

Internships

An internship is a temporary job, arranged through your paralegal program, for which you receive either academic credit or pay or both. It's really important to get out there, whether it's through a part-time job or through an internship, to get the practical experience. Otherwise, having that certificate means nothing.

Internships can provide you with the single most valuable part of your legal assistant education. They allow you to leave the rarified halls of an educational institution to see what the real world is like. If you are interested in specializing in a particular area of the law, an internship provides an invaluable education. One thing you should be prepared for, however, is the possibility that you won't like an area of the law as much as you thought you might. In my opinion, this doesn't make an internship any less valuable; indeed, it's better to waste a semester at a job you don't like than spend several years at it.

Before you choose an internship, however, you will take many classes and exams. Keep yourself open, as you take your substantive law classes, to the possibility of being surprised. You may never dream that criminal law or real estate law will interest you. Once you study them, however, you may find them fascinating.

Getting the Most out of Your Classes

The law is a discipline in which concepts build upon one another. For this reason, the law lends itself well to an outline style of note-taking. For example, your notes from an evidence or trial practice course lecture on admitting evidence at trial might look like this:

I. Admitting Evidence

  A. Only if relevant—if it tends to make a fact more or less likely than without it

    1. FRE 401—all rel. ev. admitted

    2. All rel. ev. must be:

      a. Probative—relationship between ev. and fact

      b. Material—link between fact and sub. law

    3. May be excluded if prob. value is outweighed by danger of:

      a. unfair prejudice—HOW DECIDE??

      b. confusion of issues

      c. misleading jury

      d. delay, waste of time or needless (because cumulative)

  B. Direct v. circumstantial ev.

If you haven't had much experience with outline formats, the table of contents of your textbook can be an effective starting point. Notice that this student has made use of abbreviations to make note-taking go faster. Students in this course have already been introduced to the Federal Rules of Evidence, which is abbreviated FRE (line I.A.1.). Also, this student has developed a habit of abbreviating repeated concepts rather than writing them out each time. So the word *relevant* becomes "rel." and the word *evidence* becomes "ev." "Sub. law" (line I.A.2.b.) is *substantive law*, a concept that repeats in several classes. Some of these abbreviations you will come up with on your own; some have become standard in the law.

Common Legal Abbreviations

K = contract

Δ = defendant

∏ = plaintiff

v. = *versus*, as in *Brown v. Board of Education* (lawyers usually say the letter *v* rather
than the word *versus*)

e.g. = for example

i.e. = that is

∴ = therefore

Most compilations of laws and cases are referred to in some abbreviated fashion,
such as:

FRE = Federal Rules of Evidence

CFR = Code of Federal Regulations

Notice that this student also made a note to find out more about I.A.3.a., *unfair prejudice*. This concept was not entirely clear to the student, and this note serves as a reminder to investigate further. You can use different colored highlighters for the plaintiff, the defendant, and the judge, state law versus federal law, and the new rules versus the old. Remember, you are taking notes to give yourself a concise and clear summary of each class session. Whatever method makes it most clear for you is a good method.

Because learning the law involves building concepts one upon another, it is important to attend class regularly. It is also vital to be prepared, but if for some reason you are unable to prepare, don't use that as an excuse not to attend class. You need to do both, but one is better than neither. Each instructor conducts class differently, but to the extent that it is appropriate, participate in class. It is also helpful to read over your notes briefly as soon after class as possible to make sure you understand everything you've written.

Preparing for Exams

Begin preparing for an exam by reading over your notes. Look for any areas that you indicated you didn't understand at the time, and make sure you understand them now. If you don't, talk to your instructor or do some extra reading until the concept is clear. Then try making an outline of the class. If you are an outlining expert, you've essentially done this—all you have to do is put each day's notes in order. But if, like most of us, your notes are a little sloppier, you might want to start fresh in creating an outline. (This can provide some extra computer practice!) Sometime when you're in a bookstore, take a look at *Emanuel Law Outlines*, *Smith's Review*, or the *Black Letter Law Series*. These are commercial study aids for law students—don't be alarmed to discover they're several hundred pages long—but they will give you an idea of what an outline for an entire course looks like. (Law students' textbooks are quite different from most paralegal texts; it probably would be a waste of money for you to purchase any of these books.)

Most important, the evening before the exam, relax, eat a good dinner, and get a good night's sleep. In the morning, eat a good breakfast (and lunch, if it's an afternoon test). Try to take a walk or get some other light exercise, if you have time before the exam. Most of all, stay calm and have faith in yourself and your abilities.

Networking with Students and Instructors

Part of making the most of your training is taking advantage of the interesting people who are sitting next to you in class and who are teaching your classes. These people all have experiences and knowledge that can be a benefit to you. You can help each other by studying together and sharing informal information (sometimes called *gossip*) that is part of every educational experience. You can also share all the latest lawyer jokes. And after graduation, these are the people who will help you get your first job and keep you sane in the workplace.

If your program offers social events, take advantage of them as often as you can. If the events offered don't appeal to you, suggest others. Or arrange something on your own. Aside from the obvious benefits to you career, you might even make some great friends.

Finally, make it a point early in your academic career to get to know the people in your counseling and placement offices. They know the answers to almost all your questions and are an invaluable resource.

Your paralegal education is the first, essential step on the road to becoming a paralegal. But don't view it simply as something to get through, as an ordeal you must overcome before you can begin work and start your real life. School is the time to learn as much about the profession and yourself as you possibly can. Along the way, you will make friends and contacts—sometimes they'll be the same person—who will be equally valuable to you as you finish school and embark on your career.

THE INSIDE TRACK

Who: Audrey M. Casey, PLS, CLA

What: Former Paralegal Chair; creator of the Paralegal Program at
           Andover College

Where: Portland, Maine

Degree: Bachelor's degree in business education

INSIDER'S ADVICE

I'd tell students who say, "Oh, I hate real estate law, I'd never want to do it," that learning it and doing it are a lot different. So I'd try to have them keep an open mind about
that. A lot of their frustration comes from having to learn the theory. As a paralegal you
won't spend a lot of time analyzing contracts, you'll basically be helping to draft them
and helping to format them and doing some research on a particular contract issue. So,
if the whole theory of contracts is boring, I think it's boring to everybody, basically. But
when you're actually dabbling in your theory but also dabbling in your technology skills,
then it's a lot different.

    When I was teaching, we had one legal research and writing class, and some stu-
dents just love it and want more of it, and other students really struggle with it and feel
it's very difficult. Then we have the issue of should it be offered first, like it is in law
school, or should it not be. I know some students could handle it and could really benefit from it. But a lot of our students were high school graduates, entry level, and they
would have a really difficult time. They could learn the procedure, but could they apply,
without some background, some of these legal theories? So I continue to contend that
it's a better course for them at the end.

INSIDER'S TAKE ON THE FUTURE

Right now, everybody here takes the same law courses and are, you could say, "specializing" in the business skills they want to use on the job.

    I think legal specialization is something that schools should look at. Because we had
open admissions, we had a wide variety of people, and some of them were definitely
capable at that point in their lives of specializing. They had worked in a law firm, or they
had a lot of business experience, so they had the experience to get into a specialized position and do quite nicely there. So, I think the trend for paralegal education is going to be
specializing.

CHAPTER three

FINANCING YOUR EDUCATION

POSTSECONDARY EDUCATION of any kind and duration can be quite expensive. However, that's no reason not to go to school; if you are determined to get training, there's financial aid available for you. This chapter explains the three types of financial aid: scholarships and grants, loans, and work-study programs. You will find out how to determine your eligibility, which financial records you will need to gather, and how to complete and file forms (a sample financial aid form is included). At the end of the chapter are additional resources that can help you find the aid you need.

YOU HAVE decided on a career as a paralegal, and you have chosen a training program. Now, you need a plan for financing your training. Perhaps you or your family have been saving for your education, and you have the money to pay your way. However, if you're like most students, you don't have enough to cover the cost of the training program you'd like to attend. Be assured that it is likely you can qualify for financial aid, even if you plan to attend school only part time.

Because there are many types of financial aid, and the millions of dollars given away or loaned are available through so many sources, the process of finding funding for your education can seem confusing. Read through this chapter carefully, and check out the many resources, including websites and publications, listed in Appendix C. You will have a better understanding of where to look for financial aid, what you can qualify for, and how and when to apply.

Also take advantage of the financial aid office of the school you've chosen, or your guidance counselor if you're still in high school. These professionals can offer plenty of information and can help guide you through the process. If you're not in school and haven't chosen a program yet, look to the Internet. It's probably the best source for up-to-the-minute information, and almost all of it is free. There are a number of great sites at which you can fill out questionnaires with information about yourself and receive lists of scholarships and other forms of financial aid for which you may qualify. You can also apply for some types of federal and state aid online.

SOME MYTHS ABOUT FINANCIAL AID

The subject of financial aid is often misunderstood. Here are three of the most common myths:

Myth #1. All the red tape involved in finding sources and applying for financial aid is too confusing for me.
Fact: It's really not that confusing. The whole financial aid process is a set of ordered and logical steps. Besides, several sources of help are available. To start, read this chapter carefully to get a helpful overview of the entire process and tips on how to get the most financial aid. Then, use one or more of the resources listed within this chapter and in the appendices for additional help. If you believe you will be able to cope with college, you will be able to cope with looking for the money to finance your education, especially if you take the process one step at a time in an organized manner.

Myth #2: For most students, financial aid just means getting a loan and going into heavy debt, which isn't worth it, or working while in school, which will lead to burnout and poor grades.
Fact: Both the federal government and individual schools award grants and scholarships, which the student doesn't have to pay back. It is also possible to get a combination of scholarships and loans. It's worth taking out a loan if it means attending the school you really want to attend, rather than settling for your second choice or not going to school at all. As for working while in school, it's true that it is a challenge to hold down a full-time or even part-time

job while in school. However, a small amount of work-study employment (10 to 12 hours per week) has been shown to actually improve academic perform-ance, because it teaches students important time management skills.

Myth #3. I can't understand the financial aid process because of all the unfamiliar terms and strange acronyms that are used.

Fact: Although you will encounter an amazing number of acronyms and some unfamiliar terms while applying for federal financial aid, you can refer to the acronym list and glossary on pages 104–105 for quick definitions and clear explanations of the most commonly used terms and acronyms.

TYPES OF FINANCIAL AID

There are three categories of financial aid:

1. Grants and scholarships—aid that you don't have to pay back
2. Work-study—aid that you earn by working
3. Loans—aid that you have to pay back

Each of these types of financial aid will be examined in greater detail, so you will be able to determine which one(s) to apply for, and when and how to apply. Note that the first two types of aid are available on four levels: federal, state, school, and private.

Grants

Grants are normally awarded based on financial need. Even if you believe you won't be eligible based on your own or your family's income, don't skip this section. There are some grants awarded for academic performance and other criteria. The two most common grants, the Pell Grant and Federal Supplemental Educational Opportunity Grant (SEOG), are both offered by the federal government. In 2006, the federal government added the Academic Competitiveness grant to its list of programs.

Federal Pell Grants

Federal Pell Grants are based on financial need and are awarded only to undergraduate students who have not yet earned a bachelor's or professional degree. For many students, Pell Grants provide a foundation of financial aid to which other aid may be added. For the year 2006–2007, the maximum award was $4,050.00. You can receive only one Pell Grant in an award year, and you may not receive Pell Grant funds for more than one school at a time.

How much you get will depend not only on your Expected Family Contribution (EFC), but also on your cost of attendance, whether you're a full-time or part-time student, and whether you attend school for a full academic year or less. You can qualify for a Pell Grant even if you are only enrolled part time in a training program. You should also be aware that some private and school-based sources of financial aid will not consider your eligibility if you haven't first applied for a Pell Grant. All students who are eligible for the program will receive the full amount they qualify for.

Federal Supplemental Educational Opportunity Grants (FSEOG)

FSEOGs are for undergraduates with exceptional financial need—that is, students with the lowest Expected Family Contributions (EFCs). They give priority to students who receive Pell Grants. An FSEOG is similar to a Pell Grant in that it doesn't need to be paid back.

You can receive between $100 and $4,000 a year, depending upon when you apply, your level of need, and the funding level of the school you're attending. There's no guarantee that every eligible student will be able to receive an FSEOG. Students at each school are paid based on the availability of funds at that school and not all schools participate in this program. To increase your best chances of getting this grant, apply as early as you can after January 1 of the year in which you plan to attend school.

Academic Competitiveness Grants

First available in the 2006–2007 school year, Academic Competitiveness grants may provide up to $750 for first-year students who graduated from high school after January 1, 2006, and up to $1,300 for second-year students who graduated after January 1, 2005. In addition to being eligible for a Pell Grant, students must meet certain academic requirements.

State Grants

State grants are generally specific to the state in which you or your parents reside. If you and your parents live in the state in which you will attend school, you've got only one place to check. However, if you will attend school in another state, or your parents live in another state, be sure to check to see if you might be eligible. There is a list of state agencies in Appendix B, including telephone numbers and websites, so you can easily find out if there is a grant for which you can apply.

Scholarships

Scholarships are almost always awarded for academic merit or for special characteristics (for example, ethnic heritage, personal interests, sports, parents' career, college major, geographic location) rather than financial need. As with grants, you do not pay your award money back. Scholarships may be offered from federal, state, school, and private sources.

The best way to find scholarship money is to use one of the free search tools available on the Internet. After you enter the appropriate information about yourself, a search takes place that ends with a list of those prizes for which you are eligible. Take a look at www.fastweb.com, which calls itself "the most complete source of local scholarships, national scholarships and college-specific scholarships." You can also try www.collegedata.com, www.collegenet.com, and www.collegeaidaward.com when you search for scholarships. If you don't have easy access to the Internet, or want to expand your search, your high school guidance counselors or college financial aid officers also have plenty of information about available scholarship money. Also, check out your local library.

To find private sources of aid, spend a few hours in the library looking at scholarship and fellowship books or consider a reasonably priced (under $30) scholarship search service. See the Financial Aid Resources section at the end of this chapter to find contact information for search services and scholarship book titles. Also contact some or all of the professional associations for paralegals; some offer scholarships, while others offer information about where to find scholarships. If you're currently employed, find out if your employer has aid funds available. If you're a dependent student, ask your parents and other relatives to check with groups or organizations they belong to for possible aid sources. Consider these popular sources of scholarship money:

- ▶ religious organizations
- ▶ fraternal organizations
- ▶ clubs, such as the Rotary, Kiwanis, American Legion, or 4H
- ▶ athletic clubs
- ▶ veterans groups
- ▶ ethnic group associations
- ▶ unions

If you already know which school you will attend, check with a financial aid administrator (FAA) in the financial aid department to find out if you qualify for any school-based scholarships or other aid. Many schools offer merit-based aid for students with a high school GPA of a certain level or with a certain level of SAT scores to attract more students to their school. Check with the paralegal program's academic department to see if they maintain a bulletin board or other method of posting available scholarships.

While you are looking for sources of scholarships, continue to enhance your chances of winning one by participating in extracurricular events and volunteer activities. You should also obtain references from people who know you well and are leaders in the community, so you can submit their names and/or letters with your scholarship applications. Make a list of any awards you've received in the past or other honors that you could list on your scholarship application.

Scholarships

There are thousands of scholarships awarded to students planning to enter the paralegal profession. The following are a few samples. To find more sources, search the Internet with terms such as *paralegal and scholarship*.

Career Advancement Scholarship

Offered by the Business and Professional Women's Foundation

Career Advancement Scholarship Program

P.O. Box 4030

Iowa City, IA 52243

Number of awards: 100–200

Amount of award(s): $1,000–$2,600

Minimum age to apply: 25

Must be officially accepted into an accredited degree or certification program

Nontraditional students are encouraged to apply

Must be female

Paralegal Scholarships

The National Federation of Paralegal Associations, Inc., in conjunction with West Publishing Group and the Thompson Corporation, awards two scholarships yearly, totaling $5,000. Scholarships of $3,500 and $1,500 are presented at the annual NFPA Spring Convention. West provides a travel stipend for the two award recipients so that they may receive their awards at the NFPA Spring Convention.

Applicants must be part-time or full-time enrolled students or accepted students in a paralegal education program or college-level program with emphasis in paralegal studies. They must demonstrate they have maintained a B average.

Selection will be based upon scholastic excellence, participation in campus and paralegal program leadership activities, community service, and review of an essay on a given topic. Proven need for financial assistance may be considered. NFPA membership is not a requirement.

Lambda Epsilon Chi, the National Honor Society in Paralegal/Legal Assistant Studies

American Association for Paralegal Education (AAfPE) Scholarship

To be considered, please submit:

- AAfPE LEX SCHOLARSHIP Application
- 500-word typed essay on a given topic
- The AAfPE LEX Scholarship Certification form
- An official transcript, which will demonstrate at least a B average
- A letter of recommendation from a faculty member

NOTE: The scholarship is to be used to continue the pursuit of the student's paralegal education. The AAfPE check will be made payable to the awardee and the awardee's school.

The Internal Revenue Service offers two tax credit programs for helping to offset the cost of higher education: the Hope Credit and the Lifetime Learning Credit.

Comparison of Education Credits

Hope Credit	Lifetime Learning Credit
Up to $1,500 credit per eligible student	Up to $2,000 credit per return
Available only until the first two years postsecondary education are completed	Available for all years of postsecondary education and for courses to acquire or improve job skills
Available only for two years per eligible student	Available for an unlimited number of years
Student must be pursuing an undergraduate degree or other recognized educational credential	Student does not need to be pursuing a degree or other recognized education credential
Student must be enrolled at least half time for at least one academic period beginning during the year	Available for one or more courses
No felony drug conviction on student's record	Felony drug conviction rule does not apply

For more information, see IRS Publication 970, Tax Benefits for Education, which can be viewed online at www.irs.gov.

The National Merit Scholarship Corporation offers more than 8,000 students scholarship money each year based solely on academic performance in high school. If you are a high school senior with excellent grades and high scores on tests such as the ACT or SAT, ask your guidance counselor for details about this scholarship.

You may also be eligible to receive a scholarship from your state (again, generally the state you reside in) or school. Check with the higher education department of the relevant state or states, or the financial aid office of the school you will attend.

Work-Study Programs

When applying to a college or university, you can indicate that you are interested in a work-study program. The employment office will have information about how to earn money while getting your education. Work options include the following:

▶ on- or off-campus
▶ part time or almost full time
▶ school- or nationally based
▶ in the legal field (to gain experience) or not (just to pay the bills)
▶ for money to repay student loans or to go directly toward educational expenses

If you're interested in school-based employment, you will be given the details about the types of jobs offered (they can range from giving tours of the campus to prospective students, to working in the cafeteria, or helping other students in the financial aid office) and how much they pay.

You may also want to investigate the Federal Work-Study (FWS) program, which can be applied for on the Free Application for Federal Student Aid (FAFSA). The FWS program provides jobs for undergraduate and graduate students with financial need, allowing them to earn money to help pay education expenses. It encourages community service work and provides hands-on experience related to your course of study, when available. The amount of the FWS award depends upon:

▶ when you apply (apply early!)
▶ your level of need
▶ the funds available at your particular school

Work-study salaries are the current federal minimum wage or higher, depending on the type of work and skills required. As an undergraduate, you will be paid by the hour (a graduate student may receive a salary), and you will receive the money directly from your school; you cannot be paid by commission or fee. The awards are not transferable from year to year, and you will need to check with the schools to which you're applying: Not all schools have work-study programs in every area of study.

An advantage of working under the FWS program is that your earnings are exempt from FICA taxes if you are enrolled full time and are working less than half time. You will be assigned a job on-campus, in a private nonprofit organization, or a public agency that offers a public service. Some schools have agreements with private for-profit companies, as long as those jobs are judged relevant to your course of study. The total hourly wages you earn each year cannot exceed your total FWS award for that year and you cannot work more than 20 hours per week. Your financial aid administrator (FAA) or the direct employer must consider your class schedule and your academic progress before assigning your job.

For more information about National Work Study programs, visit the Corporation for National Service website at http://studentaid.ed.gov.

Student Loans

Although scholarships, grants, and work-study programs can help offset the costs of higher education, they usually don't give you enough money to pay your way entirely. Most students who can't afford to pay for their entire education rely at least in part on student loans. The largest single source of these loans is the federal government. However, you can also find loan money from your state, school, and/or private sources.

Try these three sites for information on the U.S. government's programs:

www.fedmoney.org
This site explains everything from the application process (you can actually download the applications you will need), to eligibility requirements and the different types of loans available.

www.finaid.org
Here, you can find a calculator for figuring out how much money your education will cost (and how much you will need to borrow), get instructions for filling out the necessary forms, and even information on the various types of military aid.

studentaid.ed.gov
The Federal Student Financial Aid homepage. The FAFSA (Free Application for Federal Student Aid) can be filled out and submitted online. Use the sample FAFSA in Appendix D to familiarize yourself with its format.

You can also get excellent detailed information about different sources of federal education funding by calling for a copy of the U.S. Department of Education's publication, *Funding Education Beyond High School*. Call the Federal Student Aid Information Center at 800-4FED-AID.

What follows are some of the most popular federal loan programs:

Federal Perkins Loans

A Perkins loan has the lowest interest (currently 5%) of any loan available for both undergraduate and graduate students, and is offered to students with exceptional financial need. You repay your school, which lends the money to you with government funds.

Depending upon when you apply, your financial need, and the amount the school is given by the federal government, you can borrow up to $4,000 for each year of undergraduate study. The total amount you can borrow as an undergraduate is $20,000. If you are a graduate/professional student, you can borrow up to $6,000 per year and $40,000 total including undergraduate Perkins Loans.

The school pays you directly by check or credits your tuition account. You have a nine-month grace period after you graduate (provided you were continuously enrolled at least half time) before you must begin repayment, with up to ten years to pay off the entire loan.

PLUS Loans (Parent Loans for Undergraduate Students)

PLUS loans enable parents with good credit histories to borrow money to pay education expenses of a child who is a dependent undergraduate student enrolled at least half time. Your parents must submit the completed forms to your school.

To be eligible, your parents will be required to pass a credit check. If they don't pass, they might still be able to receive a loan if they can show that extenuating circumstances exist or if someone who is able to pass the credit check agrees to cosign the loan. Your parents must also meet citizenship requirements.

The yearly limit on a PLUS loan is equal to your cost of attendance minus any other financial aid you receive. For instance, if your cost of attendance is $10,000 and you receive $8,000 in other financial aid, your parents could borrow up to, but no more than, $2,000. The interest rate varies, but cannot exceed 9% over the life of the loan. Your parents must begin repayment while you're still in school. There is no grace period.

Direct or FFEL Stafford Loans

Stafford loans are low-interest loans that are given to students who attend school at least half time. The lender is the U.S. Department of Education for the Direct Stafford loan and a participating lender for the FFEL Stafford loan. Stafford loans fall into one of two categories:

1. *Subsidized loans* are awarded on the basis of financial need. You will not be charged any interest before you begin repayment or during authorized periods of deferment. The federal government subsidizes the interest during these periods.
2. *Unsubsidized loans* are not awarded on the basis of financial need. You will be charged interest from the time the loan is disbursed until it is paid in full. If you allow the interest to accumulate, it will be capitalized—that is, the interest will be added to the principal amount of your loan, and additional interest will be based upon the higher amount. This will increase the amount you have to repay.

There are many borrowing limit categories to these loans, depending upon whether you get an unsubsidized or subsidized loan, which year in school you're enrolled, how long your program of study is, and if you're considered independent or dependent by the federal government. You can have both kinds of Stafford loans at the same time, but the total amount of money loaned at any given time cannot exceed $23,000. The interest rate varies, but should not exceed 8.25% for new loans. An origination fee for a Stafford loan is approximately 3% or 4% of the loan, and the fee will be deducted from each loan disbursement you receive. There is a six-month grace period after graduation before you must start repaying the loan.

State Loans

Loan money is also available from state governments. In Appendix B, you will find a list of the agencies responsible for giving out such loans, with websites and e-mail addresses when available. Remember that you may be able to qualify for a state loan based on your residency, your parents' residency, or the location of the school you're attending.

Questions to Ask before You Take Out a Loan

To get the facts regarding the loan you're about to take out, ask the following questions:

1. What is the interest rate and how often is the interest capitalized? (Your college's financial aid administrator (FAA) should be able to tell you this.)

2. What fees will be charged? (Government loans generally have an origination fee that goes to the federal government to help offset its costs, and a guarantee fee, which goes to a guaranty agency for insuring the loan. Both are deducted from the amount given to you.)

3. Will I have to make any payments while still in school? (Usually you won't, and, depending on the type of loan, the government may even pay the interest for you while you're in school.)

4. What is the grace period—the period after my schooling ends—during which no payment is required? Is the grace period long enough, realistically, for me to find a job and get on my feet? (A six-month grace period is common.)

5. When will my first payment be due and approximately how much will it be? (You can get a good preview of the repayment process from the answer to this question.)

6. Who exactly will hold my loan? To whom will I be sending payments? Who should I contact with questions or inform of changes in my situation? (Your loan may be sold by the original lender to a secondary market institution, in which case you will be given the contact information for your new lender.)

7. Will I have the right to prepay the loan, without penalty, at any time? (Some loan programs allow prepayment with no penalty, but others do not.)

8. Will deferments and forbearances be possible if I am temporarily unable to make payments? (You need to find out how to apply for a deferment or forbearance if you need it.)

9. Will the loan be canceled ("forgiven") if I become totally and permanently disabled, or if I die? (This is always a good option to have on any loan you take out.)

APPLYING FOR FINANCIAL AID

Now that you're aware of the types and sources of aid available, you will want to begin applying as soon as possible. You've heard about the Free Application for Federal Student Aid (FAFSA) (see Appendix D) in this chapter already, and have an idea of its importance. This is the form used by federal and state governments, as well as school and private funding sources, to determine your eligibility for grants, scholarships, and loans. The easiest way to get a copy is to log onto www.fafsa.ed.gov, where you can find help in completing the FAFSA, and then submit the form electronically when you are finished. You can also get a copy by calling 800-4FED-AID, or stopping by your public library or your school's financial aid office. Be sure to get an original form, because photocopies of federal forms are not accepted.

The second step of the process is to create a financial aid calendar. Using any standard calendar, write in all of the application deadlines for each step of the financial aid process. This way all vital information will be in one location, so you can see at a glance what needs to be done when. Start this calendar by writing in the date you requested your FAFSA. Then mark down when you received it and when you sent in the completed form. Add important dates and deadlines for any other applications you need to complete for school-based or private aid as you progress though the financial aid process. Using and maintaining a calendar will help the whole financial aid process run more smoothly and give you peace of mind that the important dates are not forgotten.

When to Apply

Apply for financial aid as soon as possible after January 1 of the year in which you want to enroll in school. For example, if you want to begin school in Fall 2007, then you should apply for financial aid as soon as possible after January 1, 2007. It is easier to complete the FAFSA after you have completed your tax return, so you may want to consider filing your taxes as early as possible as well. Do not sign, date, or send your application before January 1 of the year for which you are seeking aid. If you apply by mail, send your completed application in the envelope that came with the original application. The envelope is already addressed, and using it will make sure your application reaches the correct address. You cannot send it via FedEx or other overnight delivery service; the address does not accept overnight deliveries.

Many students lose out on thousands of dollars in grants and loans because they file too late. A financial aid administrator from New Jersey says:

> When you fill out the Free Application for Federal Student Aid (FAFSA), you are applying for all aid available, both federal and state, work-study, student loans, etc. The important thing is complying with the deadline date. Those students who do are considered for the Pell Grant, the FSEOG (Federal Supplemental Educational Opportunity Grant), and the Perkins Loan, which is the best loan as far as interest goes. Lots of students miss the June 30 deadline, and it can mean losing $2,480 from TAG (Tuition Assistance Grant), about $350 from WPCNJ, and another $1,100 from EOF (Equal Opportunity Fund). Students, usually the ones who need the money most, often ignore the deadlines.

After you submit your completed FAFSA, your application will be processed in two to four weeks. Then, you will receive a Student Aid Report (SAR) in the mail. The SAR will disclose your Expected Family Contribution (EFC), the number used to determine your eligibility for federal student aid. Each school you list on the application may also receive your application information if the school is set up to receive it electronically.

You must reapply for financial aid every year. However, after your first year, you may file a renewal FAFSA online. Most of the FAFSA information is carried forward from the year before and you need only to update it.

Getting Your Forms Filed

Follow these three simple steps if you are not completing and submitting the FAFSA online:

1. Get an original FAFSA. Remember to pick up an original copy of this form, as photocopies are not acceptable. Better yet, take advantage of the ease of filing your FAFSA online.

2. Fill out the entire FAFSA as completely as possible. Make an appointment with a financial aid counselor if you need help. Read the forms completely, and don't skip any relevant portions.

3. Return the FAFSA before the deadline date. Financial aid counselors warn that many students don't file the forms before the deadline and lose out on available aid. Don't be one of those students!

Financial Need

Financial aid from many of the programs discussed in this chapter is awarded on the basis of need (the exceptions include unsubsidized Stafford, PLUS, and Consolidation loans, and some scholarships and grants). When you apply for federal student aid by completing the FAFSA, the information you report is used in a formula established by Congress. The formula determines your EFC, an amount you and your family are expected to contribute toward your education. If your EFC is below a certain amount, you will be eligible for a Pell Grant, assuming you meet all other eligibility requirements.

There is no maximum EFC that defines eligibility for the other financial aid options. Instead, your EFC is used in an equation to determine your financial needs.

$$\text{Cost of Attendance} - \text{EFC} = \text{Financial Need}$$

A financial aid administrator calculates your cost of attendance and subtracts the amount you and your family are expected to contribute toward that cost. If there's anything left over, you're considered to have financial need.

Are You Considered Dependent or Independent?

Federal policy uses strict and specific criteria to make this designation, and that criteria applies to all applicants for federal student aid equally. A dependent student is expected to have parental contribution to school expenses, and an independent student is not. The parental contribution depends upon the number of parents with earned income, their income and assets, the age of the older parent, the family size, and the number of family members enrolled in postsecondary education. Income is not just the adjusted gross income from the tax return, but also includes nontaxable income such as Social Security benefits and child support.

You're an independent student for the 2006–2007 school year if at least one of the following applies to you:

▶ you were born before January 1, 1983

▶ you're married (even if you're separated)

▶ you have children who get more than half of their support from you and will continue to get that support during the award year

▶ both your parents are deceased or you're an orphan or ward of the court (or were a ward of the court until age 18)

▶ you're a graduate or professional student

▶ you're a veteran of the U.S. Armed Forces—formerly engaged in active service in the U.S. Army, Navy, Air Force, Marines, or Coast Guard or as a cadet or midshipman at one of the service academies—released under a condition other than dishonorable (ROTC students, members of the National Guard, and most reservists are not considered veterans, nor are cadets and midshipmen still enrolled in one of the military service academies.)

If you live with your parents and if they claimed you as a dependent on their last tax return, then your need will be based on your parents' income. You do not qualify for independent status just because your parents have decided not to claim you as an exemption on their tax return (this used to be the case but is no longer) or do not want to provide financial support for your college education.

Students are classified as *dependent* or *independent* because federal student aid programs are based on the idea that students (and their parents or spouse, if applicable) have the primary responsibility for paying for their postsecondary, i.e., after high school, education.

Gathering Financial Records

Your financial need for most grants and loans depends on your financial situation. Now that you've determined if you are considered a dependent or independent student, you will know whose financial records you need to gather for this step of the process. If you are a dependent student, then you must gather not only your own financial records, but also those of your parents because you must report their income and assets as well as your own when you complete the FAFSA. If you are an independent student, then you need to gather only your own financial records (and those of your spouse if you're married). Gather your tax records from the year prior to the one in which you are applying. For example, if you apply for Fall 2007, you will use your tax records from 2006.

To help you fill out the FAFSA, gather the following documents:

■ U.S. Income Tax Returns (IRS Form 1040, 1040A, or 1040EZ) for the year that just ended and W-2 and 1099 forms

■ Records of untaxed income, such as Social Security benefits, AFDC or ADC, child support, welfare, pensions, military subsistence allowances, and veterans' benefits

■ Current bank statements and mortgage information

■ Medical and dental expenses for the past year that weren't covered by health insurance

■ Business and/or farm records

■ Records of investments such as stocks, bonds, and mutual funds, as well as bank Certificates of Deposit (CDs) and recent statements from money market accounts

■ Social Security number(s)

Even if you do not complete your federal income tax return until March or April, you should not wait to file your FAFSA until your tax returns are filed with the IRS. Instead, use estimated income information and submit the FAFSA, as noted earlier, just as soon as possible after January 1. Be as accurate as you can, knowing that you can correct estimates later.

Maximizing Your Eligibility for Loans and Scholarships

Loans and scholarships are often awarded based on an individual's eligibility. Depending on the type of loan or scholarship you pursue, the eligibility requirements will be different. Finaid.org offers the following tips and strategies for improving your eligibility when applying for loans and/or scholarships.

These strategies will have the largest impact on need-based aid eligibility:

1. Save money in the parent's name, not the child's name. Or use a savings vehicle that is treated like a parent asset, such as a 529 college savings plan, prepaid tuition plan, or Coverdell Education Savings Account.
2. Pay off consumer debt, such as credit card and auto loan balances.
3. Parents should go back to school to further their own education at the same time as their children, or have multiple children in college at the same time. The more family members in college simultaneously, the more aid will be available to each. (Note: This strategy is not as effective as it once was, as whether the parents count is now an item subject to professional judgment review.)
4. Spend down the student's assets and income first.
5. Accelerate necessary expenses to reduce available cash. For example, if you need a new car or computer, buy it before you file the FAFSA.
6. If you feel that your family's financial circumstances are unusual, make an appointment with the financial aid administrator at your school to review your case. Sometimes, the school will be able to adjust your financial aid package to compensate using a process known as professional judgment.
7. Minimize capital gains.
8. Maximize contributions to your retirement fund.
9. Do not withdraw money from your retirement fund to pay for school, as distributions count as taxable income, reducing next year's financial aid eligibility. If you must use money from your retirement funds, borrow the money from the retirement fund instead of getting a distribution.
10. Minimize educational debt.

11. Ask grandparents to wait until the grandchild graduates before giving them money to help with their education.

12. Trust funds are generally ineffective at sheltering money from the need analysis process and can backfire on you.

13. Prepay your mortgage.

14. A section 529 college savings plan owned by a parent has minimal impact on financial aid, and one owned by a grandparent has no impact on financial aid.

15. Choose the date to submit the FAFSA carefully, as assets and marital status are specified as of the application date.

GENERAL GUIDELINES FOR LOANS

Before you commit yourself to any loans, keep in mind that they need to be repaid. Estimate realistically how much you will earn when you leave school, remembering that you will have other monthly obligations such as housing, food, and transportation expenses.

Once You're in School

Once you have your loan (or loans) and you're attending classes, don't forget about the responsibility of your loan. Keep a file of information on your loan that includes copies of all your loan documents and related correspondence, along with a record of all your payments. Open and read all your mail about your education loan.

Remember also that you are obligated by law to notify both your financial aid administrator (FAA) and the holder or servicer of your loan if there is a change in any of the following:

▶ name
▶ address
▶ enrollment status (Dropping to less than half time means that you will have to begin payment six months later.)
▶ anticipated graduation date

After You Leave School

After graduation, you must begin repaying your student loan immediately or begin after a grace period. For example, if you have a Stafford loan, you will have a six-month grace period before your first payment is due; other types of loans have grace periods as well. If you haven't been out in the world of work before, with your loan repayment you will begin your credit history. If you make payments on time, you will build up a good credit rating, and with good credit, it will be easier for you to obtain for other things. Get off to a good start, so you don't run the risk of going into default. If you default (or refuse to pay back your loan), any number of the following things could happen to you as a result:

▶ National credit bureaus can be notified of your default, which will harm your credit rating, making it hard to buy a car or a house.
▶ You would be ineligible for additional federal student aid if you decided to return to school.
▶ Loan payments can be deducted from your paycheck.
▶ State and federal income tax refunds can be withheld and applied toward the amount you owe.
▶ You will have to pay late fees and collection costs on top of what you already owe.
▶ You can be sued.

To avoid the negative consequences of going into default in your loan, be sure to do the following:

▶ Open and read all mail you receive about your education loans immediately.
▶ Make scheduled payments on time; interest is calculated daily, so delays can be costly.
▶ Contact your servicer immediately if you can't make payments on time; he or she may be able to get you into a graduated or income-sensitive/income-contingent repayment plan or work with you to arrange a deferment or forbearance.

There are a few circumstances under which you won't have to repay your loan. If you become permanently and totally disabled, you probably will not have to (providing the disability did not exist prior to your obtaining the aid). Likewise if you die, if your school closes permanently in the middle of the term, or if you are erroneously certified for aid by the financial aid office, you generally are released from your loan obligation. However, if you're simply disappointed in your program of study or don't get the job you wanted after graduation, you are not relieved of your obligation.

Loan Repayment

When it comes time to repay your loan, you will make payments to your original lender, to a secondary market institution to which your lender has sold your loan, or to a loan servicing specialist acting as its agent to collect payments. At the beginning of the process, try to choose the lender who offers you the best benefits (for example, a lender who lets you pay electronically, offers lower interest rates to those who consistently pay on time, or who has a toll-free number to call 24 hours a day, seven days a week). Ask the financial aid administrator at your college to direct you to such lenders.

Be sure to check out your repayment options before borrowing. Lenders are required to offer repayment plans that will make it easier to pay back your loans. Your repayment options may include:

- ▶ *Standard repayment*: full principal and interest payments due each month throughout your loan term. You will pay the least amount of interest using the standard repayment plan, but your monthly payments may seem high when you're just out of school.
- ▶ *Graduated repayment*: interest-only or partial interest monthly payments due early in repayment. Payment amounts increase thereafter. Some lenders offer interest-only or partial interest repayment options, which provide the lowest initial monthly payments available.
- ▶ *Income-based repayment*: monthly payments based on a percentage of your monthly income.
- ▶ *Consolidation loan*: allows the borrower to consolidate several types of federal student loans with various repayment schedules into one loan.

This loan is designed to help student or parent borrowers simplify their loan repayments. The interest rate on a consolidation loan may be lower than what you're currently paying on one or more of your loans. The federal government has recently changed some of the rules regarding consolidation of loans, including that a student may now be allowed to consolidate loans while still in school. For information on consolidation, contact the Direct Loan Origination Center's Consolidation Department by calling 800-557-7392 or visiting loan-consolidation.ed.gov. Or, contact a participating FFEL lender if you're applying for a FFEL Consolidation Loan.

► *Prepayment*: paying more than is required on your loan each month or in a lump sum is allowed for all federally sponsored loans at any time during the life of the loan without penalty. Prepayment will reduce the total cost of your loan.

It's quite possible—in fact, likely—that while you're still in school your FFELP loan will be sold to a secondary market institution such as Sallie Mae. You will be notified of the sale by letter, and you need not worry if this happens—your loan terms and conditions will remain exactly the same or they may even improve. Indeed, the sale may give you repayment options and benefits that you would not have had otherwise. Your payments after you finish school and your requests for information should be directed to the new loan holder.

If you receive any interest-bearing student loans, you will have to attend exit counseling after graduation, where the loan lenders will tell you the total amount of debt and work out a payment schedule with you to determine the amount and dates of repayment. Many loans do not become due until at least six to nine months after you graduate, giving you a grace period. For example, you do not have to begin paying on the Perkins Loan until nine months after you graduate. This grace period is to give you time to find a good job and start earning money. However, during this time, you may have to pay the interest on your loan.

If, for some reason, you remain unemployed when your payments become due, you may receive an unemployment deferment for a certain length of time. For many loans, you will have a maximum repayment period of ten years (excluding periods of deferment and forbearance).

THE MOST FREQUENTLY ASKED QUESTIONS ABOUT FINANCIAL AID

Here are answers to the most frequently asked questions about student financial aid:

1. *I probably don't qualify for aid—should I apply for it anyway?*
   Yes. Many students and families mistakenly think they don't qualify for aid and fail to apply. Remember that there are some sources of aid that are not based on need. The FAFSA form is free—there's no good reason for not applying.

2. *Do I need to be admitted at a particular university before I can apply for financial aid?*
   No. You can apply for financial aid any time after January 1 of the year you will be in school. However, to get the funds, you must be admitted and enrolled in school.

3. *Do I have to reapply for financial aid every year?*
   Yes, and if your financial circumstances change, you may get either more or less aid. After your first year, you will receive a "Renewal Application," which contains preprinted information from the previous year's FAFSA. Renewal of your aid also depends on your making satisfactory progress toward a degree and achieving a minimum GPA.

4. *Are my parents responsible for my educational loans?*
   No. You and you alone are responsible, unless they endorse or cosign your loan. Parents are, however, responsible for the federal PLUS loans. If your parents (or grandparents or uncle or distant cousins) want to help pay off your loan, you can have your billing statements sent to their address.

5. *If I take a leave of absence from school, do I have to start repaying my loans?*
   Not immediately, but you will after the grace period. Generally, though, if you use your grace period up during your leave, you will have to begin repayment immediately after graduation, unless you apply for an extension of the grace period before it's used up.

6. *If I get assistance from another source, should I report it to the student financial aid office?*

Yes—and, unfortunately, it's possible that your aid amount will be lowered accordingly. But you will get into trouble later on if you don't report it.

7. *Are federal work-study earnings taxable?*

Yes, you must pay federal and state income tax, although you may be exempt from FICA taxes if you are enrolled full time and work fewer than 20 hours a week.

8. *My parents are separated or divorced. Which parent is responsible for filling out the FAFSA?*

If your parents are separated or divorced, the custodial parent is responsible for filling out the FAFSA. The custodial parent is the parent with whom you lived with the most during the past 12 months. Note that this is not necessarily the same as the parent who has legal custody. The question of which parent must fill out the FAFSA becomes complicated in many situations, so you should take your particular circumstance to the student financial aid office for help.

Financial Aid Checklist

_____Explore your options as soon as possible once you've decided to begin a training program.

_____Find out what your school requires and what financial aid they offer.

_____Complete and mail the FAFSA as soon as possible after January 1.

_____Complete and mail other applications by the deadlines.

_____Gather loan application information and forms from your college financial aid office.

_____Forward your loan application to your financial aid office. Don't forget to sign it.

_____Carefully read all letters and notices from the school, the federal student aid processor, the need analysis service, and private scholarship organizations. Note whether financial aid will be sent before or after you are notified about admission, and how exactly you will receive the money.

_____Return any requested documentation promptly to your financial aid office.

_____Report any changes in your financial resources or expenses to your financial aid office so they can adjust your award accordingly.

_____Reapply each year.

Financial Aid Acronyms Key

COA	Cost of Attendance
CWS	College Work-Study
EFC	Expected Family Contribution
EFT	Electronic Funds Transfer
ESAR	Electronic Student Aid Report
ETS	Educational Testing Service
FAA	Financial Aid Administrator
FAF	Financial Aid Form
FAFSA	Free Application for Federal Student Aid
FAO	Financial Aid Office/Officer
FDSLP	Federal Direct Student Loan Program
FFELP	Federal Family Education Loan Program
FSEOG	Federal Supplemental Educational Opportunity Grant
FWS	Federal Work-Study
PC	Parent Contribution
PLUS	Parent Loan for Undergraduate Students
SAP	Satisfactory Academic Progress
SC	Student Contribution
ED	U.S. Department of Education

FINANCIAL AID TERMS—CLEARLY DEFINED

Accrued interest—Interest that accumulates on the unpaid principal balance of your loan.

Capitalization of interest—Addition of accrued interest to the principal balance of your loan that increases both your total debt and monthly payments.

Disbursement—Loan funds issued by the lender.

Grace period—Specified time after you graduate or leave school during which you need not make payments.

Deferment—A period when a borrower, who meets certain criteria, may suspend loan payments.

Forbearance—Temporary adjustment to repayment schedule for cases of financial hardship.

Default (you won't need this one, right?)—Failure to repay your education loan.

Delinquency (you won't need this one, either!)—Failure to make payments when due.

Holder—The institution that currently owns your loan.

In-school grace and **deferment interest subsidy**—Interest the federal government pays for borrowers on some loans while the borrower is in school, during authorized deferments, and during grace periods.

Interest-only payment—A payment that covers only interest owed on the loan and none of the principal balance.

Interest—Cost you pay to borrow money.

Lender (Originator)—The financial institution that puts up the money when you take out a loan. Some state agencies and schools provide loans, too.

Origination fee—Fee, deducted from the principal, which is paid to the federal government to offset its cost of the subsidy to borrowers under certain loan programs.

Principal—Amount you borrow, which may increase as a result of capitalization of interest, and the amount on which you pay interest.

Promissory note—Contract between you and the lender that includes all the terms and conditions under which you promise to repay your loan.

Secondary markets—Institutions that buy student loans from originating lenders, thus providing lenders with funds to make new loans.

Servicer—Organization that administers and collects your loan. May be either the holder of your loan or an agent acting on behalf of the holder.

Subsidized Stafford Loans—Loans based on financial need. The government pays the interest on a subsidized Stafford loan for borrowers while they are in school and during specified deferment periods.

Unsubsidized Stafford Loans—Loans available to borrowers, regardless of family income. Unsubsidized Stafford loan borrowers are responsible for the interest during in-school, deferment periods, and repayment.

FINANCIAL AID RESOURCES

In addition to the sources listed throughout this chapter, additional resources may be used to obtain more information about financial aid:

Telephone Numbers

Federal Student Aid Information Center	800-4FED-AID
(U.S. Department of Education) Hotline	(800-433-3243)
TDD Number for Hearing-Impaired	800-730-8913
For suspicion of fraud or abuse of	800-MIS-USED
federal aid	(800-647-8733)
Selective Service	847-688-6888
U.S. Citizenship and Immigration	
Service (USCIS)	(800-375-5283)
Internal Revenue Service (IRS)	800-829-1040
Social Security Administration	800-772-1213
National Merit Scholarship Corporation	708-866-5100
Sallie Mae's College AnswerSM Service	800-222-7183
Career College Association	202-336-6828
ACT: American College Testing Program	916-361-0656
(about forms submitted to	
the need analysis servicer)	
College Scholarship Service (CSS)	609-771-7725;
	TDD 609-883-7051
Need Access/Need Analysis Service	800-282-1550
FAFSA on the WEB Processing/	800-801-0576
Software Problems	

Websites

studentaid.ed.gov/students/publications/student_guide
Funding Education Beyond High School: The Guide to Federal Student Aid is a free informative brochure about financial aid and is available online at the Department of Education's Web address listed here.

www.fafsa.ed.gov

This site offers students help in completing the FAFSA.

www.career.org

This is the website of the Career College Association (CCA). It offers a limited number of scholarships for attendance at private proprietary schools. You can also contact CCA at 10 G Street, NE, Suite 750, Washington, D.C. 20002-4213.

www.salliemae.com

Website for Sallie Mae that contains information about loan programs.

Books and Pamphlets

Pamphlets

Funding Education Beyond High School: The Guide to Federal Student Aid
Published by the U.S. Department of Education, this handbook is about federal aid programs. To get a printed copy, call 800-4FED-AID.

Books

College Board. *2007 Scholarship Handbook* (New York: College Board, 2006).

Davis, Kristin. *Financing College: How to Use Savings, Financial Aid, Scholarships, and Loans to Afford the School of Your Choice* (Washington, D.C.: Kiplinger Books, 2007).

National Scholarship Research Service. *The Scholarship Book, 12th Edition: The Complete Guide to Private-Sector Scholarships, Fellowships, Grants, and Loans for the Undergraduate* (Upper Saddle River, NJ: Prentice Hall Press, 2006).

Petersons. *College Money Handbook 2007* (Lawrenceville, NJ: Thomson Peterson's, 2006).

Petersons. *Scholarships, Grants, & Prizes 2007* (Lawrenceville, NJ: Thomson Peterson's, 2006).

Sandler, Corey. *Cut College Costs Now!: Surefire Ways to Save Thousands of Dollars* (Cincinnati: Adams Media Corporation, 2006).

Tanabe, Gen and Kelly Tanabe. *501 Ways for Adult Students to Pay for College* (Los Altos, CA: Supercollege, LLC, 2006).

Tanabe, Gen and Kelly Tanabe. *Get Free Cash for College: Secrets to Winning Scholarships* (Los Altos, CA: Supercollege, LLC, 2006).

Other Related Financial Aid Books

Annual Register of Grant Support (Chicago: Marquis, annual).

A's and B's of Academic Scholarships (Alexandria, VA: Octameron, annual).

Chronicle Student Aid Annual (Moravia, NY: Chronicle Guidance, annual).

College Blue Book. Scholarships, Fellowships, Grants, and Loans (New York: Macmillan, annual).

College Financial Aid Annual (New York: Prentice Hall, annual).

Directory of Financial Aids for Minorities (San Carlos, CA: Reference Service Press, biennial).

Directory of Financial Aids for Women (San Carlos, CA: Reference Service Press, biennial).

Financial Aid for the Disabled and Their Families (San Carlos, CA: Reference Service Press, biennial).

Leider, Robert and Ann Leider. *Don't Miss Out: The Ambitious Student's Guide to Financial Aid* (Alexandria, VA: Octameron, annual).

Peterson's Guides. *Paying Less for College* (Princeton, NJ: Peterson's Guides, annual).

THE INSIDE TRACK

Who: Lisa Cain

What: President, Legal Concierge, Inc.

Where: Dallas, Texas

INSIDER'S STORY

I got interested in the legal profession as a fluke—I got laid off by a company that I was working for, and when I went to the Unemployment Commission, they asked me if becoming a paralegal was a career that I might be interested in, and if so, they would show me how to get started. So, I went for it. I started by looking at all the different paralegal programs in my area, and I chose the best one. After I received my certification, I conducted my job search by networking. I simply walked into firms and began to build a rapport with someone, anyone who smiled back at me, I would ask who would be the best person to talk to and then leave that person a note that usually said something like, "I came by, and I have an interest in your firm. Would you please take a minute to meet with me?" There are all sorts of job-hunting resources, but I still think networking is the best of all avenues. Walking right into a place might seem aggressive, but most employers like that attitude in prospective employees, especially in the legal profession. And it worked; I landed a job pretty quickly as a litigation paralegal with a prestigious firm.

That first firm that I went to work for threw me onto a huge telecommunications case right away. They let me oversee all of the logistics—taking care of the attorneys' needs, catering, flights, condos, hotels, plus overseeing and dealing with all of the vendors, from copy companies to caterers. It was a fabulous experience, and one that would serve me well in the future.

I recently branched out and started my own business serving other litigation paralegals, attorneys, and litigation support managers at many firms. I now own a business called Legal Concierge, Inc. (www.mylegalconcierge.com). We handle all of the logistics for a trial team getting ready to go to trial. We go into a city and have everything in place before the trial team gets there. We can have the war room set up, all accommodations in place, and all vendors in place, ready to go. We handle everything so that the trial paralegals do not have to pull off their positions on the case and take away from their billable hours. Our slogan is *"We focus on the details so that you can focus on the case."*

I would advise anyone interested in becoming a paralegal to go for it, but know that excellent people skills, meticulous organizational skills, quick mental abilities, good common sense, and loyalty are essential for success. I also recommend that new paralegals do an internship or work for temp agencies, as they can be very enlightening as to what kind of law you might want to practice. Be prepared to work hard—working under pressure is a given at most firms; it takes a while to get really good at what you want to do, and patience is a must. But you'll be satisfied in the end. I love my work; there are many perks, and the people that I work with are intelligent and have a lot of interesting experiences to talk about. I like working with sharp people who inspire me to push myself. This profession does that for me.

CHAPTER five

HOW TO FIND YOUR FIRST JOB

STARTING THE hunt for your first job in a new field can be daunting. Especially if you are completely new to the legal profession, you may need some help identifying the places to begin and the ways to approach people. Every profession has its little quirks and tweaks; this chapter shows you what you can do to make finding your first job a little easier.

HUNTING FOR a job usually involves three phases: You need to decide whom you are going to contact, you have to advertise yourself, and you have to sell yourself. Deciding whom to contact entails identifying potential employers and narrowing the field to those you think you would most like to work for and those most apt to hire you. Advertising yourself includes writing and sending out resumes and cover letters, but also networking and other methods of bringing your skills to the attention of the right people. Finally, selling yourself involves sitting down face to face with the person who has the authority to hire you and marketing yourself to convince that person you are right for the job.

BEFORE YOU BEGIN SEARCHING

What can you expect the paralegal job market to look like by the time you finish your training and are ready to launch your career? Expectations are that the market for paralegals will continue to grow over the next several years. According to *The Occupational Outlook Handbook, 2006–2007*, published by the U.S. Department of Labor:

> Employment for paralegals and legal assistants is projected to grow much faster than average for all occupations through 2014. Employers are trying to reduce costs and increase the availability and efficiency of legal services by hiring paralegals to perform tasks formerly carried out by lawyers. Besides new jobs created by employment growth, additional job openings will arise as people leave the occupation. Despite projections of rapid employment growth, competition for jobs should continue as many people seek to go into this profession; however, experienced, formally trained paralegals should have the best employment opportunities.

> Private law firms will continue to be the largest employers of paralegals, but a growing array of other organizations, such as corporate legal departments, insurance companies, real estate and title insurance firms, and banks hire paralegals. Corporations in particular are boosting their in-house legal departments to cut costs. Demand for paralegals also is expected to grow as an expanding population increasingly requires legal services, especially in areas such as intellectual property, healthcare, international law, elder issues, criminal law, and environmental law.

> Paralegals who specialize in areas such as real estate, bankruptcy, medical malpractice, and product liability should have ample employment opportunities. The growth of prepaid legal plans also should contribute to the demand for legal services. Paralegal employment is expected to increase as organizations presently employing paralegals assign them a growing range of tasks and as paralegals are increasingly employed in small- and medium-size

establishments. A growing number of experienced paralegals are expected to establish their own businesses. Job opportunities for paralegals will expand in the public sector as well. Community legal-service programs, which provide assistance to the poor, elderly, minorities, and middle-income families, will employ additional paralegals to minimize expenses and serve the most people. Federal, state, and local government agencies, consumer organizations, and the courts also should continue to hire paralegals in increasing numbers.

To a limited extent, paralegal jobs are affected by the business cycle. During recessions, demand declines for some discretionary legal services, such as planning estates, drafting wills, and handling real estate transactions. Corporations are less inclined to initiate certain types of litigation when falling sales and profits lead to fiscal belt tightening. As a result, full-time paralegals employed in offices adversely affected by a recession may be laid off or have their work hours reduced. However, during recessions, corporations and individuals are more likely to face other problems that require legal assistance, such as bankruptcies, foreclosures, and divorces. Paralegals who provide many of the same legal services as lawyers at a lower cost tend to fare relatively better in difficult economic conditions.

Things look good, then, for paralegals in the future, although, as this report notes, competition for paralegal jobs will increase as the number of jobs increases. In this chapter, you'll find out what you can do to help make yourself a prime candidate for a top-notch paralegal job.

Internships

Internships give you valuable experience for your resume, and they often turn into permanent jobs. Law firms often use internships to hire their new lawyers; it's natural that they would rely on the same method to hire paralegals. It provides an opportunity for you to get a look at them and for them to get a look at you with very little obligation. However, if everybody likes what they see, it is to everyone's benefit to hire a former intern for a permanent position. Many internships turn into permanent jobs, so choose an internship that is the kind of work you think you want to do for the next several years.

Temporary Agencies

Some paralegals enjoy doing a variety of legal work and may work through temporary agencies for years. For others, it provides a passage to full-time work. Thus, it can be an excellent start to your career.

Temporary work gives you the opportunity to gain valuable experience. It also allows you to look over several different workplaces and get an idea of where you'd like to work permanently. And as with an internship, it gives employers a chance to get to know you. Many people gain permanent employment through temporary assignments. If, when you graduate from your program, you don't yet know for sure what kind of paralegal work you want to do, working for a temporary agency can be very valuable. If the perfect job doesn't seem to be forthcoming, temp work can lead you into it.

CONDUCTING YOUR SEARCH

Before you look for a job, you need to know what kind of job you are looking for. This means not just *paralegal* but *criminal defense paralegal* or *intellectual property paralegal* or *real estate paralegal*. Or perhaps, for you, it's a paralegal in a small firm or a paralegal with a corporation or the government. Look for your dream job from the start, but of course, you should keep your feet on the ground; you probably aren't going to be hired right out of paralegal school to manage a legal assistant department and supervise several more experienced paralegals. But it is worth spending some time pursuing the kind of job you think you would love.

One person you should definitely get to know as a paralegal student is the placement director. This is the person whose job it is to help you find a job when you graduate. A good placement office will have directories of law firms and other businesses in the local area, information about job fairs, and copies of any industry publications that list paralegal job openings. A top placement director also maintains contacts with the legal and business communities so that your school's placement office will be one of the first places to hear about a job opening and can give you valuable general information about the market in your area.

Researching the Field

Before you read this book, you probably assumed that all paralegals worked directly for lawyers. You now know this isn't true. However, most paralegals do work for law firms, so here's how to find information on attorneys and law firms in your area or the area you are interested in moving to.

Law Firms

The *Martindale-Hubbell Law Directory* is a multivolume set that includes the names, addresses, and phone numbers of all lawyers and law firms in the United States. This information is listed by attorney name, firm name, location, and specialty. The directory also lists lawyers employed by corporations and governments. If your placement office doesn't have a copy, check your nearest law library. You can also access Martindale-Hubbell on the Internet at www.martindale.com. Another Internet directory is the FindLaw Lawyer Directory at lawyers.findlaw.com.

Your state, county, or city bar association also compiles a directory of attorneys. In most cases, it will list the lawyers by name and by area of practice, and many are available online. And don't overlook something as obvious as the phone book. Many yellow pages have a section for "attorneys" or "lawyers" that includes lists by practice area as well as alphabetical lists. In addition, many of your professors probably are or were practicing attorneys, and they may know which firms in your area fit your picture of the ideal firm. There is a list of state bar associations in Appendix B of this book; to find a local bar, just look in the phone book under the name of the city or county "bar association."

Corporations

If you are considering work as a corporate paralegal, your placement office and public library should have a variety of directories to help you locate potential employers. If you are interested in a particular corporation, there are also directories like *Standard & Poor's Corporate Records* in which you can find the name of the company's chief legal officer and a wealth of other information about the company. You can find S & P Corporate Records at your library or online at www2.standardandpoors.com. Finally, for corporations, check general news indexes, such as the *Reader's Guide to Periodical Literature*, for articles about a corporation or industry in which you are particularly interested.

Nonprofit Organizations

There are a variety of regional directories of nonprofit organizations. One good national directory is Daniel Lauber's *Nonprofits and Education Job Finder*. Also check out www.idealist.org and www.nonprofitcareer.com. If you have been involved in a particular cause, as a paralegal or just as a citizen, ask around among the other volunteers and paid staff for ideas on locating organizations you might be interested in working for.

Government Agencies

Rules and regulations for finding and applying for federal government jobs are changing all the time. Your placement office should be on top of the changes when you begin job hunting, so check with them to verify the information that follows.

If you remember the days when, in order to get a federal civil service job, you had to get a rating and then get on the register and then wait for a call about an opening, you'll be happy to hear that times have changed. The whole process is much more decentralized, with most agencies doing their own hiring. In a majority of cases, the jobs are still rated, but the rating is done by the personnel office of the individual agency, following guidelines administered throughout the government by the Office of Personnel Management. The point is, if you want to work for a particular department or agency of the federal government, you should start with that agency to find out if they have openings and to whom you should apply.

Many government agencies maintain a website that includes job openings. The Department of Justice, for example, is at www.doj.gov. Industry-specific periodicals, such as those listed later in this section, often list federal government job openings, as do national newspapers. If the federal job is in a local area, such as the local office of the Federal Bureau of Investigation, it may be listed in a local newspaper. In addition, each state has at least one Federal Employment Information Center. These centers post federal job openings in your area. Many of these centers are bare-bones, offering only a recording over the telephone or several job announcements posted on the wall, but they're a place to start. State Job Service offices usually list federal government openings, and generally, you can call and talk to a live person.

If you are interested in working for state or local government, the state Job Service office is a good place to start as well. Your placement office also should be able to provide you with information about hiring procedures on the state level. In addition, most local (that is, city and county) governments post their openings in one or more central locations and advertise in local newspapers. Governments want to avoid the appearance of patronage—that is, giving someone a job to pay off a political favor. As a result, they usually advertise their openings pretty thoroughly.

Using Classified Ads

Conventional job hunting wisdom says you shouldn't depend too much on want ads for finding a job. While you shouldn't depend on them totally, there seem to be quite a few paralegal jobs advertised in the newspaper. For one thing, many law firms—especially smaller ones—see it as a relatively inexpensive way to fill positions. And even if you don't find a job through the classifieds, you can learn quite a lot about the market in your area. If you start paying attention to the ads well before you graduate, you'll be able to start a list of the places that hire paralegals.

You can get other information from the classifieds, such as typical salaries and benefits in your area. One of the hardest questions to answer on an application or in an interview is "What is your desired salary?" If you've been watching the ads, you'll have an idea of the going rate. You can also get information about temporary and part-time jobs. In some areas, temporary and part-time jobs may be a common way for paralegals to begin their careers.

Online Resources

These days, the Internet is changing and growing so fast that it's dangerous to tell you about specific sites; they could be gone by the time you read this! But the following major employment sites look like they'll be around for a while. By the way, it's always worthwhile to start with your favorite search engine (such as Yahoo or Google) to look for these and other employment sites.

Two good overview sites are The Law Engine at www.thelawengine.com and Hieros Gamos at www.hg.org. Both contain links to all kinds of helpful legal information. They lead you not only to employment sites, but also links to do legal research, find profiles of lawyers and firms, and even learn some new lawyer jokes.

Just as with classified advertisements, sometimes you will find job openings advertised on the Web that may be right for you, but there is also a wealth of information. Many websites contain legal and paralegal information; you should spend some time early in your student career visiting some of these areas. You can learn about salaries, job frustrations and pleasures, and various specialties that you may not have thought of, and you can even do some cyber-networking.

Legal Employment Sites

Here is a list of legal employment sites that contain paralegal jobs. With a few exceptions, this index includes only legal employment sites. There are also a large number of general job sites on the Web; many of them probably include paralegal jobs. The following, though, are sites that list paralegal jobs or that claim to list paralegal openings. Also, especially in the case of the nonprofit job lines, there may be situations where the job won't be listed as *paralegal* or *legal assistant* but will nonetheless be right for you.

▶ America's Job Bank (The Public Employment Service)
   (www.ajb.dni.us)
▶ Career Builder (www.careerbuilder.com)
▶ Emplawyernet (www.emplawyernet.com) (current charge is $14.95 per month)
▶ Federal Job Announcements (www.ntis.gov/jobs)
▶ Law Match (www.lawmatch.com)
▶ National Federation of Paralegal Associations
   (paralegals.legalstaff.com)
▶ Nonprofit Job Resource Center (www.nonprofitcareer.com)

Networking

The play (made into a movie) *Six Degrees of Separation* is based on the premise that everyone in the world is separated by six degrees. That is, between any two people, there are only six other people separating them. The trick, of course, is to find the right six people. Although it may take you more than six people, it works the same way in networking. You want to get from you to an employer who is hiring by way of the people you know and the people they know.

Networking is about much more than just meeting people. The point of networking is to use the relationships you have and new ones you make to help you find a job. A successful network continues to grow; it doesn't die once you get a job. As your network of acquaintances expands—one person leading you to the next and that person leading you to the next—eventually, you will get to the person who is hiring.

Networking is a major job-search tactic used by people in all industries. But no matter how widespread its use, networking remains intimidating to some, who picture it as insincere small talk or handshaking. However, when it is done properly, it is completely sincere and can provide many benefits, such as:

▶ Mentoring
▶ Making contacts within a hiring firm or company
▶ Furthering training
▶ Getting information about trends in the industry

The key to successful networking is to break down the process into easy-to-follow steps, which are reviewed over the next few pages. You will find these steps useful not only in your paralegal job search, but also in other areas of you life.

Step One: Identify Small Goals

Of course, your ultimate goal, not only for networking, but also for the entire job-search process, is to find a great job. However, you shouldn't approach day-to-day networking as a means to that larger goal. Instead, as your first step, identify smaller goals that can be met quickly. For instance, you have narrowed down your search to three law firms in your area. Now, you want to get "inside" information about these offices to decide which to apply for a job with. Or, you may simply be seeking advice from those already working in the field. Once your goals are identified, you can best determine how to meet them.

Step Two: Be Informed

If your goal is to seek advice about corporate law departments in your area, get as much information as you can first. Research the companies that hire paralegals. Understand the paralegal field in general, too. You want to sound like you have done your homework when you begin to make contacts.

This is also the step in which you begin to make a list of potential contacts that may help you meet your goal(s). If you're in school, the person at the job placement office of your school should be at the head of your list. Then, the research you do will probably mention by name the head of a corporate legal department, or hiring partner in a law firm. Newsletters from your state bar and paralegal associations may list paralegals working in your area. The students and teachers you met during your training are also good candidates for this list.

Step Three: Make a Connection

Using the list of potential contacts you developed in step two, build a network of paralegals who work at the offices you are interested in joining. Call them, or visit their offices. Although busy, most people like to talk about themselves and their jobs. They were new to the field once themselves, so if you are careful not to take up too much of their time, they will probably be glad to give you some information. Begin by introducing yourself, showing that you are informed (step two) and interested in what they have to say.

Step Four: Ask for What You Want

If your contact indicates that he or she is willing to help you, be honest and direct about what you want. If your goal is to find out inside information about the office in which a contact works, tell him or her that you are thinking of applying to work there. Then, ask questions such as:

▶ "How do you like the office?"
▶ "What are the benefits of working here?"
▶ "What is the office atmosphere like?"
▶ "Where else have you worked, and how does this office compare?"

Sending a thank-you note to someone who helps you is a nice touch that makes you stand out in that person's mind.

Step Five: Expand Your Network

One of the most valuable pieces of information you can get from a contact is another contact. After you've gotten the information you need to meet your step-one goal(s), simply ask if he or she would mind sharing with you the name of another person who might also be able to help you.

Also consider requesting informational interviews at firms that interest you. An informational interview is one in which you meet with someone to find out about the company and which may be an excellent opportunity to:

▶ learn more about how the firm works
▶ gain interview experience
▶ make a contact that might help you get a job in the future

You can also expand your circle of contacts by joining professional organizations while you're still a student. Both the National Association of Legal Assistants and the National Federation of Paralegals have discounted student memberships; most other professional organizations do so as well. Be sure to join both national organizations and their local chapters. Although the national organizations can give you valuable information, it's on the local level that you will accomplish more of your networking goals. Go to local meetings and ask questions—remind people that you're a student and soon-to-be job hunter—and volunteer for committees. The members of your local paralegal group will most likely know about job openings before anyone else does.

Step Six: Organize Yourself

You have probably already written down your goals and made lists of contacts. Once you've spoken with some of them, organization becomes even more important. You will need to keep track of your contacts, as well as the information you receive from them. When you need to connect with this person again in the future, you will be able to easily access your information. There are software packages that can help you keep track of your networking contacts, or you can simply use a notebook and organize yourself.

For each contact, note:

- ▶ Name
- ▶ Address
- ▶ E-mail address
- ▶ Phone number (work, pager, cellular phone, residence)
- ▶ Fax number
- ▶ Company name
- ▶ Job title
- ▶ First meeting—where, when, the topics you discussed
- ▶ Last contact—when, why, and how

Step Seven: Maintain Your Contacts

It is important to maintain your contacts once you have established them. Try to reach people again within a couple of weeks of meeting them. You can send a note of thanks, ask a question, or send a piece of information related to your conversation with them. This contact cements your meeting in their minds, so they will remember you more readily when you call them again in the future. If you haven't communicated with your contacts for a few months, you might send them a note or e-mail about an article you read, or relevant new technology or law to keep your name fresh in their minds.

As a group, paralegals are usually good at networking and supporting one another. It's a good idea to keep lists of agencies at which you can get jobs, and share them with paralegals you know. Many paralegals volunteer, partly to learn and partly to network. If you're doing volunteer work, it looks good on your resume and you meet people. Some paralegals go on to get good jobs through the people they meet through volunteer work.

THE INSIDE TRACK

Who: Jessica Beckett

What: Law Student and Former Legal Assistant

Where: O'Melveny & Myers

               San Francisco, California

INSIDER'S STORY

After I graduated from Brown University in Providence, Rhode Island, I had the itch to leave the East Coast where I was born and raised, and head out west, so I packed everything up and moved to San Francisco. At that time I was pretty much set on becoming an attorney, but I wanted to be absolutely sure before I made the commitment to go to law school. I also wanted to take a year or so off before I returned to school; being a paralegal seemed like the best way to go—I thought I could make some contacts and also learn what it was like to work at a law firm. The only problem was that I lacked real office experience, which is what many firms look for in paralegals. I learned very quickly that I had to play up the research and organizational skills that I used in college. My earliest interviews were disasters, but with each consecutive interview that I went on, I learned a bit more, until I was finally fully prepared to impress my interviewer. I think interviewing with law firms is probably one of the hardest things to do because often you are interviewed by attorneys, and many of them make you feel you are be cross-examined. If you're not prepared, they'll know right away.

I started off my job-hunting process by posting my resume on Monster.com, and I got a couple of responses. For me, though, networking seemed to work the best. My father is an attorney, so through him it was easy for me to find people at local firms. Once I had some names, I contacted them and asked if I could talk to them on the phone to learn more about working at a law firm. Once I felt comfortable with them, I asked if they were hiring and usually sent them a copy of my resume. I got several interviews this way. Eventually I found my job through someone I knew at a firm who told me they were hiring. I was hired as a paralegal in the Transactional Department at O'Melveny & Myers in San Francisco. I did mostly corporate and real estate work.

My work was standard paralegal stuff: Preparing closing binders at the end of a deal; organizing documents in preparation for a closing; organizing files of documents for storage after a deal; preparing the closing room for the day of execution; drafting agreements; and contacting the clients to get documents. In the corporate work, I frequently had to prepare tables that reflected stock options or shares and figure out what percentage of shares various parties owned. This involved quite a bit of work with math. It wasn't the most exciting work. To be honest, sometimes I found the work incredibly boring. At times I wished the attorneys would give me more challenging projects that required more thought and analysis, but until the attorneys really trust you, you will spend most of your time putting together closing binders and organizing filed documents. This can be very tedious, but it's important work, and it has to be done. The satisfying thing is that if you develop a good working relationship with an attorney, you can end up doing the work of a first- or second-year attorney as a paralegal, which is exciting and more challenging. For me, that was important because it solidified my decision to go to law school.

I would recommend being a paralegal to anyone in my position. Working as a paralegal at a firm really gives you a clear idea of whether or not you are cut out to be an attorney. For me it was a positive experience—I will be attending the law school at UC Hastings in San Francisco this fall.

CHAPTER five

JOB-SEARCH SKILLS AND INTERVIEWING

ONCE YOU'VE narrowed your job search and located some job openings, the process of selling yourself to a potential employer begins. Your first contact with a potential employer may be on paper, in the form of a resume and cover letter. If you make a good impression on paper, your next contact will be in person, in the form of an interview.

WHETHER YOU are responding to an advertisement, following up on a networking opportunity, or making a cold contact, your resume is usually the first means by which a potential employer learns about you. Your resume is the advertisement you write to help sell yourself, and it helps to think of it that way. Think about ads you've seen in the newspaper or a magazine that made you want to go to a store and look at the item. Maybe you didn't end up buying it, but the ad made you consider it. That's what you want a resume to do for you.

A successful advertisement catches your attention by combining several elements: composition, clarity, content, and concentration. Falling short in any of these areas can cause a reader to pass over the ad; you want to make sure that a prospective employer will not be tempted to pass over *your* ad.

There are many sources available to learn about writing resumes; this chapter addresses the specific issue of resumes for paralegals.

Even if you've written dozens of resumes in your day, it is probably worth your while to find a good resume-writing book or article to help you draft a resume for your new paralegal career. Your placement office may have a bank of former students' resumes that you can look at as well. Books such as *Resumes That Get You Hired* (LearningExpress, 2006) contain excellent general guidelines. And there are plenty of online resources to help you create a winning resume, including the following:

- ▶ ABA Resume Writing (www.abastaff.com/resources/resume.html)
- ▶ Accent Resume Writing (www.accent-resume-writing.com)
- ▶ Creative Professional Resumes (www.resumesbycpr.com)
- ▶ Free Resume Tips (www.free-resume-tips.com)
- ▶ Professional Association of Resume Writers (www.parw.com)
- ▶ Proven Resumes (www.provenresumes.com)
- ▶ eResumes & Resume Writing Services (www.eresumes.com)
- ▶ Resumania (www.resumania.com)
- ▶ Resume Broadcaster (www.resumebroadcaster.com)
- ▶ Resumedotcom (www.resumedotcom.com)

Once you have a rough draft, consider the four important elements of resume writing.

WHAT SHOULD A RESUME LOOK LIKE?

If your resume doesn't look acceptable on a very basic level, it will probably get no more than a quick glance. You can find all kinds of advice about lengths of resumes, the kinds of paper they should be on, and what fonts you should use, as well as some suggestions for resumes that are real "eye catchers." When looking for a job in the legal field, keep in mind that it is a profession that is, in large part, defined by tradition and, therefore, fairly conservative. This doesn't mean in the political sense; and it doesn't mean you can't find a law firm where T-shirts are the preferred office attire. What it means is that much of what lawyers do every day has been done a million times before by other lawyers, and most lawyers take a certain comfort in tradition.

So make conservative choices when it comes to your resume. Forgo the neon red paper and avoid parchment. Stick with something tried and true, such as white, cream, or gray. Many larger law firms will want to scan your resume into their computer system to make it accessible to all the partners. Employment agencies will want to do this, too. To help with the scanning process, send out originals of your resume, not photocopies. Light-colored, $8\frac{1}{2} \times 11$ paper, printed on one side only, will scan more easily. Try to avoid using tabs and any graphics or shadings. Don't use vertical or horizontal lines. Finally, don't staple the pages of your resume. If your resume is fairly conservative, it should scan fine. There's more information on computers and resumes in the next section.

Don't use an off-the-wall font. Would you want to read this whole page if it was printed like this?

Stick to more common computer fonts, such as Times New Roman. Ignore advice on how to make your resume stand out from all the rest. Especially avoid composing your resume so that it looks like a pamphlet or a pleading or a court decision. Like many other nontraditional tactics, it will send the message that you don't believe you can get an interview on your merits, so you've resorted to flashy advertising. Legal employers feel the same way about flashy resumes as the rest of us feel about that guy who comes on TV late at night screaming about stereos or used cars and causes us to dive for the remote's mute button.

Some resume advisers will tell you that you should never send out a resume that is more than one page long. I'm not convinced that is necessarily true. If, however, you have prior work experience and you draft a resume that is more than two pages, or you went straight from high school to paralegal training and you draft a resume that is more than one page, it probably means you are including irrelevant information or are being unnecessarily verbose. Read the rest of these suggestions and then try to cut it down. In the end, though, the content of your resume and how effectively you get it across to a prospective employer is what matters; if you need two or three pages to do that, use them.

SAY IT CLEARLY AND CONCISELY

No matter how gorgeous your resume is, it won't do any good if a prospective employer finds it difficult to read. There is only one hard and fast rule of resume writing: Never send out a resume that contains mistakes. Proofread it several times and use your spell-check. For most people, writing a resume is an ongoing process, so remember to check it over every time you make a change. There is absolutely no excuse for sending out a resume with misspelled words or grammatical errors. After you proofread it, ask one or two friends to read it over, too. If you are uncertain about a grammatical construction, change it.

In addition to checking spelling and grammar, you want to make sure that your resume is well written. Resume writing is quite different from other kinds of writing, and it takes some practice. For one thing, most resumes don't use complete sentences. You'd rarely write, "As manager of the housewares department, I managed 14 employees and was in charge of ordering $2.5 million worth of merchandise annually." Instead, you'd write, "Managed $2.5 million housewares department with 14 employees." Still, all the other rules of grammar apply to writing a resume. Tenses and numbers need to match, and double negatives and other awkward constructions are not acceptable. It is also important to be concise when writing a resume. It creates the impression that you are an efficient person.

The ability to communicate well is vital in the law field, and it is a skill that legal employers value highly. If they read something on your resume that causes them to say "Huh?" you won't look good. In addition to effective communication, paralegals need to demonstrate their talents in organization and analysis. These three skills can easily be reflected in your resume.

You demonstrate your communication abilities not only by making sure everything is spelled correctly and is grammatically accurate, but also by how well you write your resume. Word choice contributes to the clarity and persuasiveness of your resume. Experts have long recommended using verbs (action words) rather than nouns to promote yourself in a resume.

MAKING YOUR RESUME COMPUTER FRIENDLY

More and more job applicants are posting their resumes on the Internet, and many large firms are scanning resumes into their computer system, which allows people to call your resume up on their computers. Once your resume is on the Internet or in a computer system, potential employers will access it by searching for keywords. Keywords are simply words or phrases that indicate areas of expertise within an industry, in this case, the legal profession. They tend to be nouns, not verbs.

In addition to Internet-posting and in-house scanning, you need a resume that can be successfully sent via e-mail. If you're going to be applying for jobs online or submitting your resume via e-mail, you will need to create an electronic resume (in addition to a traditional printed resume).

When e-mailing your electronic resume directly to an employer, as a general rule, the document should be saved in an ASCII, Rich Text, or plain text file. Contact the employer directly to see which method is preferred.

When you send a resume via e-mail, the message should begin as a cover letter (and contain the same information as a cover letter). You can then either attach the resume file to the e-mail message or paste the resume text within the message, depending on what the employer asks for. Be sure to include your e-mail address as well as your regular mailing address and phone number(s) within all e-mail correspondence. Never assume an employer will receive your message and simply hit "respond" using their e-mail software to contact you. It doesn't hurt to put the most important information in the top one-third of your resume—in case the potential employer doesn't print it out.

Guidelines for Creating an Electronic Resume to Be Saved and Submitted in ASCII Format

■ Set the left and right margins on the document so that 6.5 inches of text will be displayed per line. This will ensure that the text won't automatically wrap to the next line (unless you want it to).

■ Use a basic, 12-point text font, such as Times New Roman.

- Avoid using bullets or other symbols. Instead, use an asterisk (*) or a dash (-). Instead of using the percentage sign (%) spell out the word *percent*.

- Use the spell-check feature of the software used to create your electronic resume and then proofread the document carefully. Just as applicant-tracking software is designed to pick out keywords from your resume that showcase you as a qualified applicant, these same software packages used by employers can also instantly count the number of typos and spelling errors in your document and report that to an employer as well.

- Avoid using multiple columns, tables, or charts within your document.

- Within the text, avoid abbreviations—spell everything out. For example, use the word *Director*, not *Dir.*, or *Vice President* as opposed to *VP*. In terms of degrees, however, it's acceptable to use terms like *MBA*, *BA*, *PhD*, and so on.

Properly formatting your electronic resume is critical to having it scanned or read properly; however, it's what you say within your resume that will ultimately get you hired. According to Rebecca Smith, author of *Electronic Resumes & Online Networking* (Career Press, 2nd Edition) and the companion website (www.eresumes.com), "Keywords are the basis of the electronic search and retrieval process. They provide the context from which to search for a resume in a database, whether the database is a proprietary one that serves a specific purpose, or whether it is a Web-based search engine that serves the general public. Keywords are a tool to browse quickly without having to access the complete text. Keywords are used to identify and retrieve a resume for the user.

"Employers and recruiters generally search resume databases using keywords—nouns and phrases that highlight technical and professional areas of expertise, industry-related jargon, projects, achievements, special task forces, and other distinctive features about a prospect's work history."

The emphasis is not on trying to second-guess every possible keyword a recruiter may use to find your resume. Your focus is on selecting and organizing your resume's content to highlight those keywords for a variety of online situations. The idea is to identify all possible keywords that are appropriate to your skills and accomplishments that support the kind of jobs you are looking for. But to do that, you must apply traditional resume-writing principles to the concept of extracting those keywords from your resume. Once you have written your resume, then you can identify your strategic keywords based on how you imagine people will search for your resume.

The keywords you incorporate into your resume should support or be relevant to your job objective. Some of the best places within your resume to incorporate keywords are when listing:

► Job titles
► Responsibilities
► Accomplishments
► Skills
► Certifications

Industry-related buzzwords, job-related technical jargon, licenses, and degrees are among the other opportunities you will have to come up with keywords to add to your electronic resume. If you are posting your resume on the Internet, look for the categories that websites use and make sure you use them, too. Be sure the word *paralegal* appears somewhere on your resume, and use accepted professional jargon. Don't, for example, write that you are interested in doing trial work. Someone scanning your resume will probably look for the word *litigation* instead.

For scanned resumes, *manager* is a better bet than *managed*. Verbs such as *initiated, inspired*, and *directed* probably won't be keywords either. However, you can still use them—just be sure they aren't taking the place of other possible keywords or can't be substituted with other possible keywords.

Keywords are often connected by *and* rather than *or*. If an employer is looking for someone interested in being a litigation paralegal in a criminal law firm, your resume won't come up if it contains only *litigation paralegal* and not *criminal*. It may be helpful to look at some of the resumes posted on the Internet; think about the keywords you would use to search for them. The successful hits you get will indicate the words you should be using.

An excellent resource for helping you select the best keywords to use within your electronic resume is *The Occupational Outlook Handbook* (published by the U.S. Department of Labor). This publication is available, free of charge, online (www.bls.gov/oco/ocos114.htm); however, a printed edition can also be found at most public libraries.

WHAT GOES ON A RESUME?

When you are just starting out, it is tempting to try to put everything you can think of on your resume to try to make it look more substantial. Don't. Stick to what's important and pertinent. Surrounding the important information with a lot of white space will make it stand out more, and that's good—it's a basic principle of advertising.

Don't include hobbies or interests. Quite frankly, a potential employer doesn't care whether you enjoy constructing card houses and practicing bird calls. Under no circumstances should you include personal information such as age, gender, religion, health or marital status, or number of children. For one thing, it's illegal for employers to ask about those things, and it's illegal for a reason: It has nothing to do with how well a person can do a job. The only personal information that belongs on your resume is your name, address, phone number, cell phone number, and e-mail address, along with a fax number if you have one. And, by the way, your name and contact information should be on every page you send, in case the pages get separated.

People often overlook or discount volunteer work when composing their resumes. Don't! For one thing, you gain skills and experience from these jobs just as you do from jobs you are paid for. Volunteering also indicates that you work well with others and that you are committed to your community. (Keep this in mind as you go through your paralegal training; if you are short on experience, you might think about volunteering.) Also, make sure your resume includes any memberships and activities in professional organizations; they help demonstrate your commitment to the profession.

Another way to make yourself look more experienced is by including your internship. Some new graduates overlook this, considering it "just part of school." But for most newly graduated paralegals, it is their only legal experience and perhaps their only work experience. The point of an internship is to give you on-the-job training. You learned things on that internship that will help you on a new job; be sure to include them.

Make sure you don't overlook any previous experience. Applicants who are changing careers sometimes think the things they did in their previous work life don't apply to being a paralegal, but that's just not true. Any job you held taught you something that will make you a better legal assistant. At the very least, it taught you the responsibility of showing up for work regularly and on time. No doubt you also learned about working with others and organizing your time. Beyond that, many jobs provide you with experience that will be highly valued by legal employers. Careers such as medicine, accounting, real estate, human resources, and insurance, as well as many others, will be considered hiring plusses by potential employers.

In addition to work experience, you may have life experience that should be emphasized for legal employers. Did you help a spouse in a business? Were you a candidate for public office? Any number of experiences can add to your attractiveness as a paralegal candidate. Especially if you don't have a great deal of work experience, be creative with other things you've done in your life. "Be creative" doesn't mean "lie." Just sit down and think about the things you've done; which have taught you lessons that are valuable for a paralegal to know? Find a way to include those experiences on your resume or in your cover letter.

HOW TO TAILOR YOUR RESUME

Each time you send out a resume, whether in response to an ad or following up on a networking lead or even a cold contact, you should concentrate on tailoring your approach for the employer you are contacting. It was recommended that you should spend some time pursuing your dream job; well, it may be that you have a couple of dream jobs, and no doubt you will also be watching out for the close-to-dream-job opening. Let's say you're interested in being a civil litigation paralegal, but you're particularly interested in insurance litigation, because every summer in high school, you worked in your mom's insurance office and you really enjoyed it. You'd probably also be willing to take a position in the human resources office of an insurance company or anywhere in a large firm that does insurance work, just to get your foot in the door. Insurance litigation is your dream job; the others are your close-to-dream jobs. And if enough time passes, you'll be happy to take any litigation position in any kind of office. Right there, you need at least four resumes.

The resume for the insurance litigation job stresses the work you did in your mom's office, the litigation skills you learned at your internship, and how well you did in civil procedure in paralegal school. Although it depends on what format you are using, you may very well stress them in that order. For a litigation position in a large firm that handles insurance, you'd probably stress your internship and education—but make sure your insurance experience stands out, too. For the human resources job, you'd emphasize your insurance experience and any employment law classes or experience. Finally, for the basic entry-level job, you'd want to construct your resume to show that you are a generalist.

Most books that tell you how to write a resume include advice about the information you should gather before you start. If you keep all of that information at hand, it won't be that difficult to construct a resume that targets a particular job—that concentrates your information so that a prospective employer will see that you are a likely candidate for this opening. In many cases, a few changes to a basic resume are enough to make it appropriate for a particular job opening. One good way to approach tailoring your resume for a particular opening is to sit for a minute and imagine what you think the job would be like. Imagine, based on the description of the job, the major things you will be expected to do day to day. Then look at your experience and education and decide how to present your information so that the employer will know that you are capable of doing those tasks.

Finally, make sure you get your resume to the appropriate person in the appropriate way. If you got the person's name through a networking contact, your contact may deliver it or suggest that you deliver it in person; most likely, though, you should mail it. If you are making a cold contact—that is, if you are contacting a firm that you found through your research but that is not actively looking to fill a position—make sure you find out the name of the hiring partner or head of the paralegal department and send your resume to that person. If you are responding to an ad, make sure you do what the ad says. If it directs you to e-mail your resume, e-mail it. If it indicates you should send a writing sample, make sure you include one. (If you are using a sample you wrote on a job or internship, you must black out all names and any other identifying information.) Demonstrate your ability to attend to detail.

Content

Use the following questionnaire to gather the information you will need for your resume.

Contact Information

The only personal information that belongs on your resume is your name (on every page, if your resume exceeds one page in length), address, phone number, fax number, and e-mail address.

Full name: _____

Permanent street address: _____

City, state, zip: _____

Daytime telephone number: _____

Evening telephone number: _____

Pager/cell phone number (optional): _____

Fax number (optional): _____

E-mail address: _____

Personal website address/online portfolio URL: _____

School address (if applicable): _____

Your phone number at school (if applicable): _____

Job/Career Objective(s)

Write a short description of the job you're seeking. Be sure to include as much information as possible about how you can use your skills to the employer's benefit. Later, you will condense this answer into one short sentence.

_____

_____

_____

What is the job title you're looking to find? (i.e., *paralegal*) _____

_____

Educational Background

Be sure to include your internships in this section. For most recent graduates, it is their only legal experience and perhaps their only work experience.

Include the skills you learned that will be applicable to the position for which you're applying.

List the most recent college or university you've attended:_____

_____

City/state:_____

What year did you start?_____

Graduation month/year:_____

Degree(s) and/or award(s) earned:_____

Your major:_____

Your minor(s):_____

List some of your most impressive accomplishments, extracurricular activi-
    ties, club affiliations, etc.:_____

List computer courses you've taken that help qualify you for the job you're
    seeking:_____

_____

_____

Grade point average (GPA):_____

Other colleges/universities you've attended:_____

_____

City/state:_____

What year did you start?_____

Graduation month/year:_____

Degree(s) and/or award(s) earned:_____

Your major:_____

Your minor(s):_____

List some of your most impressive accomplishments, extracurricular activi-
    ties, club affiliations, etc.:_____

List computer courses you've taken that help qualify you for the job you're
    seeking:_____

_____

_____

Grade point average (GPA):_____

High school attended:_____

City/state:_____

Graduation date:_____

Grade point average (GPA):_____

List the names and phone numbers of one or two current or past professors/teachers (or guidance counselors) you can contact about obtaining a letter of recommendation or list as a reference:_____

_____

_____

Personal Skills and Abilities

Your *personal skill set* (the combination of skills you possess) is something that differentiates you from everyone else. Skills that are marketable in the workplace aren't always taught in school, however. Your ability to manage people, stay cool under pressure, remain organized, surf the Internet, use software applications, speak in public, communicate well in writing, communicate in multiple languages, or perform research are all examples of marketable skills.

When reading job descriptions or help wanted ads, pay careful attention to the wording used to describe what the employer is looking for. As you customize your resume for a specific employer, you will want to match up what the employer is looking for with your own qualifications as closely as possible. Try to utilize the wording provided by the employer within the classified ad or job description.

What do you believe is your most marketable skill? Why?_____

_____

_____

List three or four specific examples of how you have used this skill in the past while at work. What was accomplished as a result?

1._____

2._____

3._____

4._____

What are keywords or buzzwords that can be used to describe your skill?_____

_____

What is another of your marketable skills? _____

Provide at least three examples of how you've used this skill in the workplace:

1. _____

2. _____

3. _____

What unusual or unique skill(s) do you possess that help you stand out from other applicants applying for the same types of positions as you?

_____

_____

How have you already proven this skill is useful in the workplace?

_____

What computer skills do you possess? _____

What computer software packages are you proficient in (such as Microsoft Office—Word, Excel, PowerPoint, FrontPage, etc.)? _____

_____

_____

Thinking carefully, what skills do you believe you currently lack?

_____

What skills do you have that need to be polished or enhanced to make you a more appealing candidate? _____

_____

What options are available to you to either obtain or brush up on the skills you believe need improvement (for example, evening/weekend classes at a college or university, adult education classes, seminars, books, home study courses, on-the-job-training, etc.)? _____

_____

_____

In what time frame could you realistically obtain this training?

_____

_____

Work/Employment History

Complete the following employment-related questions for all of your previous employers, including part-time or summer jobs held while in school, as well as temp jobs, internships, and volunteering. You probably won't want to reveal your past earning history to a potential employer, but you may want this information available as reference when you begin negotiating your future salary, benefits, and overall compensation package.

Most recent employer: _____

City/state: _____

Year you began work: _____

Year you stopped working (write "present" if still employed): _____

Job title: _____

Job description: _____

_____

Reason for leaving: _____

What were your three proudest accomplishments while holding this job?

1. _____

2. _____

3. _____

Contact person at the company who can provide a reference: _____

_____

Contact person's phone number: _____

Annual salary earned: _____

Employer: _____

City/state: _____

Year you began work: _____

Year you stopped working (write "present" if still employed): _____

Job title: _____

Job description: _____

_____

Reason for leaving: _____

What were your three proudest accomplishments while holding this job?

1. _____

2. _____

3. _____

Contact person at the company who can provide a reference:_____

_____

Contact person's phone number:_____

Annual salary earned:_____

Military Service (if applicable)

Branch served in:_____

Years served:_____

Highest rank achieved:_____

Decorations or awards earned:_____

Special skills or training you obtained:_____

Professional Accreditations and Licenses

List any and all of the professional accreditations and/or licenses you have earned thus far in your career. Be sure to highlight items that directly relate to the job(s) you will be applying for:

_____

_____

Hobbies and Special Interests

You may have life experience that should be emphasized for legal employers. Did you help a spouse in a business? Were you a candidate for public office? Any number of experiences can add to your attractiveness as a paralegal candidate. If you don't have a great deal of work experience, this part of your resume is very important. Think about the things you've done that have taught you lessons that are valuable for a paralegal to know. If you can't find a way to include those experiences on your resume, mention them in your cover letter.

List any hobbies or special interests you have that are not necessarily work related, but that potentially could separate you from the competition. Can any of the skills utilized in your hobby be adapted for the workplace?

_____

_____

_____

What nonprofessional clubs or organizations do you belong to or actively participate in?

_____

_____

_____

Personal/Professional Ambitions

You may not want to share these on your resume, but answering the following questions will help you focus your search and prepare for possible interviewing topics.

What are your long-term goals?

Personal: _____

_____

_____

Professional: _____

_____

_____

Financial: _____

_____

_____

For your personal, professional, and then financial goals, what are five smaller, short-term goals you can begin working toward achieving right now that will help you ultimately achieve each of your long-term goals?

Short-term personal goals:

1. _____
2. _____
3. _____
4. _____
5. _____

Short-term professional goals:

1. _____
2. _____
3. _____
4. _____
5. _____

Short-term financial goals:

1. _____

2. _____

3. _____

4. _____

5. _____

Will the job(s) you will be applying for help you achieve your long-term goals and objectives? If yes, how? If no, why not? _____

_____

_____

_____

Describe your current personal, professional, and financial situation.

_____

_____

_____

What would you most like to improve about your life overall? _____

_____

_____

_____

What are a few things you can do, starting immediately, to bring about positive changes in your personal, professional, or financial life? _____

_____

_____

_____

Where would you like to be personally, professionally, and financially five and ten years down the road? _____

_____

_____

_____

What needs to be done to achieve these long-term goals or objectives?

_____

_____

_____

What are some of the qualities about your personality that you're most proud of? _____

_____

_____

_____

What are some of the qualities about your personality that you believe need improvement? _____

_____

_____

What do others most like about you? _____

_____

_____

What do you think others least like about you? _____

_____

_____

If you decided to pursue additional education, what would you study and why? How would this help you professionally? _____

_____

_____

_____

If you had more free time, what would you spend it doing? _____

_____

_____

_____

List several accomplishments in your personal and professional life that you're most proud of. Why did you choose these things?

1. _____
2. _____
3. _____
4. _____
5. _____

What were your strongest and favorite subjects in school? Is there a way to incorporate these interests into the job(s) or career path you're pursuing?

_____

_____

_____

What do you believe is your biggest weakness? Why wouldn't an employer hire you? _____

_____

_____

What would be the ideal atmosphere for you to work in? Do you prefer a large corporate atmosphere, working at home, or working in a small office?

_____

_____

_____

List five qualities about a new job that would make it the ideal employment opportunity for you:

1. _____
2. _____
3. _____
4. _____
5. _____

What did you like most about the last place you worked? _____

_____

What did you like least about the last place you worked? _____

_____

What work-related tasks are you particularly good at? _____

_____

_____

What type of coworkers would you prefer to have? _____

_____

_____

When it comes to work-related benefits and perks, what's most important to you? _____

_____

_____

_____

When you're recognized for doing a good job at work, how do you like to be rewarded?_____

_____

_____

If you were to write a help wanted ad describing your dream job, what would the ad say?_____

_____

_____

Common Resume Errors to Avoid

- Stretching the truth. A growing number of employers are verifying all resume information. If you're caught lying, you won't be offered a job, or you could be fired later if it's discovered that you weren't truthful.

- Including any references to money. This includes past salary or how much you're looking to earn within your resume and cover letter.

- Including on your resume the reasons that you stopped working for an employer, switched jobs, or are currently looking for a new job. Do not include a line in your resume saying, "Unemployed" or "Out of Work" along with the corresponding dates to fill a time gap.

- Having a typo or grammatical error in a resume. If you refuse to take the time necessary to proofread your resume, why should an employer assume you'd take the time needed to do your job properly if you're hired?

- Using long paragraphs to describe past work experience. Use a bulleted list instead. Most employers will spend less than one minute initially reading a resume.

Following are two sample resumes. The first is for an applicant who wants to highlight both previous experience as a tax preparer and educational background. The second is for an applicant who has more education than experience.

Pat Paralegal

1234 Broadway
Mytown, ST 00000
Phone and fax: 007-555-5678
E-mail: pat89@online.com

OBJECTIVE

To work as a paralegal in a position that allows me to utilize and enhance my specialized computer skills and tax preparation experience.

EXPERIENCE

September–November 2006

Paralegal Intern, Zelda County Attorney's Office, 180 West Bubba Street, Mytown, ST 00000; 007-555-3456

Duties:

Answered multiline telephones

Greeted the public

Assisted with scheduling meetings, events, and appointments

Assisted with filing of pleadings

Performed legal research on CD-ROM, online, and in the library

Wrote legal memoranda

Shepardized cases

Filed documents

January 2002–April 2006

Tax Consultant, H&R BLOCK, 1440 Ivy Road, Mytown, ST 00000; 007-555-1040

Duties:

Interviewed clients

Prepared individual income tax returns, including out-of-state returns

Researched and applied IRS rules and regulations

January 2001–Present

Volunteer, Dogs and Cats Shelter, RR 1, Mytown, ST 00000, 007-555-9876

Duties:

Interview adopters

Write column for newsletter

EDUCATION

Associate of Arts, Paralegal Studies, May 2007
Paralegal College, 7890 Troubadour Street, Mytown, ST 00000

Associate of Science, Computer Technology, December 2005
Community College, Eli Hills Campus, Mytown, ST 00000

SKILLS

Fluent in Spanish

Linda Legal Assistant

1234 Broadway • Mytown, ST 00000
Phone and fax: 007-555-5678 • Email: pat89@online.com

OBJECTIVE

Entry-level paralegal position that allows me to utilize and enhance my specialized computer skills and paralegal education.

EDUCATION

Bachelor of Arts, Paralegal Certificate, May 2006, State University, Mytown, ST 00000

RELEVANT COURSES

Legal Research and Writing
Business Law
Litigation
Family Law
Criminal Law

EXPERIENCE

September–December 2006, Paralegal Intern, Zelda County Attorney's Office, 180 West Bubba Street, Mytown, ST 00000, 007-555-3456

Duties:

Answered multiline telephones
Greeted the public
Assisted with scheduling meetings, events, and appointments
Assisted with filing of pleadings
Performed legal research on CD-ROM, online, and in the library
Wrote legal memorandum
Shepardized cases
Filed documents
Updated website

September 2004–August 2005, Sales Associate, The Store, 345 Route 66, Mytown, ST 00000, 007-555-6543

Duties:

Operated cash register
Stocked shelves
Assisted customers

January 1993–present, Volunteer, Dogs and Cats Shelter, RR 1, Mytown, ST 00000, 007-555-9876

Duties:

Interview adopters
Write column for newsletter
Bathe dogs

SKILLS

Fluent in Spanish

WRITING A COVER LETTER

You should never send out a resume without a cover letter. The cover letter aims your resume directly at the available job; your resume, in turn, describes in detail why you are the person for the job. If your cover letter is a failure, your resume will get only a cursory glance at best. Your cover letter should give the impression that you are a good candidate for the job.

Most people seem to feel that writing cover letters is a real pain. You should view it, however, as another opportunity to demonstrate your writing skills, as well as your ability to organize and analyze. Although you tailor your resume to some degree for different job openings, employers expect that you will send the same resume to several potential employers. The cover letter, on the other hand, should be personalized and directed to the particular job opening.

How to Format Your Cover Letter

Your cover letter needs to grab the attention of the reader, but not because it's so bizarre that it will be posted on the office bulletin board for everyone to laugh at. As with your resume, avoid fancy fonts and stationery; choose something that matches or coordinates with your resume. Your cover letter should always be printed on good paper. Consider using letterhead with your name, address, phone and fax numbers, and e-mail address. You don't have to spend a lot of money to have letterhead stationery printed; you can make it on your computer.

A cover letter should be composed in the same way as a business letter. It should include your address (preferably in the letterhead), the date, the name and address of the person the letter is sent to, and a salutation. At the end of the body of the letter, you should include a closing (such as "Sincerely" or "Respectfully"), your signature, and your name typed out below. Other formatting choices are up to you—for example, whether you prefer block paragraphs or indented paragraphs and whether you write "enc." at the bottom, indicating there is material (your resume) enclosed with the letter.

Rarely do you need a cover letter that is more than one page. On occasion, an advertisement for a job will ask for a resume and a detailed statement of interest (or words to that effect). Sometimes, ads will even ask you to address specific questions or issues in your letter, such as your goals, what you can contribute to the organization, etc. In such cases, you may need to write a letter that is more than one page. Normally, however, your letter should be contained on one page.

Write Clearly and Concisely

You should never send out a cover letter with a grammatical or spelling error. Even when you are pressed for time and rushing to get a letter out, make sure to spell-check it and proofread it carefully. If writing letters doesn't come naturally to you—and writing cover letters doesn't come naturally to most of us—have someone read it over. It should be accurate, clear, and concise. It serves as a letter of introduction, an extension of your advertisement. Your cover letter needs to convince a prospective employer that *you* are one of the people who should be interviewed for this position.

Your cover letter should begin with some sort of introduction, followed by an explanation of why you are right for this job and a closing paragraph. As with your resume, it is vital that your cover letter be well written; however, it requires a different writing style. Sentence fragments don't work in a cover letter. In addition, a resume offers a somewhat formal presentation of your background, but a cover letter should let a bit of your personality come through. It should be written in an almost conversational tone. It shouldn't be quite as informal as the tone of this book—for example, don't use contractions or slang in a cover letter—but you should view it as your first chance to "chat" with a prospective employer. The resume tells employers what you know and what you can do; the cover letter should tell them a little bit about who you are.

What to Include in Your Cover Letter

Much more than a resume, a cover letter is targeted to a particular job. The concentration on a particular job opening is the major component of a cover letter. A cover letter should never read like a form letter; the best way to avoid that is by writing a new letter for every job you apply for. A cover let-ter does more than just repeat the information in your resume. It tells the prospective employer why you are the one for a particular job.

In the first paragraph, you should indicate why you are writing this letter at this time. You may write something like

- ▶ "I would like to apply for the litigation paralegal position advertised in the April 11 *Sunday Post*."
- ▶ "I am writing in response to your ad in the February 1 *Sunday Times*."
- ▶ "I am interested in obtaining an entry-level paralegal position with your firm."
- ▶ "If you are looking for a legal assistant with insurance experience and top-notch paralegal training, you will be interested in talking to me."
- ▶ "We met last July at the NALA Convention. I will be graduating from my paralegal program in May."

The first paragraph also usually indicates that your resume is enclosed for consideration, although this may also be in the closing paragraph.

In the body of the cover letter, you want to explain why your training and experience make you the right person for the job. The cover letter provides you with the opportunity to include something that is not on your resume. For example, life experience can be difficult to incorporate into a resume, but it is much easier to talk about in a letter. Also, the body of the letter should highlight and summarize the information in your resume. You have to assume that the employer is going to read your resume, so don't just repeat things. For example, instead of writing, "Before paralegal school, I worked at The Store for two years, and before that at The Shop for three years," try something like, "I have five years of retail experience in which I interacted with the public on a daily basis." The body of the letter is your opportunity to explain why the employer should care about your experience and training.

In the body of the letter, you can also include information about how soon you are available for employment or why (if it's the case) you are applying for a job out of town. You may also include the specifics that you are looking for in a job—if they are either nonnegotiable or flattering to the employer. You should definitely make some direct reference to the specific position and organization. Here are some examples:

▶ "I will graduate on May 16 and will be available for employment immediately. A position with your firm appeals to me because I understand you do a great deal of plaintiff employment work, and that is a field I am very interested in. Employment law was one of the electives I chose as a student. In addition, at this time I am looking for part-time employment and I believe you currently have a part-time opening."

▶ "Although my internship was with the County Attorney's Office, I have come to realize that while that work was intensely interesting, I would prefer a position in the private sector that will afford me the opportunity to call on my real estate experience and my paralegal training. I believe your firm is the place for me and I am certain I would be an asset to you."

▶ "As you look at my resume, you will notice that although I am just now finishing my paralegal training, I offer a background in administration and problem solving. Because your company has recently undergone a major expansion, I believe you would find me a valuable addition to your staff."

Finally, the last paragraph (some people prefer it to be two short paragraphs) should thank the person, make a reference to future contact, and offer to provide further information.

▶ "Thank you for your consideration. Please contact me at the address or phone number above if you need any further information."

▶ "I look forward to meeting you to discuss this job opening."

▶ "Thank you, and I look forward to speaking with you in person."

▶ "I would welcome the opportunity to discuss the match between my skills and your needs in more detail. You can contact me at the address or phone number above, except for the week of the 27th, when I will be out of town. Thank you for your time."

A cover letter provides the opportunity for you to sell yourself for a particular job, and it should be tailored that way. The letter should indicate some knowledge about what makes this job better than all the other jobs and what makes you a better candidate than all the other candidates.

SURVIVING YOUR INTERVIEW

When job hunting, you'll send out carefully worded resumes and cover letters. But some of the time, you'll either get a polite brush-off or no response at all. After a while, you might become frustrated. Then, miracle of miracles, someone wants to interview you, and you immediately revive your dream of fleeing the country to aid rebels trying to overthrow the corrupt government of some small nation—anything to get out of town!

Although we really want to get an interview, when we get one, we'd rather do almost anything else—go to the dentist, give the cat a bath, clean the oven, *anything*. The tips on the next few pages won't necessarily make your next interview 100% painless, but you can get through it and come out a winner.

Preparing for Your Interview

When you study the law, you will hear judges and lawyers talk about a "level playing field." This means that two parties are equal in contract negotiations or applying for a job or whatever. Generally, in the law, we think a level playing field is a good thing, although it can be tough to achieve. If you prepare for your interview adequately, you'll go a long way toward leveling the field between you and the "big bad" interviewer. As with writing resumes and cover letters, there are many fine sources of information about job interviews; this book goes over some things that are specific to paralegal job hunting, especially when you're after your first job in the field.

Most interviewers will ask, "Why do you want to work here?" Sometimes, the true answer to that question is, "I don't necessarily want to work *here*; I'd be just as happy down the street, but you've got the opening." This is not a good answer. Every time you get an interview, you should prepare an answer to it.

If you managed to get an interview without researching the firm ahead of time, do so now. (If you researched the firm before you applied, as you should have, make sure you saved everything so you can use it now.) Keep researching until you find something that makes you excited about working there. That can sometimes be difficult, but there will be something. Don't forget to keep an eye on the newspapers; if you read about an interesting local case and they mention an attorney, find out where that lawyer works; someday, that may provide you with a reason you want to work at this firm.

Even if you're not asked why you want to work at a firm, find an opportunity to let your interviewer know you've done your research. Is it a fairly new firm or has it been around forever? Is it the largest or one of the smallest firms in town? Did it just win (or lose) a big case?

Of course, before your interview, you'll check the exact address and find out how to get there and where to park. You'll try on your interview outfit and make sure it's comfortable for both walking and sitting. The night before, make sure you'll be armed with everything you need by reviewing the following list.

► Bring your resume (a few copies) and a list of references. I suggest carrying them in a decent briefcase. Remember, it's called a briefcase because it's for carrying briefs; it's a legal thing.

► Make sure you have a decent-looking pen that works and a legal pad, in case you want to take notes.

► Also, have a writing sample with you, even if no one has mentioned it specifically.

► You should also have copies of your transcripts in your briefcase.

► Bring an extra pair of pantyhose; men, of course, may prefer to have an extra tie.

Answering Tough Questions

There are two important things to keep in mind while job hunting. One is that even if you apply and interview for a job, you don't have to take it; and the other is that good interviewers will be trying to sell *you* on coming to work for *them*.

Understanding that you aren't required to take a job just because it's offered makes the interview seem less like a life-or-death situation and more like an opportunity to get to know at least one person at this firm. There are other jobs out there, and although job hunting isn't much fun, you *will* find a job. Realizing that interviewers should be trying to sell you on coming to work for them is helpful, too. Although conducting job interviews is a skill that some people never master, good interviewers want to find a good person to fill the job opening. They already think you're a possibility; even though they may end up hiring someone else, during the interview, they should be convincing you that you would be very happy working there.

Neither of these points takes away from the fact that you have to sell yourself. But in preparing for the interview, keep in mind that you have certain requirements of your own and that you are meeting these potential employers to find out if the two of you are a match.

Greet your interviewer with a firm handshake and an enthusiastic smile. Speak with confidence throughout your interview and let your answers convey your assumption that you will be offered the job. For example, phrase your questions this way: "What would my typical day consist of?" "How many paralegals work here, and what are their areas of expertise?" Answer questions in complete sentences; however, don't ramble on too long in answering any one question. Many hiring managers will ask questions that don't have a right or wrong answer; they ask such questions to evaluate your problem-solving skills.

The world won't end if you stumble or don't know how to answer a question or forget your phone number, but that doesn't mean you shouldn't prepare. At a minimum, get out your resume and look at it and think about what you would want to know about this person. For example, you may be asked why you want to be a paralegal. You'll probably be asked which areas of the law you like best and least. And once you answer, you may be asked why. If you are changing careers, you may be asked why you're changing and what you liked and didn't like about your former career. Spend some time thinking about and practicing ways to answer these questions.

As you look at your resume, note any unusual aspects that might elicit questions. For example, I once worked as a cab driver; as long as that was on my resume, I *always* got asked about it. I was relieved when this experience was more than ten years old and I could leave it off and start talking about other things. If you have a gap in your work history, be prepared to explain why. Be prepared to talk about the kinds of legal computer software you are familiar with, as well as the kinds of work you've done in an internship or a previous job.

If you are not fresh out of paralegal school but are leaving one position for another, you will no doubt be asked why. You will probably be asked about your billable hours at your previous paralegal job, and you may be expected to discuss what went well or poorly at that job, how you handled difficult clients or attorneys, and what you hope will be different about your new job.

The toughest of the tough questions that you will have to deal with are the illegal ones—and, yes, attorneys sometimes ask them. A potential employer is not allowed to ask you about your marital status, whether you have kids or plan to, your age, your religion, or your race (these kinds of questions *may* be asked on anonymous affirmative action forms). Nor can an interviewer employ sneaky techniques to find out (such as "I bet your husband and kids are really proud of you!"). If someone does ask you such a question, you can say, "It's illegal for you to ask me that" and then sit silently until the interviewer says something. Or try to get a handle on why they are asking, and address that. So the answer to "Do you have children?" becomes "If you're asking if I can travel and work overtime, that's generally not a problem." Or you can say something like, "I don't understand the question; what is it you want to know?"

Remember that illegal questions aren't always obvious. Most interviewers know enough not to say, "How old are you, anyway?" But they might say, "Will it bother you if your supervisor is younger than you?" If you encounter this kind of situation, think long and hard before you accept a position with this firm. Also, if you were referred to this interview through an employment agency or your school's placement office, notify that source that you believe you were asked illegal questions.

What follows are some general guidelines to follow when answering questions in an interview:

- ▶ Use complete sentences and proper English.
- ▶ Don't be evasive, especially if you're asked about negative aspects of your employment history.
- ▶ Never imply that a question is "stupid."
- ▶ Don't lie or stretch the truth.
- ▶ Be prepared to answer the same questions multiple times. Make sure your answers are consistent, and never reply, "You already asked me that."
- ▶ Never apologize for negative information regarding your past.

▶ Avoid talking down to an interviewer or making them feel less intelligent than you are.

Asking Questions

When we think about the kinds of questions an interviewee should ask in an interview, we often concentrate on what kinds of questions we think we are expected to ask. But the main goal is to ask the things you really want to know. One exception is that you should probably save questions about salary and benefits for a second interview; a first interview is an opportunity to learn more about the firm.

Beyond that, ask about almost anything. You may want to know about the kinds of assignments you can expect, whether you will be able to follow cases from start to finish, whether you'll have the opportunity to specialize, who manages paralegals and determines their assignments. These are all legitimate questions. You may also have questions about the resources of the firm, such as the computers and library. The number of billable hours you will be expected to produce is certainly something you will want to know.

If the firm is large, you can ask about its structure. For example, is there a paralegal department or are paralegals assigned to attorneys? Do paralegals have secretarial support? Is there a paralegal training program in place? If the firm is small, you may ask how long it has employed paralegals, whether it plans to hire more in the future, and whether paralegals are expected to do significant clerical work. In any size firm, you can ask about chances for promotion.

You can ask what a typical day for a paralegal at the firm is like. Imagine you have been offered this job and another. Think about what you would like to know about this job that would help you decide which one to take.

By the way, you don't need to wait to be asked, "Do you have any questions?" It is perfectly appropriate to ask questions when they fit into the interview. For example, if the interviewer tells you that each paralegal and attorney has a computer, it's a good time to ask what software they use and whether the firm subscribes to an online service.

The following are common interview questions, along with suggestions on how you can best answer them:

▶ What can you tell me about yourself? (Stress your skills and accomplishments. Avoid talking about your family, hobbies, or topics not relevant to your ability to do the job.)

▶ Why have you chosen to pursue a career as a paralegal? (Give specific reasons and examples.)

▶ In your personal or professional life, what has been your greatest failure? What did you learn from that experience? (Be open and honest. Everyone has had some type of failure. Focus on what you learned from the experience and how it helped you grow as a person.)

▶ Why did you leave your previous job? (Try to put a positive spin on your answer, especially if you were fired for negative reasons. Company downsizing, a company going out of business, or some other reason that was out of your control is a perfectly acceptable answer. Remember, your answer will probably be verified.)

▶ What would you consider your biggest accomplishments at your last job? (Talk about what made you a productive employee and valuable asset to your previous employer. Stress that teamwork was involved in achieving your success and that you work well with others.)

▶ What are your long-term goals? (Talk about how you have been following a career path, and where you think this preplanned career path will take you in the future. Describe how you believe the job you're applying for is a logical step forward.)

▶ Why do you think you're the most qualified person to fill this job? (Focus on the positive things that set you apart from the competition: what's unique about you, your skill set, and past experiences. What work-related experiences do you have that relate directly to this job?)

▶ What have you heard about this firm that interests to you? (Focus on the firm's reputation. Refer to positive publicity, personal recommendations from employees, or published information that caught your attention. This shows you've done your research.)

▶ What can you tell about yourself that isn't listed in your resume? (This is yet another opportunity for you to sell yourself to the employer. Take advantage of the opportunity.)

Avoiding Common Interview Mistakes

Once you get invited by a potential employer to come in for an interview, do everything within your power to prepare, and avoid the common mistakes often made by applicants. Remember that for every job you apply for, there are probably dozens of other paralegals who would like to land that same position.

The following are some of the most common mistakes applicants make while preparing for or participating in job interviews, with tips on how to avoid making these mistakes.

> ▶ Don't skip steps in your interview preparation. Just because you've been invited for an interview, you can't afford to "wing it" once you get there. Prior to the interview, spend time doing research about the company, its products/services, and the people you will be meeting with.

> ▶ Never arrive late for an interview. Arriving even five minutes late for a job interview is equivalent to telling an employer you don't want the job. On the day of the interview, plan on arriving at least ten minutes early, and use the restroom before you begin the actual interview.

> ▶ Don't neglect your appearance. First impressions are crucial. Make sure your clothing is wrinkle-free and clean, that your hair is well groomed, and that your makeup (if applicable) looks professional. Always dress up for an interview, even if the dress code at the company is casual. Also, be sure to brush your teeth prior to an interview, especially if you've eaten recently.

> ▶ Prior to an interview, avoid drinking any beverages containing caffeine. Chances are, you will already be nervous about the interview. Drinking coffee or soda won't calm you down.

> ▶ Don't go into the interview unprepared. Prior to the interview, use your research to compile a list of intelligent questions to ask the employer. These questions can be about the company, its products/services, its methods of doing business, the responsibilities of the job you're applying for, and so on. When it's time for you to answer questions, always use complete sentences.

> ▶ Never bring up salary, benefits, or vacation time during the initial interview. Instead, focus on how you (with all of your skills, experience,

and education) can become a valuable asset to the company you're interviewing with. Allow the employer to bring up the compensation package to be offered.

▶ Refrain from discussing your past earning history or what you're hoping to earn. An employer typically looks for the best possible employees for the lowest possible price. Let the employer make you an offer first. When asked, tell the interviewer you're looking for a salary/benefits package that's in line with what's standard in the industry for someone with your qualifications and experience. Try to avoid stating an actual dollar figure.

▶ During the interview, avoid personal topics. There are questions that an employer can't legally ask during an interview situation or on an employment application (as mentioned on page 155). In addition to these topics, refrain from discussing sex, religion, politics, and any other highly personal topics.

▶ Never insult the interviewer. An interviewer may ask what you might perceive to be a stupid or irrelevant question. In some cases, the interviewer is simply testing to see how you will respond. Some questions are asked to test your morals or determine your level of honesty. Other types of questions are used simply to see how you will react in a tough situation. Try to avoid getting caught up in trick questions. Never tell an interviewer that his or her question is stupid or irrelevant.

▶ Throughout the interview, avoid allowing your body language to get out of control. For example, if you're someone who taps your foot when you're nervous, make sure you're aware of your habit so you can control it in an interview situation.

▶ If your job interview takes place over lunch or dinner, refrain from drinking alcohol of any kind.

Follow-Up Procedures

You should follow up your interview with a letter. There is some disagreement about the form this letter should take. When I was in law school, we were told that. Sending a handwritten thank-you letter to everyone you meet in an interview is the tradition many lawyers are used to. On the other hand,

ter on letterhead looks more professional. If your handwriting is
ecipherable, you should definitely type your thank-you letters.
that, check with your placement office and fellow paralegal job
etermine the tradition in your area. You should do what is commonly accepted in your area and makes you feel most comfortable. Note that
there may be times when you have no choice but to handwrite a letter (if you
are out of town or at a professional conference, for example).

Whatever your letter looks like, it should include a warm thank-you
for the interviewer's time and should reiterate your enthusiasm for the
job. You should also say something specific to your interview to give it a
personal touch. Thank-you letters are generally quite short. Here are a
few examples.

▶ "I enjoyed meeting with you yesterday to discuss the paralegal position at Barrister, Counselor, and Solicitor. In addition to providing a
   good deal of information, you made me very enthusiastic about the
   position. I was very pleased to have the opportunity to meet Mr. Law;
   I can see that he will be difficult to replace. I am gratified to be considered for the position."

▶ "Thank you so much for the time you spent with me yesterday. I
   really appreciated the tour of the office and the information you
   shared about the paralegal position. By the way, I double-checked
   when I got home, and the case I was trying to think of was *Marbury
   v. Madison*."

▶ "The legal assistant position we discussed yesterday certainly sounds
   like a challenging one. After reviewing the information you gave me
   about your needs for this job, I am convinced that I am the right person for the position. Thank you for the time and consideration you
   gave me. I look forward to hearing from you again soon."

Basically, a follow-up letter reminds employers who you are and makes
you stand out from the crowd, clarifies (but only if necessary) anything that
you were unable to make clear in the interview, and lets employers know
that you really want this job.

As you begin your job hunt, keep in mind that you are not just looking
for a job but also you're looking for a good job, one you will enjoy and feel

challenged by. At each stage of the hunt—researching the market, sending out resumes and cover letters, having interviews, and accepting or rejecting offers—keep in mind the principles of job hunting. You need to decide who you are going to contact, you have to advertise yourself, and you have to sell yourself. Remember that each of these involves particular activities and particular ways of thinking about yourself and what you want, as well as marketing yourself to appeal to employers. Once you've finished paralegal school and an internship, you have a lot to offer to any legal employer. Keep that in mind throughout the process: You're not begging for a job; you're trying to find an employer who will be a match for your skills and talents.

THE INSIDE TRACK

Who: Manolo Murillo
What: Immigration Paralegal
Where: Los Angeles, California

INSIDER'S STORY

I was born in Bakersfield, California, shortly after my parents emigrated there from Mexico City. Growing up in a largely Hispanic community in southern California, the subjects of immigration and citizenship were often an issue among family and friends.

I had been working for a law firm as a paralegal for three years when I met an immigration lawyer who was starting his own law firm in my hometown, and he needed a legal assistant. I had often thought to myself exactly what he told me—our community lacked a really good lawyer to assist the hardworking people that desired citizenship. It seemed to me (and I viewed it firsthand when my father went through the naturalization process when I was a teen) that many of the so-called immigration specialists were more interested in taking advantage than actually helping out. After a short time assisting the lawyer and helping out people from all over the world, it didn't take me long to realize that I made the right choice by entering into the immigration field.

I have been working as a paralegal for ten years now, seven of them assisting in immigration law. Our firm's clients are usually Latin American or Mexican, and we often work pro bono—helping hardworking people like my parents is all the payment I need. On occasion, I will also conduct free information seminars at a local church.

Believe it or not, I originally became a paralegal because I wanted to make a lot of money. If I stayed with the big firm, I would be making much more than I am now. But I quickly learned that helping people out was much more rewarding than monetary gain. Working so closely with the lawyer and his clients made me want to be able to fully practice law, so I applied to law school, got accepted, and will be attending UCLA law school this coming fall. Being a paralegal opened up my eyes to my life's calling and gave me invaluable experience for my future career as a lawyer.

CHAPTER six

HOW TO SUCCEED ONCE YOU'VE FOUND THE JOB

THE KEY to success in any new endeavor is understanding what the people around you expect of you, what you can expect of them, and how those expectations can be made to work together so that you will not only succeed but be comfortable and maybe even enjoy yourself as well. In this chapter, you'll find tips on fitting into the legal work environment as well as resources from which you can get general information about fitting into your working environment and dealing with difficult people.

CONGRATULATIONS! YOU'VE worked hard to get the paralegal training you need, and gone through the job-search process. Now, you're employed in your first job as a legal assistant. Succeeding in your new position is your next goal. You have an understanding of a paralegal's basic duties and how to perform them, but your training didn't cover how to manage work relationships or how to acclimate yourself to a new work environment. There is much to learn regarding how to perform well on the job, beyond what you were taught in the classroom. Many of these topics will be touched on, including finding and learning from a mentor so that you will be armed with the knowledge you need to succeed.

The first thing you need to know is that the law as a profession in the United States underwent a tremendous change in the last half of the twentieth century. The modern Civil Rights movement, which began in the 1960s, and the modern women's movement, which began in the 1970s, caused societal upheavals that affected the legal community. Within the legal profession, two developments in the 1970s led to great changes as well: the plain-language movement and the poverty law movement, which led to the establishment of the Legal Services Corporation.

Prior to these changes, the law was often a profession for well-off young men who needed a career but didn't want to be bankers. Not surprisingly, most of their clients were well off, too. Some of them used legal training as a springboard into politics, and there have certainly been various crusading lawyers throughout history. But before these new developments, the majority of people went through their whole lives without consulting an attorney, except, perhaps, to write a will.

The various social movements of the last half of the twentieth century opened the legal profession to women, people of color, and poor people, and resulted in a lot of changes in the legal culture. However, the law as a profession was deeply infused with tradition, and to some extent, these new people applied these traditions to themselves. So there have been some major changes and some mere adaptations.

The plain-language movement and Legal Services Corporation have had a greater impact. The plain-language movement suggested that the written product of lawyers did not have to be full of "heretofore" and "party of the first part" and other overblown language whose only purpose was to bury the plain meaning of a document and make people feel that they had to have lawyers to handle even routine matters. The purpose of the plain-language movement was to get lawyers to begin writing documents in plain language that any average person can understand.

The Legal Services Corporation is a nonprofit corporation established by Congress in 1974 to address the needs of poor people who did not have access to legal advice when they needed it, thus leaving themselves vulnerable to those who could afford a lawyer. Legal Services deals with big discrimination cases but also represents tenants and spouses who would otherwise be unrepresented in legal proceedings. The paralegal profession grew directly out of Legal Services (and other privately funded poverty law organizations). To provide more people with legal services for less money, paralegals began doing some of the tasks that lawyers had done in the past.

FITTING INTO THE WORKPLACE CULTURE

Two results of all these changes have direct impact on paralegals and the way they fit into various legal cultures. People who have entered the legal profession in the last several decades have introduced new ways of doing things. Many of the old traditions have remained but have been adapted. For example, it would be difficult for a law firm today to state that "all partners and associates must wear ties," because many partners and associates are now women. However, in most law firms, both men and women dress conservatively. Until you find out otherwise, you should dress and behave on your new job in accordance with the idea that you are working in an old, established profession.

Of course, if you go to work for the legal services/environmental law/nonprofit crowd, you will find a much less conservative, much more casual work culture. In offices like these, except on days when you go to court, jeans and T-shirts may be appropriate attire. Somewhere between the old, established firms and the politically active organizations are the small firms and solo practitioners, where style is determined much more by the individuals in the firm than anything else. The safest thing is to take your cue from those around you. You may not meet any other paralegals in the interview and hiring process, but if you do, dress according to their style for your first couple of days. If you're uncertain at first, wear businesslike attire. Once you've worked in a place for a while, you'll know what's acceptable.

Fitting into the workplace culture is about a lot more than what you wear, however. Law firms have very well-established traditions, and it will be to your benefit to figure them out. There may, for example, be unspoken rules about who works for whom and when you drop everything to do a particular partner's bidding. In particularly traditional firms, you may be expected to call the attorneys Mr. or Ms. Or maybe that's only required for the partners, not the associates. In a legal services office, the attorneys are probably known by their first names.

There are two ways to ensure that you will fit into your workplace culture. Realize that there *is* a culture and that you may not know what it is. Then keep your eyes open and act the way other people act. If no one brings a sack lunch and eats it in the law library, don't immediately take it upon yourself to start a new trend. The other way to learn the ropes is to get yourself a mentor as soon as possible (see the section titled Finding a Mentor on pages 174–175).

POWER IN NUMBERS

In addition to the changes to the profession that resulted from the influx of new attorneys, the poverty law movement and the plain-language movement led directly to a greater number of paralegals. These movements empowered legal consumers so that they realized they didn't always need to hire an attorney to accomplish a legal objective. With some information, people who have not been to law school can write divorce decrees, articles of incorporation, and bankruptcy petitions. However, most people still feel unsure about doing these things on their own, and paralegals fill the gap. Either within a legal organization or on their own, paralegals can assist their clients with many of the rudimentary legal activities. What they cannot do— as you know by now—is practice law. Once legal decisions are made, however, they can take over most aspects of a case. They also can tell you when you do need to consult an attorney.

An unfortunate result of this growth of the paralegal profession is that some attorneys are suspicious of paralegals. The number of such attorneys is shrinking all the time; nonetheless, the tension still exists. The concern among attorneys is that paralegals can easily slip over the line and begin practicing law. As you go through your paralegal studies, you'll see that this can be a difficult line to draw. Especially as you become a more experienced paralegal, you'll be tempted to answer when your client says, "Do you think I should do X or Y?" But legally, you can't answer those questions.

Lawyers aren't just worried about losing business to paralegals, they're worried that people will receive bad legal advice. Over the years, though, paralegals have conducted themselves in such a professional manner and have been so conscientious about understanding their role that lawyers are, for the most part, now welcoming paralegals into the legal culture.

But as a result of this tradition of tension, you may encounter (particularly in a large organization) an attorney who, at best, doesn't understand what paralegals do, or, at worst, is openly hostile to paralegals. The ones who don't understand may just need to be gently reminded that you are not a legal secretary—that other, very competent and talented people in the firm do *that* job. The hostile ones, obviously, are more difficult.

In the end, you will fit in on your first paralegal job the same way you have any time you went to a new school or did something for the first time.

You'll watch people around you and behave as they do, and when you can't figure something out, you'll ask somebody. And you will find that lawyers aren't necessarily scary.

MANAGING WORK RELATIONSHIPS

Basic Rules

When it comes to building and maintaining professional relationships, some basic rules apply to any workplace.

Sometimes peace is better than justice

You may be absolutely, 100% sure you are right about a specific situation. Unfortunately, you may have coworkers who doubt you or who flatly disagree with you. This is a common occurrence in the workplace.

In some situations, you need to assert your position and convince the disbelievers to trust your judgment. Your previous track record and reputation will go a long way in helping convince people to trust your opinions, ideas, and decisions. However, carefully consider the gravity of the situation before you stick your neck out.

In other words, in a work environment, choose your battles wisely. For instance, go ahead and argue your position if you can prevent a catastrophe. On the other hand, if you are having a debate about an issue of taste, opinion, or preference, you may want to leave the situation alone or accept the decisions of your superiors. Let your recommendation(s) be known, but do not argue your point relentlessly. Sometimes, you will be right and people will not listen to you. Always be open to compromise and be willing to listen to and consider the options and ideas of others.

Don't burn bridges

If you are in a disagreement, if you are leaving one employment situation for another, or if a project is ending, always leave the work relationship on a good note. Keep in mind that your professional reputation will follow you throughout your career. It will take years to build a positive reputation, but only one mistake could destroy it.

When changing jobs, don't take the opportunity to vent negative thoughts and feelings before you leave. Although it might make you feel good in the short term, it will have a detrimental, lasting effect on your career and on people's perception of you. Someone you insulted could become your boss some day or be in a position to help you down the line. The legal field is a close-knit community, and many people know one another, either in person or by reputation.

If you wind up acting unprofessionally toward someone, even if you don't ever have contact with that person again, he or she will have contact with many other people and possibly describe you as hard to work with or rude. Your work reputation is very important; don't tarnish it by burning your bridges.

When changing employment situations, do so in a professional manner. There are countless reasons that someone leaves one job to pursue a career with another firm, but to maintain a good reputation within the industry, it's important to act professionally when you actually quit. Getting into a fight with your boss, shouting "I quit!" and then stomping out of the building forever is never the best way to handle things. Even if you think your boss is incompetent, in the heat of anger, never let your negative feelings cause you to act unprofessionally.

Instead, if you get into a major disagreement with your employer, don't make a decision to quit impulsively. Spend a few days thinking about your decision. If you decide it's time to move on, start looking for a new job before actually tendering your resignation with your current employer. As a general rule, even if you're not getting along with your boss or coworkers, it's never a good idea to quit your current job until you've lined up a new one.

Once you've actually landed that new job, be prepared to give your current employer the traditional two weeks notice. Arrange a private meeting with your boss or with the appropriate person within the company, and offer your resignation in person, following it up in writing with a friendly and professional letter. Some people give notice and then use their accumulated vacation or sick days to avoid showing up for work. This is not appropriate behavior. Even if your new employer wants you to start work immediately, they will almost always understand that, as a matter of loyalty and professional courtesy, it is necessary for you to stay with your current employer for those two weeks after giving your notice.

During those last two weeks on the job, offer to do whatever you can to maintain a positive relationship with your coworkers and boss, such as offering to train your replacement. Make your exit from the firm as smooth as possible. Purposely causing problems, stealing from the employer, or sabotaging business deals are all unethical and totally inappropriate actions. Some firms will request your immediate departure when you quit, and will cut off your computer access and escort you out of the building, especially if you're leaving on a negative note. Prior to quitting, try to determine how past coworkers were treated, so you will know what to expect.

As you actually leave the company for the last time, take with you only your personal belongings and nothing that is considered the company's property. Make a point to return directly to your boss your office keys and any company-owned equipment that was in your possession. If possible, for your protection, obtain a written memo stating that everything was returned promptly and in working order.

Keep your work and social lives separate

You were hired to do a job, not to meet new friends and potential dates. Although it's important to be friendly and form positive relationships with the people you work with, you should understand the risks associated with becoming too close. Personal relationships can interfere with your job performance, and your job performance can weaken or destroy a relationship. Consider that you might be asked to rate a coworker's job performance, and the coworker happens to be your best friend. Unless your friend is perfect in every way, you will have to compromise either the rating you were asked to give or your friendship. You may also find yourself in the position of having to take work direction from a buddy, or fire someone with whom you've become good friends. All of these challenges can be difficult.

The challenges associated with at-work romances, however, can lead to disaster. Imagine these situations again, substituting a romantic partner for the friend. What was difficult before seems nearly impossible. Not only are you endangering your job performance and the relationship, but you may also be setting yourself up to lose your job. Many firms and corporations frown upon office romances, and some firms have strict policies against them. If your coworkers find out about your romance, depending upon where you work, you could end up looking for another job.

Lawyers

Most of us spend more waking hours with the people we work with than with our families and friends. It's to everyone's advantage to find ways to get along. One of the most difficult people to work with is the attorney who doesn't believe paralegals should exist. Fortunately, the number of lawyers who feel that way is shrinking, if for no other reason than that paralegals have been around for quite a while and most attorneys have worked with at least one paralegal and had a positive experience. If you do run into an anti-paralegal lawyer, the best way to handle the relationship is to do your job very well. It is also imperative that you never, ever do anything that this individual can interpret as practicing law.

Lawyers are often accused of being a little overloaded on ego. You may be able to exploit that. If you have to deal with an anti-paralegal lawyer, maybe you can make that person your expert on helping you understand and define the practice of law. In the process, that attorney may learn that many of the things a lawyer does are not, strictly, the practice of law, and that a paralegal can take them over with no harm done. Then again, the lawyer may be one of those people who doesn't like change and will never get used to working with paralegals. The good news is you will probably find this person in a large organization only; a single anti-paralegal attorney in a small firm would probably have enough power to keep paralegals from being hired at all.

Sexual Harassment

Sometimes, as mentioned earlier, attorneys break the law (remember Watergate?). It's worth noting again, but this time, referring to sexual harassment. The courts generally define sexual harassment based on the way the recipient feels about the behavior. If something is making you uncomfortable, it is probably inappropriate and you should report it. Most firms have a policy about sexual harassment in place, and that policy should include the way you are expected to report it. And remember, men can be the victims of sexual harassment and women can be the perpetrators.

Coworkers

You're apt to run into other kinds of difficult coworkers. Any number of books can give you advice about coworkers who backstab, undercut, or short-circuit you. In general, the best advice is to learn about the personnel structure of the firm you are working in. There may be a paralegal manager, or perhaps you work under the supervision of a particular partner. Make sure you know whom to talk to if problems with your coworkers reach that level of seriousness.

The Client Relationship

In a great many paralegal jobs, more of your time will be spent with clients than with coworkers. Often, when people come to see a lawyer, it is because they are facing a crisis. Perhaps they have been arrested or threatened, are getting divorced, or are contemplating death. They need legal representation to defend themselves, protect their rights, negotiate a settlement, or write a will. None of these are things most of us look forward to doing. Even in corporate law, your clients may be facing crises involving hostile takeovers or product liability suits. For most of us, when things get bad enough that we hire a lawyer, we want the lawyer to wave a magic legal wand and make all the bad go away. Unfortunately, that's not how it works.

Many attorneys have little training in client counseling—and it's too rarely part of the paralegal curriculum. Remember, the operative word is *counseling*. If at all possible, a client should leave a meeting with a lawyer or paralegal feeling better than before. That can be tricky for you, because when you interview a client, you are forcing thoughts to the surface that most people would rather keep tucked away. Imagine how you would feel if someone asked you questions like these:

- ▶ And after he threatened your life, what did he do?
- ▶ Tell me about all your debts and assets.
- ▶ Did the police read you your rights?
- ▶ Are you afraid your ex-spouse will harm your child?

A situation that leads to such questions is probably one that clients would rather not think about. And there you are, making them think about it. It can be harrowing.

You need great counseling and communication skills to handle these kinds of situations. If these don't come naturally to you, you are well advised to get as much training as you can and learn as much on your own as you can. In addition to reading books, watch the people you work with who seem to be good at counseling and follow their example. Always remember that your clients probably wish they didn't have to be seeing you; but it's nothing personal.

Your clients probably have little knowledge about what paralegals are and what they do. As a result, clients either may not want to talk to you, feeling you are somehow a poor substitute for a lawyer, or they may pressure you for legal opinions. In the first instance, a professional demeanor on your part will go a long way toward gaining a reluctant client's confidence. You may sometimes have to say, "Your lawyer trusts me to handle this matter. Please give me a chance to show you that trust is justified." In the second instance, remember that engaging in the unauthorized practice of law could jeopardize your job and your career. Don't do it; explain, kindly, that it's not your place to give legal advice and that the client should ask the attorney, or you can pass the question along. That doesn't mean you can never answer a question; of course, you will and should exercise your independent judgment. Just don't let a weeping client convince you that just this time it's okay to suggest which bankruptcy chapter to file.

Managing Your Time

Effective time management is crucial to a law practice. A great deal of a lawyer's—and, therefore, a paralegal's—schedule is determined by someone else. If you have 20 days to respond to a complaint, its due date is determined by the date the complaint was filed. Even when your client is initiating the action, you have to wait for the client to come to you with a problem. The stereotype of ambulance-chasing lawyers aside, attorneys really don't sit around thinking, "Gee, maybe I can talk someone into getting divorced; I haven't done a good divorce decree in a while!" In addition to courts and clients, government agencies determine when documents need to be filed. In some cases, a judge or other hearing officer then tells you when the hearing will be. Of course, they try to accommodate everyone's schedule, but ultimately, the judge decides when the trial will be.

If you miss any such deadlines, it can mean an ethical violation for the attorney you work for and even a malpractice suit. And you can bet that of all the work lawyers want to give up to paralegals, calendaring is at the top of the list. Very often, it will be up to you to let your boss know that something is due to be filed.

As a paralegal, you may be responsible for keeping the scheduling software up to date. There is a variety of computer programs to do the trick. The best advice is to never, ever think you'll remember something without writing it down. In large firms, there may be one person whose job is doing the entire calendar; in other firms, you will be responsible, but only for particular attorneys or certain cases. However it is handled, the information has to get to the right place; a computer program doesn't know you have a response due next week unless you tell it so. Make sure you come up with some surefire method for doing your part of the calendaring.

Budgeting Time for Projects

Remember that most of a law office's schedule is determined by someone else. Then remember that you will probably be working for more than one attorney. Now picture several attorneys handing you projects that take three days and are all due tomorrow. Suddenly, finals week doesn't look so bad, does it?

Relax. Just because somebody says something is due tomorrow doesn't mean it really is. Often, it just makes people feel important to say, "I need this right away!" Also, no matter how much you want to please your bosses, you can't take on more than one three-day project and have them all done tomorrow (whether you could do one is questionable as well). Deep down in most every lawyer is a reasonable person who knows that. You're not going to be fired if you say, "I can't do that" to the second and third requests. Finally, just because someone asked you first doesn't mean that person's task is more urgent. The key to working these things out is to get everybody together (as much as possible) and figure out which project really has to be done tomorrow and which can wait or be done by someone else. You'll save yourself some time if you get that kind of information at the outset; don't wait until you're swamped. Then, when one attorney says, "You have to do this first! It's due next week!" you can say, "Yes, but this is due tomorrow."

The main points of organization are communication and knowledge. Find out as much as you can about each assignment, and keep your bosses informed about your progress. For your own sanity, bear in mind that people who like crises seem to be drawn to the law. Some people believe—whether it's true or not—that they are more productive when they work in "crisis mode." An unusually high number of these people seem to become lawyers. If you are one of those types, you'll fit right in; if not, you'll quickly become valued as "the rock," the calm, organized person everyone else can count on.

FINDING A MENTOR

A mentor is a person who is almost as dedicated to advancing your career as you are. In addition, a mentor needs to have the knowledge and experience to help you advance. The typical mentor is an attorney or a senior paralegal at the firm where you work. But a mentor also can be a professor or someone you met through a professional organization. Mentors can be invaluable in helping you succeed in your career—and that means "succeed" in the broadest sense, not just as in getting a promotion. A good mentor not only advises and helps you advance in your career, but also is interested in helping you fit in at your job and listening when you need to talk out a problem. A mentor is a combination of friend and teacher.

By now, you're probably thinking, "Sounds good; how do I find one of them?" That, of course, is the difficult part. Aggressively seeking out a mentor may lead to a very insincere—and, therefore, uncomfortable—relationship. Instead, just keep the idea of a mentor in the back of your mind. If the paralegal in the next office, who's worked at the firm for several years, asks you to lunch, go. Then ask a lot of questions. Ask what is best and worst about working there, ask about interesting cases from the past, ask how the paralegal department has evolved. In other words, demonstrate that you are interested and that you believe this person has a lot of answers. No matter how well you seem to hit it off the first time, try a few more times. Next time, ask the other paralegal out to lunch. If you hit it off, you may have found yourself a mentor.

If you don't, you've gained a lot of useful information about the firm, including, maybe, some ideas about other people you could try out as mentors.

Never become so single-minded in your search for a mentor that you forget to keep your eyes open for friends. They can come in quite handy, too. Be aware, too, that older, more traditional firms may be quite hierarchical, and approaching an attorney to be your mentor may be a faux pas. However, an attorney can make a great mentor, especially because paralegals sometimes decide they want to become attorneys.

Becoming a Mentor

You should also strive to *be* a mentor as much as you can. When you are fresh out of paralegal school and on your new job, it may be hard to imagine that you can be much help to anybody else. Although you probably can't help much with information about the job, you may know other helpful things, such as the best place to get a haircut, or who makes the best pizza in town, or where the best parking spaces are. If you open up that way to others, they are likely to open up to you. Over time, you will have enough knowledge about the job to be a paralegal mentor; in the meantime, do what you can to create relationships.

It's a mistake to think of mentoring as a one-way process in which the senior person is helping the junior person along. Mentoring is multidirectional; it works best when those involved aim to advance themselves while looking out for each other. If a senior paralegal is mentoring you and you hear about a job opening that is exactly what your mentor is looking for, you pass on that information. And the person mentoring you will be pleased to see you mentoring others. The plain truth is, nobody gets ahead without some help. Mentoring is just a way of acknowledging that.

PROMOTING YOURSELF

Believe it or not, there are still some people out there who aren't sure just what a paralegal does. If you end up working for one of those people, you may find that your job feels quite dead-end after a while. When some attorneys first get a paralegal, they are told, "Oh, paralegals are great; they can do all your research!" So your first assignment is to do some research, and you do a good job, so your next assignment is to do some more research, and pretty soon, you realize that's all you ever do. Now every time this attorney gives you a research assignment, you sigh and think, "I do have other skills, you know." A better response is to offer something concrete that you can do. "After I finish, I can draft the complaint for you. I can have that done by next Thursday." That makes the attorney think, "Paralegals do more than research?" Most attorneys are swamped enough that they'll be willing to let you try something new.

In addition, keep your ears open for the litany that every lawyer spouts on a fairly regular basis. It goes something like this: "I am so busy. I have a telephone hearing at 11 and a deposition this afternoon, and I have to finish an answer to a complaint by the filing deadline tomorrow!" At this point, you can say, "I can draft the answer for you and have it first thing in the morning. You can see if there need to be any changes, and then I can file it before the end of the business day." You have just volunteered your way into more responsibility and a chance to show off your writing skills.

No matter how well you work with others and how organized you are, in the end, you will be judged by the product you put out. You want to develop a reputation as someone who gets an assignment, does it right, and does it on time. To accomplish this, whenever someone gives you a task, make sure you know exactly what is expected of you. When an attorney tells you to do research for a memo, ask him or her if you are to draft the memo or if the research should be organized in a particular way. And when the attorney tells you the research is needed "next week," find out if there is an appointment with the client and whether it is on Monday or Friday. If you don't have this kind of information, you may manage to do the assignment, but the attorney may be disappointed in the end. It never hurts to get things in writing, either.

Maintain a Record of Your Work

As your career progresses, find a way to keep track of the work you do. Please note that you should never make unauthorized copies of work and sock it away in your own file; to do so could lead to breaches in client confidentiality. But you can keep a record of the work you do. On your calendar or elsewhere, write down when assignments were given and just what they were, as well as when and if they were modified and when you completed them. That way, when your performance is reviewed and some attorney says, "I think you were late on the X research last month," you can look at your records and point out that you were told to put that work aside when another, more pressing, matter came up. It also allows you to chart, both for yourself and your bosses, the path your career has taken at the firm.

Some larger firms use forms for requesting in-house paralegal services. The information on these forms and their degree of detail varies a great deal, but in essence, their purpose is to outline the tasks required of the paralegal department. When you are the only paralegal working on a case, that request form will be given to you; when several paralegals will work on the case, each will be given a copy indicating which tasks are assigned to which person. If you keep a file of copies of these request forms—and make any notes on them about verbal instructions you received—you'll be well on your way to having a complete record of the work you've done.

Handle Criticism in a Positive Way

When you do receive criticism about your job performance—and we all do, sometimes—try to remain calm and listen carefully to what is being said. First, pay attention to positive comments. Most of us tend to zero in on the one bad thing and discount all the good. Let's say your critique is something like "Your research and organization on this memo are excellent; I do think you need to work a bit on your writing skills, however." Most of us walk away thinking, "My writing stinks!" So make sure you hear the part about your excellent research and organization.

Second, ask for concrete help to rectify the situation. Don't say, "Thanks. I'll work on my writing." Instead, ask for specific information. Is the problem spelling, grammar, legalese? Too wordy, too terse? Ask for suggestions. There are books on legal writing; or maybe it's just a question of remembering to use the spell-check on the final copy. Then follow the advice you are given, and ask the person for help in the future. See if you can find a time when things aren't so busy to go over your brief and make specific suggestions for changes; maybe this attorney would be willing to read some earlier drafts in the future and give you feedback.

Good Luck

As mentioned throughout this book, the paralegal profession is growing, and it doesn't look likely to slow down anytime soon. Not only are there more and more paralegals, but paralegals also are moving in many new directions. The paralegal career pays quite well, is well respected, and affords you opportunities for advancement. But the best thing about working in the legal profession, no matter what area you're in and no matter how routine your work may be, is that every once in a while, you make a huge difference in someone's life, whether it be in a big area such as tobacco or breast-implant litigation or a small area such as getting the used-car dealer to take back a lemon and refund the money. Or getting a sign-language interpreter for a deaf student. Or stopping the hostile takeover of a small corporation. These are only small victories in the grand scheme of things; to your client, they mean everything. And you helped make it happen. Pretty awesome.

THE INSIDE TRACK

Who: Cindy Lopez
What: Founder, NJParalegal.com, Paralegal Career Consultant
Where: New Jersey

INSIDER'S STORY

I knew the legal profession was where I was meant to be while I was attending Brookdale Community College in New Jersey two nights a week, and working full-time at a law office toward my AAS degree in Paralegal Studies.

When I graduated and received my degree, I did an internship and used temp agencies for employment; I recommend both to any student or new paralegal. The internship gave me great insight into the inner workings of a law office. The temp positions helped me see what type of law I preferred, and gave me the experience of working in large, medium, and small firms, giving me the opportunity to decide in what setting I would ultimately prefer to work. For me, I realized that I preferred working for a small firm, or even a sole practitioner—the office is usually less strict, and it is often like a family environment. It's a great situation because in those types of settings you have the ability to develop a good relationship with your boss, and access his or her expertise and professional knowledge. And if they gain confidence in you, they will often be more willing to give you more challenging work and responsibilities. Something else that I did, and I recommend to do, was to join my college's Paralegal Alumni Association; it served me as an important resource and a foundation for networking.

I love being a paralegal, but over the years I definitely encountered some challenges. When I started out, I did not realize that where you are located has a direct influence upon many things in the profession. For example, in New York's tri-state area, the closer to New York City you go, the better the salary, the positions, etc. However, where I'm based in central to southern New Jersey, paralegals are rarely hired or recognized as having a "profession" at all. Most of the employers in the area hire legal secretaries for clerical work and recent law school graduates for research, drafting of pleadings, and so on; even in the larger firms, it is difficult to get the title of "paralegal." I quickly realized the need for paralegals to network and to push for recognition. That's when I came up with the idea for NJParalegal.com. I envisioned it as an online community for paralegals to find jobs, schools, associations, career tips, newsletters, support, sharing, and more. And that is what it is has become.

I strived for change through legal community involvement and education. I became a member of the Legal Assistants' Association of New Jersey (LAANJ), the New Jersey State Bar Association, and my local chamber of commerce. My mission was dedicated to the support and recognition of the paralegal profession in New Jersey.

My advice for new or prospective paralegals is simple: Know what you are getting yourself into. As a paralegal you will hardly ever be bored or twiddling your thumbs. It is a fast-paced profession with plenty of deadlines. Some people love that kind of environment, some people can't stand it—you have to realize what type of person you are. Also, as a paralegal you will be expected to know three things: 1) the legal process and rules, 2) the documents, and 3) your clients. As in any career, you will find the work rewarding and challenging if you truly like what you are doing. And, if your belief system coincides with your area of law, you will find this is also a field where there is opportunity to "make a difference" in the lives of others!

Appendix A

Directory of Paralegal Training Programs

ONLINE

Many of the programs listed by state also offer distance learning.

American Institute for Paralegal Studies
800-553-2420
www.aips.com

Blackstone Paralegal Studies School
800-826-9228
www.blackstonelaw.com

Kaplan University
866-527-5268
www.kaplanuniversityonline.com

Keiser College
866-534-7371
www.keisercollege.edu

Herzing College
866-508-0748
www.herzingonline.com

Florida Metropolitan University Online
888-741-4270
http://fmuonline.edu

Penn Foster Career School
800-275-4410
www.pennfoster.edu

Professional Career Development Institute
800-417-2407
www.pcdi.com

Tidewater Tech Online
877-281-2121
www.tidewatertechonline.com

UMass Online
508-856-5203
www.umassonline.net

Washington Online Learning Institute
800-371-5581
www.woli.com

ALABAMA

Virginia College at Huntsville
Paralegal Studies Program
2800a Bob Wallace Avenue
Huntsville, AL 35805
256-533-7387
www.vc.edu/huntsville/program.cfm?ID=23

Auburn University at Montgomery
Legal Assistant Education Program
P.O. Box 244023
Montgomery, AL 36124-4023
334-244-3692
www.aum.edu/jps

Faulkner University
Legal Studies Program
5345 Atlanta Hwy
Montgomery, AL 36109-3398
334-386-7304
http://www.faulkner.edu

Gadsden State Community College
Paralegal Program
P.O. Box 227
Gadsden, AL 35902-0227
256-549-8200
www.gadsdenst.cc.al.us

Northeast Alabama Community College
P.O. Box 159
Rainsville, AL 35986
256-228-6001
www.nacc.cc.al.us

Samford University
Legal Assistant Education Program
SU Box 2200
Birmingham, AL 35229
205-726-2011
www.samford.edu

South University
Legal Studies/Paralegal Studies
5355 Vaughn Road
Montgomery, AL 36116-1120
800-688-0932
www.southuniversity.edu/campus/Programs/
    index.asp?progid=6

Virginia College at Birmingham
Paralegal Studies
P.O. Box 19249
Birmingham, AL 35219-9249
877-213-7589
www.vc.edu

Wallace State Community College
Paralegal Program
P.O. Box 2000
Hanceville, AL 35077-2000
866-350-9722
www.wallacestate.edu

ALASKA

University of Alaska Anchorage
Paralegal Certificate Program
Justice Center 3211 Providence Drive
Anchorage, AK 99508
907-786-1810
http://justice.uaa.alaska.edu

University of Alaska Fairbanks
Paralegal Studies
510 Second Avenue
Downtown Center
Fairbanks, AK 99701
907-455-2835
http://www.tvc.uaf.edu/programs/paralegal
/index.html

University of Alaska Southeast
Paralegal Studies
11120 Glacier Highway
Juneau, AK 99801
907-465-6347
www.uas.alaska.edu/academics/assoc/aas/
paralegal_studies.html

ARIZONA

Everest College
Legal Assistant Program
2525 W Beryl Avenue
Phoenix, AZ 85021-1641
888-741-4270
www.everest-college.com/main_programs_
detail.php?schoolProgram=Paralegal

Lamson College
Legal Assistant Program
1126 N Scottsdale Road #17
Tempe, AZ 85281-1700
800-915-2194
www.lamsoncollege.com

Long Technical College
Paralegal Studies Program
4646 East Van Buren, Suite 350
Phoenix, AZ 85008
602-252-2171
www.longtechnicalcollege.com/east_valley/
c_paralegal.html

Mohave Community College
Legal Assistant Studies
1971 Jagerson Avenue
Kingman, AZ 86401
928-757-4331
www.mohave.edu/pages/1.asp

Phoenix Career College
General Practice Paralegal Program
111 West Monroe #800
Phoenix, AZ 85003
602-252-2171
www.careercolleges.com/campaign/235/
Phoenix-Career-College.html#Programs

Phoenix College
Legal Assisting Program
1202 W Thomas Road
Phoenix, AZ 85013
602-285-7500
www.pc.maricopa.edu/index.php?page=
29&subpage=707

Pima Community College
Legal Assistant Paralegal Studies
1255 North Stone Avenue
Tucson, AZ 85709-3030
520-206-7352
www.pima.edu/program/paralegal/index.shtml

Yavapai College
Paralegal Studies
1100 East Sheldon Street
Prescott, AZ 86301
800-922-6787
www2.yc.edu

ARKANSAS

University of Arkansas—Fort Smith
Legal Assistance/Paralegal Program
5210 Grand Avenue
P.O. Box 3649
Fort Smith, AR 72913-3649
479-788-7000
www.uafortsmith.edu/Degrees/AAS-
LegalAssistanceAndParalegal

CALIFORNIA

California Polytechnic State University
Paralegal Studies Certificate Program
Extended Education
One Grand Avenue
San Luis Obispo, CA 93407-9750
805-756-2053
www.calpoly.edu/index.html

California State University-Hayward
Paralegal Studies Certificate Program
25800 Carlos Bee Boulevard
Warren Hall Room 804
Hayward, CA 94542-3012
800-730-2784
www.extension.csuhayward.edu/html/par.htm

California State University, Los Angeles
Certificate Program in Paralegal Studies
5151 State University Drive
Los Angeles, CA 90032
323-343-4967
www.calstatela.edu/exed/certificate/
paralegal.htm

Cerritos Community College
Paralegal Program
11110 Alondra Boulevard
Norwalk, CA 90650
562-860-2451 ext. 2703
www.cerritos.edu

City College of San Francisco
Paralegal/Legal Studies
50 Phelan Avenue C-106
San Francisco, CA 94112
415-239-3508
http://www.ccsf.edu/Departments/index.shtml

Coastline Community College
Paralegal Studies Program
11460 Warner Avenue
Fountain Valley, CA 92708
714-546-7600 ext. 17319
http://coastline.cccd.edu/page.asp?Link
 ID=377

College of the Sequoias
Paralegal Program
915 S Mooney Boulevard
Visalia, CA 93277
559-730-3840
www.cos.edu

Cuyamaca Community College
900 Rancho San Diego Parkway
El Cajon, CA 92019
619-660-4362
www.cuyamaca.edu/paralegal

De Anza College
Paralegal Program
21250 Stevens Creek Boulevard
Cupertino, CA 95014
408-864-8563
www.deanza.edu

El Camino College
Legal Assistant Program
16007 Crenshaw Boulevard
Torrance, CA 90506
310-660-3773
www.elcamino.edu

Fresno City College
Paralegal Studies Program
1101 E University Avenue
Fresno, CA 93741
559-442-4600 ext. 8485
www.fresnocitycollege.edu/business/paralegal

Fullerton College
Paralegal Studies Program
321 East Chapman Avenue
Fullerton, CA 92832-2095
714-992-7000
www.fullcoll.edu

Los Angeles City College
Legal Assistant/Paralegal Studies
855 North Vermont Avenue
Los Angeles, CA 90029
323-953-4000 ext. 2751
www.lacitycollege.edu/academic/
 departments/law/index.html

Los Angeles Mission College
Paralegal Studies Program
13356 Eldridge Avenue
Sylmar, CA 91342
818-364-7720
www.lamission.edu

Maric College
2022 University Drive
Vista, CA 92083
760-630-1555
www.mariccollege.edu/california_legal_
 program.html

Miramar College
Legal Assistant Program
10440 Black Mountain Road
San Diego, CA 92126
619-388-7427
www.miramarcollege.net

Mt. San Antonio College
Paralegal Studies Program
1100 North Grand Avenue
Walnut, CA 91789
909-594-5611 ext. 4907
http://paralegal.mtsac.edu

MTI College
Legal Assistant Program
5221 Madison Avenue
Sacramento, CA 95841
916-339-1500
www.mticollege.edu

Palomar College
Business Education
1140 West Mission Road
San Marcos, CA 92069
760-744-1150
www.palomar.edu

Pasadena City College
Legal Assisting Program
1570 East Colorado Boulevard
Pasadena, CA 91106-2003
626-585-7817
www.pasadena.edu

Platt College
Paralegal Program
3700 Inland Empire Boulevard
Ontario, CA 91764
909-941-9410
www.plattcollege.com

Saint Mary's College
Paralegal and Law Studies Program
SMC P.O. Box 3052
Moraga, CA 94575
925-631-4509
www.stmarys-ca.edu

San Francisco State University
Paralegal Studies College of Ext. Learning
425 Market Street
SFSU Downtown Center
San Francisco, CA 94105
415-405-7770
www.cel.sfsu.edu/paralegal

Santa Ana College
Paralegal Program
1530 W 17th Street
Santa Ana, CA 92706
714-564-6813
www.sac.edu/degrees/sac/Paralegal.htm

Sonoma State University
Paralegal Program
1801 East Cotati Avenue
Extended Education
Rohnert Park, CA 94928
707-664-2394
www.sonoma.edu/exed/certificates/aa/-
    attnindex.html

Southwestern College
900 Otay Lakes Road
Chula Vista, CA 91910
619-421-6700 ext. 5711
www.swc.cc.ca.us

University of California, Irvine
Paralegal Certificate Program
P.O. Box 6050
Irvine, CA 92716-6050
949-824-2282
https://unex.uci.edu/certificates/
   business_mgmt/paralegal/index.asp

University of California, Los Angeles
   Extension
Attorney Assistant Training Program
10995 Le Conte Avenue
Room 517
Los Angeles, CA 90024
310-825-0741
www.uclaextension.edu/aatp

University of California, Riverside
Legal Assistantship Certificate Program
1200 University Avenue
Riverside, CA 92507-4596
951-827-4105
www.ucrextension.net/law

University of California, San Diego
Legal Assistant Program
UCSD Extension
9500 Gilman Drive #0172B
La Jolla, CA 92093
858-882-8008
www.paralegal.ucsd.edu

University of California, Santa Barbara Ext.
Legal Assistantship Certificate Program
6950 Hollister Avenue
Goleta, CA 93117
805-893-4200
www.unex.ucsb.edu

University of La Verne
Legal Studies Program
1950 Third Street
La Verne, CA 91750
909-593-3511
www.ulv.edu/legalstudies

University of San Diego
Paralegal Program
5998 Alcala Park
Alcala West 1-204
San Diego, CA 92110
619-260-4579
www.sandiego.edu/paralegal

University of West Los Angeles
School of Paralegal Studies
1155 W Arbor Vitae Street
Inglewood, CA 90301-2902
310-342-5208
www.uwla.edu/sps/index.html

West Valley College
Paralegal Program
14000 Fruitvale Avenue
Saratoga, CA 95070
408-741-4635
www.westvalley.edu/wvc/careers/
   paralegal.html

Western College
Paralegal Studies
10900 E 183rd Street
Suite 290
Cerritos, CA 90703-5342
562-809-5100
www.westerncollegesocal.com

COLORADO

Arapahoe Community College
Paralegal Degree/Certificate
5900 South Sante Fe Drive
Littleton, CO 80160-9002
303-797-5878
www.arapahoe.edu

Community College of Aurora
Paralegal/Legal Assistant Program
16000 East CentreTech Parkway C208
Aurora, CO 80011-9036
303-340-7502
www.ccaurora.edu

Denver Career College
Paralegal Program
500 East 84th Avenue
Suite W-200
Thornton, CO 80229
800-848-0550
www.denvercareercollege.com

Institute of Business and Medical Careers
1609 Oakridge Drive
Fort Collins, CO 80525
970-223-2669
www.ibmcedu.com/showpage.asp?
    section=924163165&sub=834177509&id=
    834177509

Parks College
9065 Grant Street
Denver, CO 80229
303-457-2757
www.parks-college.com/main_programs_
    detail.php?schoolProgram=Paralegal

Pikes Peak Community College
Legal Assistant Program
100 West Pikes Peak Avenue
Colorado Springs, CO 80903
719-527-6033
www.ppcc.edu

Center for Legal Studies
22316 Sunset Drive
Golden, CO 80401-9537
303-273-9777
www.legalstudies.com

CONNECTICUT

Briarwood College
Paralegal Program
2279 Mount Vernon Road
Southington, CT 06489
860-628-4751
www.briarwood.edu/index.html

University of Hartford
Legal Studies
1265 Asylum Avenue
Hartford, CT 06105
860-768-5652
http://admission.hartford.edu/legalstudies

Manchester Community College
Paralegal Program
Great Path
P.O. Box 1046
Manchester, CT 06045-1046
860-512-2642
www.mcc.commnet.edu/academic/
   degrees/para.php

Naugatuck Valley Community Technical
   College
Legal Assistant Program
750 Chase Parkway
Waterbury, CT 06708
203-596-8744
www.nvctc.commnet.edu

Norwalk Community College
Legal Assistant Program
188 Richards Avenue
Norwalk, CT 06854
570-348-6288
www.nctc.commnet.edu

Quinnipiac University
Legal Studies Department
275 Mt. Carmel Avenue
Hamden, CT 06518
203-582-8712
www.quinnipiac.edu/x301.xml

Sacred Heart University
Legal Assistant Program
5151 Park Avenue
Fairfield, CT 06825
203-371-7999
www.sacredheart.edu

University of New Haven
Legal Studies
300 Boston Post Road
West Haven, CT 06516
203-932-7373
www.newhaven.edu/show.asp?durki=428

Branford Hall Career Institute
995 Day Hill Drive
Windsor, CT 06095-1722
860-683-4900
www.branfordhall.edu/main/paralegal.html

DELAWARE

Wesley College
Paralegal Studies Program
120 North State Street
Dover, DE 19901
302-736-2300
www.wesley.edu

Widener University
Law Center Legal Education Institute
4601 Concord Pike
Wilmington, DE 19803
302-477-2100
www.law.widener.edu/lei_lnc/index.shtml

DISTRICT OF COLUMBIA

George Washington University
G W Solutions
Legal Assistant Program
2121 Eye Street NW
Washington, D.C. 20052
202-994-1000
www.gwu.edu

Georgetown University

1437 37th Street NW

Poulton Hall 2nd Floor

Washington, D.C. 20057

202-687-6245

http://scs.georgetown.edu/psp

FLORIDA

Barry University

Legal Studies

11300 NE Second Avenue

Miami Shores, FL 33161-6695

305-899-3100

www.barry.edu

Broward Community College

Legal Assisting Program

111 East Las Olas Boulevard

Fort Lauderdale, FL 33301

954-201-7400

www.broward.edu

Florida Community College at Jacksonville

Legal Studies Institute

3939 Roosevelt Boulevard

Jacksonville, FL 32205

904-381-3400

www.fccj.org

Florida Gulf Coast University

10501 FGCU Boulevard South

Fort Myers, FL 33965-6565

941-590-7817

http://cps.fgcu.edu/cj/ls/index.html

Florida International University

Legal Studies Institute

University Park Campus, GL-120

11200 SW 8 Street

Miami, FL 33199

305-348-2492

http://caps.fiu.edu/legal

Hillsborough Community College

2112 North 15th Street

Tampa, FL 33605

813-253-7753

www.hccfl.edu

International College

Paralegal Program

2655 Northbrooke Drive

Naples, FL 34119

239-513-1122

www.internationalcollege.edu/Paralegal/

pardegree.htm

Manatee Community College

Legal Assisting Paralegal Programs

5840 26th Street West

Bradenton, FL 34207

941-752-5000

www.mccfl.edu/pages/1.asp

Miami-Dade Community College

Legal Assistant Program

300 NE 2nd Avenue

Room 3704

Miami, FL 33132

305-237-3048

www.mdc.edu/wolfson/academic/Legal

Assistant

Nova Southeastern University
Paralegal Assistant Studies Program
3301 College Avenue
Parker Building #370
Fort Lauderdale, FL 33314
954-262-7948
www.nova.edu

Palm Beach Community College
Legal Assisting Paralegal
4200 Congress Ave
Lake Worth, FL 33461
561-207-5405
www.pbcc.cc.fl.us

Pensacola Junior College
418 West Garden Street
Pensacola, FL 32501
850-484-1367
www.pjc.edu

Santa Fe Community College
Legal Assistant Program
3000 NW 83rd Street
Gainesville, FL 32605
352-395-5139
www.santafe.cc.fl.us

Seminole Community College
Legal Assisting Paralegal Program
100 Weldon Boulevard
Sanford, FL 32773-6199
407-328-2269
www.scc-fl.edu

South University
Paralegal Studies/Legal Studies
1760 North Congress Avenue
West Palm Beach, FL 33409
561-697-9200
www.southuniversity.edu/campus/
    WestPalmBeach

St. Petersburg College
Legal Assisting Program
2465 Drew Street
Clearwater, FL 33765
727-791-2530
www.spcollege.edu/bachelors/legal_curr.php

University of Central Florida
Legal Studies Program
P.O. Box 161600
Dept of Criminal Justice
Orlando, FL 32816-1600
407-823-5364
www.cohpa.ucf.edu/crim.jus

University of North Florida
Legal Studies Institute
4567 St. Johns Bluff Road South
Jacksonville, FL 32224
904-620-1000
www.unf.edu

University of West Florida
Legal Studies
11000 University Parkway
Pensacola, FL 32514
850-474-2344
www.uwf.edu/uwfMain

Valencia Community College
Paralegal Studies
P.O. Box 3028
Orlando, FL 32802-3028
407-299-5000
http://valenciacc.edu/departments/east/
business/paralegal/program.asp

GEORGIA

Athens Technical College
Paralegal Studies Program
800 U.S. Highway 29 North
North Athens, GA 30601-1500
706-355-5000
www.athenstech.edu

Brenau University
Conflict Resolution and Legal Studies
500 Washington Street SE
Gainesville, GA 30511
770-534-6179
www.brenau.edu/sfah/humanities/CR/
program.htm

Clayton College & State University
Paralegal Studies Program
2000 Clayton State Boulevard
Morrow, GA 30260
678-466-4000
www.clayton.edu

Gainesville College
Paralegal Program
P.O. Box 1358
Gainesville, GA 30503
770-718-3639
www.gsc.edu

South University
709 Mall Boulevard
Savannah, GA 31406
912-201-8000
www.southuniversity.edu

HAWAII

Kapi'olani Community College
Legal Education Department
4303 Diamond Head Road
Honolulu, HI 96816
808-734-9000
http://legal.kcc.hawaii.edu

IDAHO

Eastern Idaho Technical College
1600 South 25th East
Idaho Falls, ID 83404
208-524-3000
www.eitc.edu

Idaho State University
Campus Box 8380
Pocatello, ID 83209
208-282-5846
www.isu.edu

ILLINOIS

Elgin Community College
Paralegal Program
1700 Spartan Drive
Elgin, IL 60123
847-697-1000
www.elgin.cc.il.us

Illinois Central College
Paralegal Studies Program
1 College Drive
East Peoria, IL 61635-0001
309-999-4502
www.icc.edu

Illinois State University
Legal Studies Program
4600 Department of Politics and
    Government
Normal, IL 61790
309-438-8638
www.politicsandgovernment.ilstu.edu/
    paralegal/Paralegal.htm

Kankakee Community College
Paralegal/Legal Assistant Studies Program
P.O. Box 888
Kankakee, IL 60901
815-802-8100
www.kcc.edu

Loyola University Chicago
Institute for Paralegal Studies
820 N Michigan Avenue
Chicago, IL 60611
312-915-6820
www.luc.edu/paralegal

MacCormac College
Paralegal Studies
29 East Madison Street
Chicago, IL 60602
312-922-1884
www.maccormac.edu

Northwestern Business College
Paralegal Program
4829 North Lipps Avenue
Chicago, IL 60630
773-777-4220
www.northwesternbc.edu/paralegal

Rockford Business College
Paralegal-Legal Office Assistant Program
730 North Church Street
Rockford, IL 61103
815-965-8616
www.rbcsuccess.com

Roosevelt University
Lawyer's Assistant Program
430 South Michigan Avenue
Chicago, IL 60605
312-341-3500
www.roosevelt.edu/paralegal

South Suburban College
Paralegal/Legal Assistant Program
15800 South State Street
South Holland, IL 60473
708-596-2000 ext. 2579
www.ssc.cc.il.us/acad/career/depts/
    legalstudies/paralegal.htm

Southern Illinois University
Paralegal Studies Program
Faner Hall Room 4425 Mail Code 4540
Southern Illinois University Carbondale
1000 Faner Drive
Carbondale, Illinois 62901
www.siu.edu/~para

Southwestern Illinois College
Paralegal Studies
2500 Carlyle Avenue
Belleville, IL 62221
618-222-5494
www.southwestern.cc.il.us/instruction/
    paralegal

William Rainey Harper College
Paralegal Studies Program
1200 W Algonquin Road
Palatine, IL 60067
847-925-6407
www.harpercollege.edu/catalog/career/
    para/index.htm

INDIANA

Ball State University
Legal Assistance Studies
Department of Political Science
Muncie, IN 47306
765-285-8800
www.bsu.edu

Calumet College of St Joseph
Paralegal Program
2400 New York Avenue
Whiting, IN 46394
219-473-4254
www.ccsj.edu/academics/programs/
    par/index.html

Indiana University/Purdue University
    Indianapolis
Certificate in Paralegal Studies
425 University Boulevard
Indianapolis, IN 46202
www.iupui.edu/~polisci/paralegal.htm

Indiana University South Bend
IU South Bend Paralegal Studies
1700 Mishawaka Avenue
P.O. Box 7111
South Bend, IN 46634-7111
219-237-4261
www.iusb.edu/~cted/spring/Paralegal.htm

Ivy Tech State College
Paralegal Program
3800 North Anthony Boulevard
Fort Wayne, IN 46805
260-480-4254
www.ivytech.edu/fortwayne/pubserv/
    paralegal/index.html

Ivy Tech State College Region 6
4301 South Cowan Road
Muncie, IN 47302
765-289-2291 ext. 417
www.ivytech.edu/eastcentral

Saint Mary-of-the-Woods College
Paralegal Studies Program
Guerin Hall
Saint Mar-of-the-Woods, IN 47876
812-535-5235
www.smwc.edu/cgi-bin/site.pl?3208&dw
    Content_contentID=474&menuID=
    1&weight=155

University of Evansville
Legal Studies Program
1800 Lincoln Avenue
Evansville, IN 47722
812-479-2389
http://lps.evansville.edu

Vincennes University
Legal Assistant/Paralegal Program
1002 N First Street
Vincennes, IN 47591
812-888-5764
www.vinu.edu/academicresources/majors/
    factsheet.aspx?fsh_lKey=153

IOWA

Des Moines Area Community College
Legal Assistant Program
1100 7th Street
Des Moines, IA 50314
515-248-7208
www.dmacc.edu

Kirkwood Community College
Legal Assistant/Paralegal Program
6301 Kirkwood Boulevard SW
Cedar Rapids, IA 52404
319-398-5576
www.kirkwood.edu

KANSAS

Johnson County Community College
Paralegal/Legal Nurse Consultant Program
12345 College Boulevard
Overland Park, KS 66210-1299
913-469-8500 ext. 3184
www.johnco.cc.ks.us/home/depts/1206

Northeast Kansas Technical College
1501 West Riley
Atchison, KS 66002
913-367-6204
    www.universities.com/On-Campus/www.
    Northeast_Kansas_Technical_College.html

Washburn University
Legal Studies Program
1700 College, Benton Hall
Topeka, KS 66621
785-231-1010
www.washburn.edu/sas/olt/legal-assist

Wichita State University
Legal Assistant Program
1845 North Fairmont Avenue
Wichita, KS 67260 316-978-7123
http://webs.wichita.edu/?u=barton&p=/
    coursepages/legalasstcourses

KENTUCKY

Beckfield College
16 Spiral Drive
Florence, KY 41022
859-371-9393
www.beckfield.edu/Web%20Pages/
    Paralegal_Program.htm

Daymar College
Paralegal Studies
3361 Buckland Square
Owensboro, KY 42301
877-258-7796
www.daymarcollege.edu

Eastern Kentucky University
Paralegal Programs
McCreary 113
Richmond, KY 40475-3102
859-622-1025
www.paralegal.eku.edu

Morehead State University
Paralegal Studies Program
350 Rader Hall, University Boulevard
Morehead, KY 40351
606-783-2655
www.morehead-st.edu/ggh/index.
    aspx?id=1801

Sullivan University
The Institute for Legal Studies
3101 Bardstown Road
Louisville, KY 40205
502-456-6505
www.sullivan.edu

Sullivan University Lexington Campus
The Institute for Paralegal Studies
2355 Harrodsburg Road
Lexington, KY 40504
859-276-4357
www.sullivan.edu/lexington/Index.htm

University of Louisville
Paralegal Studies Program
Ford Hall Room 104
Louisville, KY 40292
502-852-3249
www.louisville.edu/a-s/polsci/paralegal

Western Kentucky University
Bowling Green Community College
Paralegal Studies Program
2355 Nashville Road
Suite B
Bowling Green, KY 42101
270-780-2539
www.bgcc.wku.edu/ParalegalStudies-
    home.htm

LOUISIANA

Herzing College
Associate of Science in Paralegal
2400 Veterans Boulevard #410
Kenner, LA 70062
504-733-0074
www.herzing.edu/neworleans/programs

Louisiana State University
Paralegal Studies Program
177 Pleasant Hall
Baton Rouge, LA 70803-1520
225-578-6325
www.doce.lsu.edu

Tulane University
Paralegal Studies Program
125 Gibson Hall
New Orleans, LA 70118
504-865-5555
www.uc.tulane.edu

University of New Orleans
Paralegal Studies Program
226 Carondelet Street #310L
New Orleans, LA 70130-2933
504-539-9500
http://training.uno.edu/paralegal.htm

MAINE

Andover College
Paralegal Program
901 Washington Avenue
Portland, ME 04103
207-774-6126
www.andovercollege.com/paralegal.asp

University of Maine—Augusta
Legal Technology Department
46 University Drive
Augusta, ME 04330-9410
207-621-3000
www.uma.edu

MARYLAND

Anne Arundel Community College
Paralegal Studies Program
101 College Parkway
Arnold, MD 21012
410-777-2222
www.aacc.cc.md.us

Community College of Baltimore County
Dundalk Campus Paralegal Studies
    Program
7200 Sollers Point Road
Baltimore, MD 21222
410-285-9794
www.ccbcmd.edu

Frederick Community College
7932 Opossumtown Pike
Frederick, MD 21702
301-846-2819
www.frederick.edu

Harford Community College
Paralegal Studies Program
401 Thomas Run Road
Bel Air, MD 21015
410-836-4000
www.harford.edu

University of Maryland University College
3501 University Boulevard E
Adelphi, MD 20783
301-985-7733
www.umuc.edu/prog/ugp/majors/lgst.shtml

Villa Julie College
Paralegal Department
1525 Greenspring Valley Road
Stevenson, MD 21153
410-602-7423
www.vjc.edu/academics/index.aspx?id=1605

MASSACHUSETTS

Anna Maria College
Paralegal Studies Program
50 Sunset Lane
Paxton, MA 01612
508-849-3380
www.annamaria.edu

Bay Path College
Legal Studies
588 Longmeadow Street
Longmeadow, MA 01106
413-565-1238 www.baypath.edu/
    academics_legal.htm

Elms College
Paralegal and Legal Studies Department
291 Springfield Street
Chicopee, MA 01013
413-594-2761
www.elms.edu/academics/undergraduate/
    bl_Paralegal.htm

North Shore Community College
Paralegal Program
1 Ferncroft Road
Danvers, MA 01923
978-762-4000
www.northshore.edu/departments

Northeastern University
Paralegal Professional Program
360 Huntington Avenue
269 Ryder Hall
Boston, MA 02115
617-373-2000
www.northeastern.edu/welcome.html

Northern Essex Community College
Paralegal Program
100 Elliot Street
Haverhill, MA 01830
978-556-3000
www.necc.mass.edu/programsassociate
    degree/paralegal.shtml

Suffolk University
Paralegal Studies Programs
41 Temple Street
Boston, MA 02114
617-573-8228
www.suffolk.edu/cas/ehs/undergrad_
    paralegal.html

MICHIGAN

Davenport University
Paralegal Program
123 West Main Street
Kalamazoo, MI 49006
269-382-2835
www.davenport.edu

Davenport University—Grand Rapids
Paralegal Studies
415 East Fulton Street
Grand Rapids, MI 49503
616-451-3511
www.davenport.edu

Delta College
Legal Support Professional Program
1961 Delta Road
University Center, MI 48710
989-686-9000
www.delta.edu

Eastern Michigan University
Legal Assistant Program
14 Sill Hall
Ypsilanti, MI 48197
734-487-1849
www.emich.edu

Ferris State University
Legal Assistant Program
BUS 358
119 South Street
Big Rapids, MI 49307
616-591-2427
http://catalog.ferris.edu/programs/92

Grand Valley State University
Legal Studies Program
401 West Fulton
Grand Rapids, MI 49504
616-336-7147
http://www4.gvsu.edu/ls

Henry Ford Community College
Legal Assistant Program
5101 Evergreen Road
Dearborn, MI 48128
313-845-9693
https://reg.henryford.cc.mi.us/site_manager/
    catalog_manager/programs/view_
    program1.asp?id=97&view=s

Kellogg Community College
Legal Assistant Paralegal Program
450 North Avenue
Battle Creek, MI 49017
616-965-3931
www.kellogg.edu/socialscience/
    legalassitant/index.html

Lake Superior State University
School of Business, Economics and Legal
    Studies
650 West Easterday Avenue
Sault Ste. Marie, MI 49783
908-635-2104
www.lssu.edu/degrees/degree.php?id=5168

Lansing Community College
Legal Assistant Program
P.O. Box 40010
Business Dept
Lansing, MI 48901-7210
517-483-1957
www.lcc.edu/business/legal_asst

Macomb Community College
Legal Assistant Program
14500 East 12 Mile Road
Warren, MI 48088
810-286-2058
www.macomb.edu/academics/departments/
    lega/default.asp

Madonna University
Legal Assistant Department
36600 Schoolcraft Road
Livonia, MI 48150
734-432-5549
www.madonna.edu/pages/paralegal.cfm

Northwestern Michigan College
Legal Assistant Program
1701 East Front Street
Traverse City, MI 49686
231-995-1235
www.nmc.edu/business

Oakland Community College
Paralegal Program
2480 Opdyke Road
Bloomfield Hills, MI 48304
248-341-2000
www.oaklandcc.edu

Oakland University
Legal Assistant Program
2200 North Squirrel Road
Rochester, MI 48309-4401
248-370-2100
http://www4.oakland.edu

MINNESOTA

Hamline University
Paralegal Legal Assistant Program
1536 Hewitt Avenue
Saint Paul, MN 55104
651-523-2745
www.hamline.edu/cla/admission/postbac/
    paralegal.html

Inver Hills Community College
Paralegal Program
2500 East 80th Street
Inver Grove Heights, MN 55076-3224
612-450-8567
www.inverhills.edu/AcademicPrograms/
    CareerPrograms/Paralegal.asp

Minnesota Paralegal Institute
Post-Baccalaureate Certificate Program
12450 Wayzata Boulevard
Minnetonka, MN 55305
952-542-8417
www.mnparalegal.com

Minnesota School of Business/Globe
    College
5910 Shingle Creek Parkway
Brooklyn Center, MN 55430
763-566-7777
www.msbcollege.edu/programs/aas_
    paralegal.html

Minnesota State University Moorhead
Paralegal Department
1104 7th Avenue South
Moorhead, MN 56563
218-477-2587
www.mnstate.edu/paralegal

North Hennepin Community College
Paralegal Program
7411 85th Avenue North
Brooklyn Park, MN 55445
763-424-0915
www.nh.cc.mn.us

Winona State University
Paralegal Program
P.O. Box 5838
Winona, MN 55987
507-457-5400
www.winona.edu/paralegal

MISSISSIPPI

Mississippi College
Paralegal Studies Program
200 South Capitol Street
Clinton, MS 39058
601-925-3000
www.mc.edu

Mississippi University for Women
Paralegal Studies Program
Cromwell Communications Building
1100 College Street
W-Box 1634
Columbus, MS 39701
662-329-7386
www.muw.edu/paralegal

University of Mississippi
Paralegal Studies Program
P.O. Box 1848
University, MS 38677
662-915-7211
www.olemiss.edu/course_cat_index/course_
    catalog2000/html/Schools/ParaLegal_
    Studies/program.htm

University of Southern Mississippi
Paralegal Studies
118 College Drive
Hattiesburg, MS 39406
601-266-1000
www.usm.edu

MISSOURI

Avila University
Paralegal Program
11901 Wornall Road
Kansas City, MO 64145
816-501-3644
www.avila.edu/catalog/degrees/paralega.htm

Hickey College
940 West Port Plaza Drive
St. Louis, MO 63146
314-434-2212
www.hickeycollege.edu/programs.htm

Maryville University
Paralegal Studies
13550 Conway Road
St. Louis, MO 63141
800-627-9855
www.maryville.edu

Missouri Western State College
Legal Studies Program
4525 Downs Drive
St. Joseph, MO 64507
816-271-4200
www.missouriwestern.edu/CJ_LS/about.htm

Patricia Stevens College
330 North 4th Street
Saint Louis, MO 63102
314-421-0949
www.patriciastevenscollege.com/program_
    paralegal.aspx

Penn Valley Metropolitan Community
    College
Paralegal Program
3201 Southwest Trafficway
Kansas City, MO 64111
816-759-4000
www.mcckc.edu/home.asp?QLinks=
    Penn+Valley

Rockhurst College
Paralegal Studies
1100 Rockhurst Road
Kansas City, MO 64110
816-501-4767
www.rockhurst.edu/academic/paralegal/
    index.asp

St. Louis Community College—Florissant
    Valley
Legal Assistant Program
3400 Pershall Road
Ferguson, MO 63135
314-513-4200
www.stlcc.cc.mo.us/fv

St Louis Community College—Meramec
Legal Studies for the Paralegal
11333 Big Bend Boulevard
St Louis, MO 63122
314-984-7500
www.stlcc.cc.mo.us/mc

Webster University
Legal Studies Department
470 East Lockwood Avenue
Saint Louis, MO 63119
314-968-7067
www.webster.edu

William Woods University
Paralegal Studies Program
200 West 12th Street
Fulton, MO 65251
573-642-2251
www.williamwoods.edu/2004catalog/
    majordetail.asp?SCMajorID=90

MONTANA

University of Great Falls
Paralegal Studies Program
1301 20th Street South
Great Falls, MT 59405
406-761-8210
http://www.ugf.edu/academics/competency
    objectives/paralegal.htm

University of Montana
College of Technology
32 Campus Drive
Missoula, MT 59812
406-243-7882
www.cte.umt.edu/departments/business/
    paralegal/default.htm

NEBRASKA

Central Community College
Paralegal Studies
3134 West Highway 34
Grand Island, NE 68802-4903
308-398-4222
http://www.cccneb.edu/igsbase/
    igstemplate.cfm?SRC=SP&SRCN=
    programchart2&GnavID=20&SnavID=
    &TnavID=&cccProgramID=85&LS=
    &PS=&KS=paralegal

College of Saint Mary
Paralegal Studies
7000 Mercy Road
Omaha, NE 68106
402-399-2405
www.csm.edu

Metropolitan Community College
Paralegal/Legal Assistant Program
P.O. Box 3777
Omaha, NE 68103
402-457-2400
www.mccneb.edu/programs/lawsfaq.asp

NEVADA

Community College of Southern Nevada
Legal Assistant Program
6375 West Charleston Boulevard
Las Vegas, NV 89146-1164
702-651-5954
www.ccsn.nevada.edu

Heritage College
Association of Arts Degree, Paralegal
    Studies
3315 Spring Mountain Road
Las Vegas, NV 89102
702-368-2338
www.heritagecollege.com/01-paralegal.html

Truckee Meadows Community College
Paralegal/Law Program
7000 Dandini Boulevard RDMT 207P
Reno, NV 89512-3999
775-772-4337
www.tmcc.edu/paralegal

NEW HAMPSHIRE

Hesser College
3 Sundial Avenue
Manchester, NH 03103
603-668-6660
www.hesser.edu/legal_paralegal.htm

McIntosh College, Inc.
23 Cataract Avenue
Dover, NH 03820
603-742-1234
www.mcintoshcollege.edu/programs/
    paralegal.asp

New Hampshire Technical Institute
Certificate Program in Paralegal Studies
31 College Drive
Concord, NH 03301-7412
603-271-6484
www.nhti.edu/academics/academic
    programs/degparaleg.html

NEW JERSEY

Atlantic Cape Community College
Paralegal Studies Program
5100 Black Horse Pike
Mays Landing, NJ 08330-2699
609-343-4941
www.atlantic.edu/program/degrees/aas
    Degrees/paralegalDegree.htm

Bergen Community College
Legal Assistant Program
400 Paramus Road
Paramus, NJ 07652
201-447-7100
www.bergen.cc.nj.us

Berkeley College
Paralegal Studies
44 Rifle Camp Road
West Patterson, NJ 07424
973-278-5400
www.berkeleycollege.edu

Brookdale Community College
Paralegal Studies Program
765 Newman Springs Road
Lincroft, NJ 07738-1597
732-224-2337
www.brookdale.cc.nj.us/fac/legalstudies

Burlington County College
601 Pemberton Browns Mills Road
Pemberton, NJ 08068
609-894-9311
http://staff.bcc.edu/paralega

Cumberland County College
Paralegal Studies Program
College Avenue
P.O. Box 1500
Vineland, NJ 08362
856-691-8600
www.cccnj.edu

Essex County Community College
Legal Assistant Studies
303 University Avenue
Newark, NJ 07102
973-877-3462
www.essex.edu

Fairleigh Dickinson University
Paralegal Studies Program
285 Madison Avenue M-DH2-02
Madison, NJ 07940
973-443-8690
http://paralegal.fdu.edu

Gloucester County College Business
    Division
1400 Tanyard Road
Sewell, NJ 08080
856-468-5000
www.gccnj.edu/academics/business_and_
    technology/programs.cfm

Mercer County Community College
Legal Assistant Program
North Broad and Academy Streets
Trenton, NJ 08608
609-586-4800
www.mccc.edu/programs_degree_
    paralegal.shtml

Middlesex County College
Paralegal Studies Program
2600 Woodbridge Avenue
Edison, NJ 08818-3050 732-906-2576
www.middlesexcc.edu/departments/
    accounting/control.cfm

Montclair State University
Paralegal Studies Program
Legal Studies Dept
1 Normal Avenue
Montclair, NJ 07043
973-655-4000
www.montclair.edu

Ocean County College
Legal Assistant Program
P.O. Box 2001
Toms River, NJ 08754
732-255-0390
www.ocean.edu/academics/programs_of_st
    udy/business_studies/index.htm

Raritan Valley Community College
Paralegal Studies
Route 28 and Lamington Road
North Branch, NJ 08876
908-526-1200
http://rvcc2.raritanval.edu/~busadm/
BusLegal.htm

Sussex County Community College
Legal Studies Program/Legal Assistant
One College Hill Road
Newton, NJ 07860
973-300-2181
http://sussex.edu/areasofstudy/divisions/
legal/npweb6.htm

Warren County Community College
Legal Studies
475 Route 57 West
Washington, NJ 07882
908-835-9222
www.warren.cc.nj.us

NEW MEXICO

Albuquerque Technical Vocational Institute
Paralegal Studies
717 University SE
Albuquerque, NM 87106
505-224-3846
www.tvi.edu/bod

Dona Ana Branch Community College
Paralegal Program
Box 30001-Dept 3DA
3400 South Espina Street
Las Cruces, NM 88003
505-527-7500
http://dabcc.nmsu.edu

New Mexico State University—Alamogordo
Paralegal Program
2400 North Scenic Drive
Alamogordo, NM 88310
505-439-3600
http://alamo.nmsu.edu

NEW YORK

Berkeley College
99 Church Street
White Plains, NY 10601
914-694-1122
www.berkeleycollege.edu/academics/
    programs/descriptions/aas_paralegal.htm

Berkeley College of New York City
Paralegal Studies Program
3 East 43rd Street
New York, NY 10017
212-986-4343
www.berkeleycollege.edu/Academics/
    Programs/Descriptions/AAS/AAS_
    Paralegal.htm

Bronx Community College
Paralegal Studies Program
University Avenue and West 181 Street
Bronx, NY 10453
718-289-5636
www.bcc.cuny.edu/business/curricul/
   curparal.htm

Corning Community College
Paralegal Studies Program
1 Academic Drive
Corning, NY 14830-3297
607-962-9222
www.corning-cc.edu

Dutchess Community College
Paralegal Program
53 Pendell Road
Poughkeepsie, NY 12601-1595
914-431-8000
www.sunydutchess.edu

Erie Community College
City Campus—Paralegal Program
121 Ellicott Street
Buffalo, NY 14203
716-851-2770
www.ecc.edu/academics/paralegal.asp

Fingerlakes Community College
Paralegal Program
4355 Lakeshore Drive
Canandaigua, NY 14424
716-394-3522
www.flcc.edu

Genesee Community College
Paralegal Program
One College Road
Batavia, NY 14020
585-343-0055
www.sunygenesee.cc.ny.us/academics/
   programs/legal/Paralegal

Hilbert College
Paralegal Studies Program
5200 South Park Avenue
Hamburg, NY 14075
716-649-7900
www.hilbert.edu

Hofstra University
Paralegal Certificate Legal Studies Program
University College of Continuing Education
250 Hofstra University
Hempstead, NY 11549
516-463-4811
www.hofstra.edu/Academics/UCCE/ucce
   LegalStudies/ucce_ls_paralegal.cfm

Interboro Institute
Paralegal Studies Program
450 West 56th Street
New York, NY 10019
212-399-0091
www.interboro.edu

LaGuardia Community College—CUNY
Paralegal Studies Program
31-10 Thomson Avenue
Long Island City, NY 11101
718-482-7200
www.lagcc.cuny.edu/majors/lawlabor.aspx

Lehman College
Paralegal Certificate Program
250 Bedford Park Boulevard West
Bronx, NY 10468-1589
718-960-8601
www.lehman.edu/ce/paralegal.html

Long Island University
Paralegal Studies Program
1 University Plaza
Brooklyn, NY 11201
718-488-1066
www.brooklyn.liu.edu/bbut05/paralegal_
    studies/paralegal_studies.htm

Long Island University/C.W. Post Legal
    Studies
Paralegal & Legal Nurse Consultant Program
720 Northern Boulevard
Brookville, NY 11548-1300
516-299-2236
www.liu.edu/cwpceps

Marist College
Fishkill Extension Center
400 Westage Business Center
Fishkill, NY 12524
845-897-9648
www.marist.edu/liberalarts/paralegal

Mercy College
Legal Studies Major
555 Broadway
Dobbs Ferry, NY 10522
914-674-7546
www.mercy.edu

Mercy College
Paralegal Studies Certificate Program
277 Martine Avenue
White Plains, NY 10601
914-948-3666 ext. 3328
http://ibs.mercy.edu/student/eozden/
    mercyceu/paralegal.cfm

Monroe Community College
Law & Criminal Justice
228 East Main Street
Rochester, NY 14604
585-262-1600
www.monroecc.edu/etsdbs/MCCatPub.nsf/3
    4872b3a38b0fb868525681700713165/4
    5be87276d4c4669852567230046b64a?
    OpenDocument

Nassau Community College
Paralegal Program
One Education Drive
Garden City, NY 11530
516-572-7501
www.ncc.edu/dptpages/legal

New York City College of Technology
Legal Assistant Studies Department
300 Jay Street N 622
Brooklyn, NY 11201
718-260-5500
www.citytech.cuny.edu/academics/
    deptsites/legalstudies/index.shtml

New York University
Diploma Program in Paralegal Studies
11 West 42nd Street
New York, NY 10036
212-790-1326
www.scps.nyu.edu/departments/
    department.jsp?deptId=30

Olean Business Institute
301 North Union Street
Olean, NY 14760
716-372-7978
www.obi.edu/plg.htm#top

Queens College/CUNY
Paralegal Studies Program
65-30 Kissena Boulevard
Flushing, NY 11367
718-997-5700
www.qc.cuny.edu/CEP

Rockland Community College
145 College Road
Suffern, NY 10901
845-574-4000
www.sunyrockland.edu/paralegal/
    paralegalpage.html

Sage Colleges
Legal Studies Program
140 New Scotland Avenue
Albany, NY 12208
518-292-1736
www.sage.edu/academics/schoolof
    professionalstudies/legalstudies/
    programs/legalstudies.php

Schenectady County Community College
Department of Business and Law
78 Washington Avenue
Schenectady, NY 12305
518-381-1366
www.sunysccc.edu/academic/buslaw/
    progpal.htm

St John's University
Paralegal Studies Program
8000 Utopia Parkway
Queens, NY 11439
718-990-7417
http://new.stjohns.edu

Suffolk County Community College
Paralegal Program
533 College Road
Selden, NY 11784
631-451-4663
http://www3.sunysuffolk.edu/index.asp

SUNY/Westchester Community College
Paralegal Studies
75 Grasslands Road
Valhalla, NY 10595-1698
914-606-6218
www.sunywcc.edu/dep/paralegal

Syracuse University
Legal Studies Program
700 University Avenue, 4th Floor
Syracuse, NY 13244
315-443-3299
http://suce.syr.edu/lap

Tompkins Cortland Community College
Paralegal Program
170 North Street
Dryden, NY 13053
607-844-8211
www.sunytccc.edu/academic/paralegal/
  main.asp

NORTH CAROLINA

Carteret Community College
Paralegal Technology
3505 Arendell Street
Morehead City, NC 28557
252-222-6290
www.carteret.edu/education/academic
  programs/paralegal/paralegalindex.htm

Central Piedmont Community College
Paralegal Technology
P.O. Box 35009
Charlotte, NC 28235
704-330-2722
www.cpcc.edu/paralegal

Fayetteville Technical Community College
Paralegal Technology Program
2201 Hull Road
Fayetteville, NC 28303
919-678-8400
www.faytechcc.edu

King's College
Paralegal Program
322 Lamar Avenue
Charlotte, NC 28204
800-768-2255
www.kingscollegecharlotte.edu/html/index_
  programs.htm

Meredith College
Paralegal Program
3800 Hillsborough Street
Raleigh, NC 27607-5298
919-760-2855
www.meredith.edu/legal

Pitt Community College
Paralegal Technology
1986 Pitt Tech Road
Winterville, NC 28590
252-493-7503
www.pitt.edu

South College—Asheville
1567 Patton Avenue
Asheville, NC 28806
828-252-2486
www.southcollegenc.com/SC03/Programs/
  Paralegalstudies.htm

South Piedmont Community College
Paralegal Technology
4209 Old Charlotte Highway
Monroe, NC 28110
704-290-5100
www.spcc.edu

Western Piedmont Community College
Paralegal Technology
1001 Burkemont Avenue
Morganton, NC 28655-4504
704-438-6194
www.wpcc.edu/acadiv/btd/lex_hm.htm

NORTH DAKOTA

Lake Region State College
1801 College Drive North
Devils Lake, ND 58301-1598
800-443-1313
www.lrsc.nodak.edu

OHIO

Capital University Law School
Paralegal Program
303 East Broad Street
Columbus, OH 43215-3200
614-236-6500
www.law.capital.edu/Paralegal

College of Mount St. Joseph
Paralegal Studies Program
5701 Delhi Road
Cincinnati, OH 45233-1670
800-654-9314
www.msj.edu/academics/majors/
    undergrad/para

Columbus State Community College
550 East Spring Street
Franklin Hall 216
Columbus, OH 43215
800-621-6407
www.cscc.edu/PARL/index.htm

Cuyahoga Community College
Paralegal Studies Program
11000 Pleasant Valley Road
Parma, OH 44130
216-987-5112
www.tri-c.edu/paralegal

Myers University
Paralegal Education Program
3921 Chester Avenue
Cleveland, OH 44115
216-377-6937
www.dnmyers.edu/paraleg/plhome.html

Edison Community College
Paralegal Studies
1973 Edison Drive
Piqua, OH 45356
937-778-8600
www.edison.cc.oh.us/legal

EHOVE Career Center
Paralegal Program
316 West Mason Road
Milan, OH 44846
419-499-4663
www.ehove.net/adulted/paralegal

Kent State University
Paralegal Studies
113 Bowman Hall
P.O. Box 5190
Kent, OH 44242-0001
330-672-2775
http://dept.kent.edu/cjst/paralegalstudies.html

Kent State University—East Liverpool
Legal Assisting Technology
400 East 4th Street
East Liverpool, OH 43920
330-382-7455
www.eliv.kent.edu/ProspectiveStudents/
AcademicPrograms/LegalAssisting
   Technology.cfm

Lake Erie College
Legal Studies Program
391 W. Washington Street
Painesville, OH 44077
800-533-4996
www.lec.edu/management_studies/legal.php

Lakeland Community College
Paralegal Program
7700 Clocktower Drive
Willoughby, OH 44094
800-589-8520
http://lakelandcc.edu/academic/business/
   paralegl

North Central State College
2441 Kenwood Circle
Mansfield, OH 44906
888-755-4899
www.ncstatecollege.edu/academics/
   business/paralegal.htm

RETS Tech Center
Legal Assisting/Paralegal Program
555 East Alex Bell Road
Centerville, OH 45459-9627
800-837-7387
www.retstechcenter.com/legal.shtml

Rhodes State College
Paralegal/Legal Assisting Program
4240 Campus Drive
Lima, OH 45804
419-995-8000
www.rhodesstate.edu/divisions/business_-_
   public_services/program.asp?id=18

Shawnee State University
Legal Assisting Program
940 Second Street
Portsmouth, OH 45662
740-355-2575
www.shawnee.edu/acad/ba/legal.html

Sinclair Community College
Paralegal Program
444 West Third Street
Dayton, OH 45402-1460
800-315-3000
www.sinclair.edu

The University of Akron
Summit College
Legal Assisting Technology
The Polsky Building Room 192
Akron, OH 44325-6501
330-972-7221
http://sc.uakron.edu/?/publicservice/la.html

University of Cincinnati Clermont
4200 Clermont College Drive
Batavia, OH 45103
513-732-5200
www.uc.edu/programs/viewprog.asp?
   progid=1276

The University of Toledo
Department of Undergraduate Legal
   Specialties
College of Health and Human Services
2801 W. Bancroft Street, Stop Code #119
Toledo, Ohio 43606
419-530-4636
www.hhs.utoledo.edu/paralegal/faq.html

Ursuline College
Legal Studies/Paralegal Education
2550 Lander Road
Pepper Pike, OH 44124
440-684-8324
www.ursuline.edu/UCAP/prog_legal_
   studies.asp

Zane State College
Paralegal Program
1555 Newark Road
Zanesville, OH 43701
800-686-8324
www.zanestate.edu/PAR/default.htm

OKLAHOMA

East Central University
Legal Studies Program
1100 East 14th Street
Ada, OK 74820-6999
580-310-5423
www.ecok.edu/academics/schools/hss/hps/
   ls/ls_home.asp

Metropolitan College
10820 East 45th Street, Building B, Suite 101
Oklahoma City, OK 73118
918-627-9429
http://64.143.91.248/prod01.htm

Rose State College
Legal Assistant Program
6420 SE 15th Street
Midwest City, OK 73110
405-733-7673
www.rose.edu/cstudent/busdiv/LA.htm

Tulsa Community College
Legal Assistant Program
909 South Boston
Tulsa, OK 74119
918-595-7000
www.tulsacc.edu/page.asp?durki=
   3731&site=85&return=3543

University of Oklahoma Law Center
Department of Legal Assistant Education
300 Timberdell Road, Room 314
Norman, OK 73019
405-325-1726
www.law.ou.edu/lae

University of Tulsa
Legal Assistant Program
600 South College Avenue
Div. of Continuing Education
Tulsa, OK 74104
918-631-2070
www.utulsa.edu

OREGON

Pioneer Pacific College

Legal Studies

27501 SW Parkway Avenue

Wilsonville, OR 97070

503-682-1862

www.pioneerpacificcollege.com/prog_
leg_para.htm

PENNSYLVANIA

Academy of Medical Arts and Business

Paralegal Specialist Program

2301 Academy Drive

Harrisburg, PA 17112

717-545-4747

www.acadcampus.com/degree.html

Bucks County Community College

Paralegal Studies

275 Swamp Road

Newtown, PA 18940

215-968-8000

www.bucks.edu/paralegal

Berks Technical Institute

2205 Ridgewood Road

Wyomissing, PA 19610

800-490-6992

www.berkstech.com/btiMainSite_content.html

Cedar Crest College

Paralegal Program

100 College Drive

Allentown, PA 18104-6196

610-437-4471

www.cedarcrest.edu/Redesign/homepage4/
home4.asp

Central Pennsylvania College

Paralegal Program

College Hill and Valley Roads

Summerdale, PA 17093

800-759-2727

www.centralpenn.edu/academics/
programs/program.asp?id=fe0L6E4PJfT
gIK9RY9b5

Clarion University of Pennsylvania

Legal Business Studies

840 Wood Street

Clarion, PA 16214

800-672-7171

www.clarion.edu

Community College of Philadelphia

Paralegal Studies Curriculum

1700 Spring Garden Street

Philadelphia, PA 19130

215-751-8010

http://faculty.ccp.edu/dept/pls

Consolidated School of Business

2124 Ambassador Circle

Lancaster, PA 17603

717-394-6211

www.csb.edu/programs.asp?sub=4&id=5

Delaware County Community College

Paralegal Studies

901 South Media Line Road

Media, PA 19063

610-359-5050

www.dccc.edu

Duquesne University
Paralegal Institute
600 Forbes Avenue
Pittsburgh, PA 15282
412-396-6000
www.leadership.duq.edu/home/main.cfm?
    SID=177&myReferer=/paralegal

Gannon University
Paralegal Program
109 University Square
Erie, PA 16541
800-426-6668
www.gannon.edu/PROGRAMS/UNDER/
    paraleg.asp

Harrisburg Area Community College
Legal Assistant Program
One HACC Drive
Harrisburg, PA 17110-2999
717-780-2300
www.hacc.edu

Lehigh Carbon Community College
Paralegal Studies
4525 Education Park Drive
Schnecksville, PA 18078
610-799-1594
www.lccc.edu

Manor College
Paralegal Studies
700 Fox Chase Road
Jenkintown, PA 19046
215-884-2218
www.manor.edu/business/legal%20
    career.htm

Marywood University
Social Sciences Department
2300 Adams Avenue
Scranton, PA 18509
570-348-6211
www.marywood.edu

McCann School of Business
Paralegal Program
2650 Woodglen Road
Pottsville, PA 17901
570-622-7622
www.mccannschool.com

Northampton Community College
Paralegal/Legal Assistant
3835 Green Pond Road
Bethlehem, PA 18020
610-861-5300
www.northampton.edu

Peirce College
Paralegal Studies
1420 Pine Street
Philadelphia, PA 19102
888-467-3472
www.peirce.edu

Pennsylvania College of Technology
Paralegal/Legal Assistant Program
One College Avenue
Williamsport, PA 17701
800-367-9222
www.pct.edu

Villanova University
Paralegal Program
800 Lancaster Avenue
Villanova, PA 19085
610-519-4310
www3.villanova.edu/continuingstudies/
    paralegal/index.html

RHODE ISLAND

Roger Williams University
Legal Studies Department
One Old Ferry Road
Bristol, RI 02809
401-254-3021
www.rwu.edu/Academics/Academic+Progra
    ms/School+of+Justice+Studies/Undergra
    duate+Program.htm

Johnson & Wales University
Center for Legal Studies
8 Abbott Park Place
Providence, RI 02903
401-598-1000
www.jwu.edu/business/deg_paraleg.htm

Community College of Rhode Island
400 East Avenue
Warwick, RI 02886
401-825-1000
www.ccri.edu/catalog/ps-
    laws.shtml#Paralegal_Studies

SOUTH CAROLINA

Aiken Technical College
Paralegal Studies
P.O. Drawer 696
Aiken, SC 29802
803-593-9231
www.aik.tec.sc.us

Central Carolina Technical College
Legal Assistant/Paralegal Major
506 North Guignard Drive
Sumter, SC 29150
803-778-7875
www.sum.tec.sc.us/cctc.asp

Florence-Darlington Technical College
Legal Assistant/Paralegal Program
2715 West Lucas Street
P.O. Box 100548
Florence, SC 29501-0548
800-228-5745
www.fdtc.edu

Greenville Technical College
Paralegal/Legal Assistant Program
506 South Pleasantburg Drive CJ 122
Greenville, SC 29607
864-250-8111
www.greenvilletech.com

Horry-Georgetown Technical College
Legal Assistant/Paralegal Program
743 Hemlock Street
Myrtle Beach, SC 29577
843-477-2006
www.hgtc.edu/academics/departments/
    Legal_Studies/Default.htm

Midlands Technical College

Legal Assistant/Paralegal Program

P.O. Box 2408

Columbia, SC 29202

803-822-3320

www.midlandstech.edu/business/legal.html

Orangeburg-Calhoun Technical College

Associate in Public Service

3250 Saint Matthews Road

Orangeburg, SC 29118-8299

803-536-0311

www.octech.edu

South University—Columbia

Paralegal Studies

3810 Main Street

Columbia, SC 29203

800-688-0932

www.southuniversity.edu

Technical College of the Lowcountry

921 Ribaut Road

Beaufort, SC 29901

843-525-8211

www.tclonline.org

Trident Technical College

Legal Assistant/Paralegal Program

P.O. Box 118067

Charleston, SC 29403-8067

843-722-5526

www.tridenttech.edu/1842.htm

SOUTH DAKOTA

National American University

Paralegal Studies

321 Kansas City Street

P.O. Box 1780

Rapid City, SD 57701

800-843-8892

www.national.edu/Academic%20Programs/
BS_paralegal_studies.html

Western Dakota Technical Institute

Paralegal/Legal Assistant

800 Mickelson Drive

Rapid City, SD 57703

605-394-4034

http://westerndakotatech.org

TENNESSEE

Chattanooga State Technical Community
College

4501 Amnicola Highway

Chattanooga, TN 37406

423-697-4404

www.chattanoogastate.edu/legal_assisting/
lamain.asp

Cleveland State Community College

Legal Assistant Program

P.O. Box 3570

Cleveland, TN 37320

423-472-7141

www.clevelandstatecc.edu

Draughons Junior College
340 Plus Park Boulevard
Nashville, TN 37217
877-258-7796
www.draughons.edu/tennesse/programs-
    legal_assisting.htm

Miller-Motte Technical College
Paralegal Program
1820 Business Park Drive
Clarksville, TN 37040
800-558-0071
www.miller-motte.com

Pellissippi State Technical Community
    College
Paralegal Studies
10915 Hardin Valley Road
P.O. Box 22990
Knoxville, TN 37933-0990
865-694-6400
www.pstcc.edu/community_relations/
    catalog/ctp/programs/ps.html

Roane State Community College
Paralegal Studies
276 Patton Lane
Harriman, TN 37748
865-354-3000
www.roanestate.edu

South College
Paralegal Studies and Legal Studies
200 Hayfield Road
Knoxville, TN 37922
865-251-1800
www.southcollegetn.edu

Southeastern Career College
719 Thompson Lane
Suite 600
Nashville, TN 37204
615-269-9900
www.southeasterncareercollege.edu/
    paralegal.html

Southwest Tennessee Community College
Paralegal Studies
5983 Macon Cove
Memphis, TN 38134
901-333-4130
www.southwest.tn.edu/paralegal

University of Memphis
Paralegal Studies
Room 218
Brister Hall
Memphis, TN 38152
901-678-2716
www.uc.memphis.edu/paralegal.htm

University of Tennessee Chattanooga
Legal Assistant Studies
615 McCallie Avenue
Department 3203
Chattanooga, TN 37403-2598
423-425-4135
www.utc.edu/Academic/CriminalJustice

Volunteer State Community College
Paralegal Studies Program
1480 Nashville Pike
Gallatin, TN 37066-3188
615-230-3303
www2.volstate.edu/academic/Business/
    Paralegal

Walters State Community College
Management/Legal Assistant Concentration
500 South Davy Crockett Parkway
Morristown, TN 37813-6899
423-585-2600
www.wscc.cc.tn.us

TEXAS

Amarillo College
Paralegal Studies Program
2201 South Washington
Amarillo, TX 79109
806-345-5522
www.actx.edu

Blinn College
Legal Assistant Program
2423 Blinn Boulevard
Bryan, TX 77805
979-209-7200
www.blinn.edu

Center for Advanced Legal Studies
3910 Kirby Drive
Suite 200
Houston, TX 77098
713-529-2778
www.paralegal.edu

Central Texas College
Paralegal Program
P.O. Box 1800
Killeen, TX 76540
254-526-1489
http://online.ctcd.edu

Del Mar College
Legal Professions Paralegal Specialty
101 Baldwin Boulevard
Corpus Christi, TX 78404
361-698-1491
www.delmar.edu/legalprof/pl

El Centro College
Paralegal Studies
801 Main Street
Dallas, TX 75202-3604
214-860-2037
www.elcentrocollege.edu

Lamar State College Port Arthur
P.O. Box 310
1500 Procter Street
Port Arthur, TX 77640
800-477-5872
www.lamarpa.edu

Lee College
Legal Assistant Program
P.O. Box 818
Baytown, TX 77522-0818
281-425-6527
www.lee.edu/businesstech/legal

McLennan Community College
Legal Assistant Program
1400 College Drive
Waco, TX 76708
254-299-8622
www.mclennan.edu

Midland College
Legal Assistance Program
3600 North Garfield
Midland, TX 79705
432-685-4500
www.midland.edu/academics/courses/legal.
   php

North Harris College
Legal Assisting Program
2700 W.W. Thorne Drive
Houston, TX 77073
281-618-5400
www.northharriscollege.com

San Antonio College
1300 San Pedro Avenue
San Antonio, TX 78212
210-733-2000
www.accd.edu/sac/sacmain/sac.htm

San Jacinto College—North
Legal Assistant Program
5800 Uvalde
Houston, TX 77049
281-458-4050
www.sjcd.edu

Southeastern Career Institute
Paralegal Program
12005 Ford Road
Northpointe Centre, Suite 100
Dallas, TX 75234
800-524-8800
www.southeasterncareerinstitute.com

San Marco Texas State University
Legal Studies Program
601 University Drive
San Marcos, TX 78666
512-245-2111
www.txstate.edu

Southwestern Professional Institute
Legal Assistant Studies Program
3033 Chimney Rock
Suite 200
Houston, TX 77056
713-781-5908
www.spi-careers.com

Stephen F. Austin State University
Legal Assistant Program
P.O. Box 13064
Nacogdoches, TX 75962-3064
936-468-4408
www.sfasu.edu/aas/criminalj/profession.htm

Tarrant County College
1500 Houston Street
Fort Worth, TX 76102
817-515-8223
www.tccd.edu

Texas A&M University at Commerce
Department of Political Science
P.O. Box 3011
Commerce, TX 75429
903-886-5081
http://orgs.tamu-commerce.edu/paralegal

Texas State University—San Marcos

601 University Drive

San Marcos, TX 78666

512-245-2111

www.txstate.edu

Texas Woman's University

Government Major—Paralegal Emphasis

P.O. Box 425589

Denton, TX 76204

940-898-2000

www.twu.edu

University of Texas at Brownsville/Texas
  Southmost College

80 Fort Brown

Brownsville, TX 78520

956-882-8200

www.utb.edu

Virginia College at Austin

Paralegal Studies

6301 East Highway 290

Austin, TX 78723

866-314-6324

www.vc.edu/austin/program.cfm?ID=16

UTAH

Everest College

Paralegal Studies

3280 West 3500 South

West Valley City, UT 84119

801-840-4800

http://everest-college.org/
  &ctk=1&kid=GOG0005931705

Utah Valley State College

800 West University Parkway

Orem, UT 84058

801-863-4636

www.uvsc.edu/legl

VERMONT

Woodbury College

Paralegal Program

660 Elm Street

Montpelier, VT 05602

802-229-0516

www.woodbury-college.edu/programs/legal

VIRGINIA

Bryant & Stratton College

Paralegal Studies

8141 Hull Street Road

Richmond, VA 23235

804-745-2444

www.bryantstratton.edu

J. Sargeant Reynolds Community College

Legal Assisting Program

P.O. Box 85622

Richmond, VA 23285-5622

804-371-3000

www.jsr.vccs.edu

Marymount University

Paralegal Studies & Legal Administration

2807 North Glebe Road

Arlington, VA 22207

703-522-5600

www.marymount.edu

National College of Business and
  Technology
Paralegal Studies
1813 East Main Street
Salem, VA 24153
540-986-1800
www.ncbt.edu/academics/acadprograms/
  assocparalegal.asp

Northern Virginia Community College
Legal Assisting Program
4001 Wakefield Chapel Road
Annandale, VA 22003
703-323-3000
www.nv.cc.va.us

Virginia Center for Paralegal Studies
411 Chatham Square Office Park
Fredericksburg, VA 22405
540-373-1900
www.virginiaparalegalstudies.com

Virginia Intermont College
Legal Studies and Legal Assisting
1013 Moore Street
Bristol, VA 24201
276-466-7856
www.vic.edu/frameset.html?/academics/
  degrees/index.shtml&1

Virginia Western Community College
Legal Assistant Program
3095 Colonial Avenue
P.O. Box 14007
Roanoake, VA 24038
540-857-8922
www.virginiawestern.edu/academics/
  programs_of_study/programs_detail.php?
  program_id=86

WASHINGTON

Edmonds Community College
Paralegal Program
20000 68th Avenue West
Lynnwood, WA 98036
425-640-1459
www.edcc.edu

Highline Community College
Paralegal Department
2400 South 240th Street
Des Moines, WA 98198
206-870-4853
http://flightline.highline.edu/cg/paralegal.html

Pierce College
Paralegal Studies Program
9401 Farwest Drive SW
Lakewood, WA 98498
253-964-6638
www.pierce.ctc.edu

Skagit Valley College
Paralegal Program
2405 East College Way
Mount Vernon, WA 98273
360-416-7734
www.skagit.edu

South Puget Sound Community College
Paralegal Program
2011 Mottman Road SW
Olympia, WA 98512
360-754-7711
www.spscc.ctc.edu

Spokane Community College
Legal Assistant Program
1810 North Greene Street
Spokane, WA 99217
509-533-7470
www.scc.spokane.edu

Tacoma Community College
6501 South 19th Street
Tacoma, WA 98466
253-566-5000
www.tacomacc.edu/inst_dept/allied_
    health/hjhs/adj_main/start.shtm

WEST VIRGINIA

Marshall Community & Technical College
Legal Assistant Program
400 Hal Greer Boulevard
Huntington, WV 25755-2700
304-696-3646
www.marshall.edu/ctc

Mountain State University
Legal Studies
P.O. Box 9003
Beckley, WV 25802
800-766-6067
www.mountainstate.edu/majors/whystudy/
    legalstudies

WISCONSIN

Chippewa Valley Technical College
Paralegal Program
620 West Clairemont Avenue
Eau Claire, WI 54701
715-833-6260
www.cvtc.edu/Programs/DeptPages/
    Paralegal

Lakeshore Technical College
Paralegal Program
1290 North Avenue
Cleveland, WI 53015
888-468-6582
www.gotoltc.com/programs/para_index.shtml

Madison Area Technical College
3550 Anderson Street
Madison, WI 53704
608-246-6100
http://matcmadison.edu/matc/ASP/show
    program.asp?programnumber=101101

Milwaukee Area Technical College
Paralegal Program
700 West State Street
Milwaukee, WI 53233
414-297-6370
www.matc.edu/student/offerings/
    paralegalaas.html

Northeast Wisconsin Technical College
Paralegal Program
2740 West Mason Street
Green Bay, WI 54307
920-498-6956
www.nwtc.edu/programs/paralegal/
    default.htm

Western Wisconsin Technical College

Paralegal Program

304 6th Street North

La Crosse, WI 54601

608-785-9571

www.western.tec.wi.us

WYOMING

Casper College

Legal Assistant Program

125 College Drive

Casper, WY 82601

307-268-2618

www.caspercollege.edu/adultstudents/

    programs/socialscience/paralegal/index.

    html

Laramie County Community College

Social Science Division Legal Assistant

    Program

1400 East College Drive

Cheyenne, WY 82007

307-778-1230

www.lccc.wy.edu/justice

Appendix B

Professional Associations

In addition to contact information for national paralegal associations and state bar associations, this appendix lists the affiliated organizations of the National Federation of Paralegal Associations. You'll also find a state-by-state listing of higher education agencies.

NATIONAL PARALEGAL ORGANIZATIONS

American Alliance of Paralegals, Inc.
16815 East Shea Boulevard
Suite 110
Box 101
Fountain Hills, AZ 85268
www.aapipara.org

American Association for Paralegal
   Education
19 Mantua Road
Mt. Royal, NJ 08061
856-423-2829
www.aafpe.org

American Bar Association Standing
   Committee on Paralegals
321 North Clark Street
Chicago, IL 60610
312-988-5000
www.abanet.org/legalservices/paralegals

Association of Legal Administrators
75 Tri-State International
Suite 222
Lincolnshire, IL 60069-4435
847-267-1252
www.alanet.org

International Paralegal Management
  Association
P.O. Box 659
Avondale Estates, GA 30002-0659
404-292-4762
www.paralegalmanagement.org

NALS—The Association of Legal
  Professionals
314 East Third Street
Suite 210
Tulsa, OK 74120
918-582-5188
www.nals.org

National Association of Legal Assistants
1516 South Boston #200
Tulsa, OK 74119
918-587-6828
www.nala.org

National Federation of Paralegal
  Associations, Inc.
P.O. Box 2016
Edmonds, WA 98020
425-967-0045
www.paralegals.org

STATE BAR ASSOCIATIONS

Alabama State Bar
415 Dexter Avenue
Montgomery, AL 36104
334-269-1515
www.alabar.org

Alaska Bar Association
P.O. Box 100279
Anchorage, AK 99510-0279
907-272-7469
www.alaskabar.org

State Bar of Arizona
4201 N. 24th Street
Suite 200
Phoenix, AZ 85016-6288
602-252-4804
www.azbar.org

Arkansas Bar Association
400 West Markham
Little Rock, AR 72201
501-375-4606
www.arkbar.org

State Bar of California
180 Howard Street
San Francisco, CA 94105
415-538-2000
www.calbar.org

Colorado Bar Association
1900 Grant Street
Suite 50
Denver, CO 80203
303-860-1115
www.cobar.org

Connecticut Bar Association
30 Bank Street
P.O. Box 350
New Britain, CT 06050
860-223-4400
www.ctbar.org

Delaware State Bar Association
301 North Market Street
Wilmington, DE 19801
302-658-5279
www.dsba.org

District of Columbia Bar
1225 19th Street, NW
Suite 800
Washington, D.C. 20036
202-223-6600
www.badc.org

Florida Bar
651 E. Jefferson Street
Tallahassee, FL 32399-2300
850-561-5600
www.flabar.org

State Bar of Georgia
104 Marietta Street NW
Suite 100
Atlanta, GA 30303
800-334-6865
www.gabar.org

Hawaii State Bar Association
1132 Bishop Street
Suite 906
Honolulu, HI 96813
808-537-1868
www.hsba.org

Idaho State Bar Association
P.O. Box 895
Boise, ID 83701
208-334-4500
www2.state.id.us/isb

Illinois State Bar Association
Illinois Bar Center
424 South Second Street
Springfield, IL 62701
217-525-1760
www.illinoisbar.org

Indiana State Bar Association
One Indiana Square
Suite 530
Indianapolis, IN 46204
317-639-5465
www.state.in.us/isba

Iowa State Bar Association
521 East Locust
Floor 3
Des Moines, IA 50309-1939
515-243-3179
www.iowabar.org

Kansas Bar Association
1200 SW Harrison Street
P.O. Box 1037
Topeka, KS 66601-1037
785-234-5696
www.ksbar.org

Kentucky Bar Association
514 West Main Street
Frankfort, KY 40601-1883
502-564-3795
www.kybar.org

Louisiana State Bar Association
601 St. Charles Avenue
New Orleans, LA 70130
504-566-1600
www.lsba.org

Maine State Bar Association
124 State Street
P.O. Box 788
Augusta, ME 04332-0788
207-622-7523
www.mainebar.org

Maryland State Bar Association, Inc.
520 West Fayette Street
Baltimore, MD 21201
410-685-7878
www.msba.org

Massachusetts Bar Association
20 West Street
Boston, MA 02111
617-338-0500
www.massbar.org

State Bar of Michigan
306 Townsend Street
Lansing, MI 48933-2083
517-346-6300
www.michbar.org

Minnesota State Bar Association
600 Nicollet Mall
Suite 380
Minneapolis, MN 55402
612-333-1183
www.mnbar.org

Mississippi Bar
643 North State Street
P.O. Box 2168
Jackson, MS 39225-2168
601-948-4471
www.msbar.org

Missouri Bar
P.O. Box 119
Jefferson City, MO 65102
573-635-4128
www.mobar.org

State Bar of Montana
7 West Sixth Avenue
Suite 2B
P.O. Box 577
Helena, MT 59624
406-442-7660
www.montanabar.org

Nebraska State Bar Association
635 South 14th Street
2nd Floor
Lincoln, NE 68501
402-475-7091
www.nebar.com

Nevada State Bar
600 East Charleston Boulevard
Las Vegas, NV 89104
702-382-2200
www.nvbar.org

New Hampshire Bar Association
2 Pillsbury Street
Suite 300
Concord, NH 03301
603-224-6942
www.nhbar.org

New Jersey State Bar Association
New Jersey Law Center
One Constitution Square
New Brunswick, NJ 08901
732-249-5000
www.njsbf.org

State Bar of New Mexico
5121 Masthead NE
Albuquerque, NM 87109
505-797-6000
www.nmbar.org

New York State Bar Association
1 Elk Street
Albany, NY 12207
518-463-3200
www.nysba.org

North Carolina Bar Association
P.O. Box 3688
Cary, NC 27519-3688
919-828-4620
www.ncbar.org

State Bar Association of North Dakota
504 North Washington Street
Bismarck, ND 58502-2136
701-255-1404
www.sband.org

Ohio State Bar Association
1700 Lake Shore Drive
P.O. Box 16562
Columbus, OH 43216-6562
614-487-2050
www.ohiobar.org

Oklahoma Bar Association
1901 North Lincoln Boulevard
Oklahoma City, OK 73152
405-416-7000
www.okbar.org

Oregon State Bar
5200 SW Meadows Road
P.O. Box 1689
Lake Oswego, OR 97035-0889
503-620-0222
www.osbar.org

Pennsylvania Bar Association
100 South Street
P.O. Box 186
Harrisburg, PA 17108-0186
717-238-6715
www.pabar.org

Rhode Island Bar Association
115 Cedar Street
Providence, RI 02903
401-421-574
www.ribar.com

South Carolina Bar Association
950 Taylor Street
Columbia, SC 29202
803-799-6653
www.scbar.org

State Bar of South Dakota
222 East Capitol Avenue
Pierre, SD 57501-2596
605-224-7554
www.sdbar.org

Tennessee Bar Association
221 4th Avenue North
Suite 400
Nashville, TN 37219-2198
615-383-7421
www.tba.org

State Bar of Texas
1414 Colorado
Austin, TX 78701
512-463-1463
www.texasbar.com

Utah State Bar
645 South 200 East
Suite 310
Salt Lake City, UT 84111
801-531-9077
www.utahbar.org

Vermont Bar Association
35-37 Court Street
P.O. Box 100
Montpelier, VT 05601-0100
802-223-2020
www.vtbar.org

Virginia State Bar
707 East Main Street
Suite 1500
Richmond, VA 23219-2800
804-775-0550
www.vsb.org

Washington State Bar Association
2101 Fourth Avenue
Suite 400
Seattle, WA 98121-2330
800-945-9722
www.wsba.org

West Virginia State Bar
2006 Kanawha Boulevard East
Charleston, WV 25311
304-558-7993
www.wvbar.org

State Bar of Wisconsin
P.O. Box 7158
Madison, WI 53707-7158
608-257-3838
www.wisbar.org

Wyoming State Bar
500 Randall Avenue
P.O. Box 109
Cheyenne, WY 82003
307-632-9061
www.wyomingbar.org

NFPA-AFFILIATED ORGANIZATIONS

ALASKA
Alaska Association of Paralegals
P.O. Box 101956
Anchorage, AK 99510-1956
907-646-8018
www.alaskaparalegals.org

CALIFORNIA
Sacramento Valley Paralegal Association
P.O. Box 453
Sacramento, CA 95812-0453
916-286-8317
www.svpa.org

San Francisco Paralegal Association
985 Darien Way
San Francisco, CA 94125
415-770-2390
www.sfpa.com

COLORADO
Rocky Mountain Paralegal Association
1660 Lincoln Street
Suite 2000
Denver, CO 80246-2000
303-370-9444
www.rockymtnparalegal.org

CONNECTICUT
Central Connecticut Paralegal Association,
   Inc.
P.O. Box 230594
Hartford, CT 06123-0594
CentralConnecticut@paralegals.org

Connecticut Association of Paralegals
P.O. Box 134
Bridgeport, CT 06601-0134
Connecticut@paralegals.org

New Haven County Association of
   Paralegals
P.O. Box 862
New Haven, CT 06504-0862
NewHaven@paralegals.org

DISTRICT OF COLUMBIA
National Capital Area Paralegals
   Association
P.O. Box 27607
Washington, D.C. 20038-7607
www.ncapa.com

FLORIDA
Tampa Bay Paralegal Association, Inc.
P.O. Box 2840
Tampa, FL 33601
813-229-3333
www.tbpa.org

GEORGIA
Georgia Association of Paralegals
1199 Euclid Avenue
Atlanta, GA 30307
404-522-1457
gaparalegal@mindspring.com

HAWAII

Hawaii Paralegal Association
P.O. Box 674
Honolulu, HI 96809
www.hawaiiparalegal.org

ILLINOIS

Illinois Paralegal Association
P.O. Box 452
New Lenox, IL 60451-0452
815-462-4620
www.ipaonline.org

INDIANA

Indiana Paralegal Association, Inc.
P.O. Box 44518
Indianapolis, IN 46204
www.IndianaParalegals.org

The Michiana Paralegal Association, Inc.
P.O. Box 11458
South Bend, Indiana 46634
Michiana@Paralegals.org

Northeast Indiana Paralegal Association
P.O. Box 13646
Fort Wayne, IN 46865
www.neindianaparalegal.org

KANSAS

Kansas Paralegal Association
P.O. Box 1675
Topeka, Kansas 66601
www.ksparalegals.org

KENTUCKY

Greater Lexington Paralegal Association,
    Inc.
P.O. Box 574
Lexington, KY 40589
www.lexingtonparalegals.org

LOUISIANA

New Orleans Paralegal Association
P.O. Box 30604
New Orleans, LA 70190
504-467-3136
neworleans@paralegals.org

MARYLAND

Maryland Association of Paralegals, Inc.
550M Ritchie Highway
PMB #203
Severna Park, MD 21146
410-576-2252
info@MDparalegals.org

MASSACHUSETTS

Central Massachusetts Paralegal
    Association
P.O. Box 444
Worcester, MA 01614
centralmassachusetts@paralegals.org

Massachusetts Paralegal Association, Inc.
P.O. Box 1381
Marblehead, MA 01945
massachusetts@paralegals.org

Western Massachusetts Paralegal
Association, Inc.
P.O. Box 30005
Springfield, MA 01103
www.wmassparalegal.org

MINNESOTA

Minnesota Paralegal Association
1711 West County Road #300N
Roseville, MN 55113
651-633-2778
www.mnparalegals.org

NEBRASKA

Rocky Mountain Paralegal Association
P.O. Box 481864
Denver, CO 80248-1864
303-370-9444
www.rockymtnparalegal.org

NEW HAMPSHIRE

Paralegal Association of New Hampshire
P.O. Box 728
Manchester, NH 03105-0728
www.panh.org

NEW JERSEY

South Jersey Paralegal Association
P.O. Box 355
Haddonfield, NJ 08033
www.sjpaparalegals.org

NEW YORK

Capital District Paralegal Association, Inc.
P.O. Box 12562
Albany, NY 12212-2562
www.cdpa.info

Long Island Paralegal Association
1877 Bly Road
East Meadow, NY 11554
516-357-9820
www.liparalegals.org/main_web/home-
page_main.htm

Manhattan Paralegal Association, Inc.
P.O. Box 4006
Grand Central Station
New York, NY 10163
212-330-8213
Manhattan@paralegals.org

Paralegal Association of Rochester, Inc.
P.O. Box 40567
Rochester, NY 14604
www.par.itgo.com

OHIO

Cleveland Association of Paralegals
P.O. Box 14517
Cleveland, OH 44114
216-556-5437
www.capohio.org

Greater Dayton Paralegal Association, Inc.
P.O. Box 10515
Mid-City Station
Dayton, OH 45402
www.gdpa.org

Paralegal Association of Central Ohio
P.O. Box 15182
Columbus, OH 43215-0182
614-470.2000
www.pacoparalegals.org

OREGON

Oregon Paralegal Association
P.O. Box 8523
Portland, OR 97207
503-796-1671
www.oregonparalegals.org

PENNSYLVANIA

Central Pennsylvania Paralegal Association
   (CPPA)
P.O. Box 11814
Harrisburg, PA 17108
cppageneral@comcast.net

Montgomery County Paralegal Association
P.O. Box 1765
Blue Bell, PA 19422
Montgomery@Paralegals.org

Philadelphia Association of Paralegals
P.O. Box 59179
Philadelphia, PA 19102-9179
215-255-8405
www.philaparalegals.com

Pittsburgh Paralegal Association
P.O. Box 2845
Pittsburgh, PA 15230
412-344-3904
www.pghparalegals.org

RHODE ISLAND

Rhode Island Paralegals Association
P.O. Box 1003
Providence, RI 02901
RhodeIsland@paralegals.org

SOUTH CAROLINA

Palmetto Paralegal Association
P.O. Box 11634
Columbia, SC 29211-1634
http://ppasc.org/cgi-bin/site.cgi?tab=1&
   pl=200

SOUTH DAKOTA

Served by:
Rocky Mountain Paralegal Association
P.O. Box 481864
Denver, CO 80248-1864
303-370-9444
www.rockymtnparalegal.org

TENNESSEE

Middle Tennessee Paralegal Association
P.O. Box 198006
Nashville, TN 37219
www.mtpaonline.com

TEXAS

Dallas Area Paralegal Association
P.O. Box 12533
Dallas, Texas 75225-0533
972-991-0853
dallasparalegals.org

UTAH

Served by:

Rocky Mountain Paralegal Association

P.O. Box 481864

Denver, CO 80248-1864

303-370-9444

www.rockymtnparalegal.org

VERMONT

Vermont Paralegal Organization

P.O. Box 5755

Burlington, VT 05402

Vermont@paralegals.org

WASHINGTON

Washington State Paralegal Association

P.O. Box 58530

Seattle WA 98138-1530

866-257-9772 (WSPA)

www.wspaonline.org

WYOMING

Served by:

Rocky Mountain Paralegal Association

P.O. Box 481864

Denver, CO 80248-1864

303-370-9444

www.rockymtnparalegal.org

STATE AGENCIES OF HIGHER EDUCATION

Alabama Commission on Higher Education

P.O. Box 302000

Montgomery, AL 36130-2000

334-242-1998

www.ache.state.al.us

Alaska Commission on Postsecondary
Education

3030 Vintage Boulevard

Juneau, AK 99801

907-465-2962

800-441-2962

http://alaskadvantage.state.ak.us

Arizona Commission for Postsecondary
Education

2020 North Central Avenue

Suite 550

Phoenix, AZ 85004-4503

602-258-2435

www.azhighered.gov

Arkansas Department of Higher Education

114 East Capitol Avenue

Little Rock, AR 72201

501-371-2000

www.arkansashighered.com

California Student Aid Commission
P.O. Box 419027
Rancho Cordova, CA 95741-9027
916-526-7590
888-224-7268
www.csac.ca.gov

Colorado Commission on Higher Education
1380 Lawrence Street
Suite 1200
Denver, CO 80204
303-866-2723
www.state.co.us/cche

Connecticut Department of Higher
    Education
61 Woodland Street
Hartford, CT 06105-2326
860-947-1800
www.ctdhe.org

Delaware Higher Education Commission
Carvel State Office Building
820 North French Street
Fifth Floor
Wilmington, DE 19801
302-577-5240
800-292-7935
www.doe.state.de.us/high-ed

State Education Office District of Columbia
441 4th Street NW
Suite 350 North
Washington, D.C. 20001
202-727-6436
http://seo.dc.gov/main.shtm

Florida Department of Education
Office of Student Financial Assistance
1940 North Monroe Street
Suite 70
Tallahassee, FL 32303
904-487-0649
www.firn.edu/doe/osfa

Georgia Student Finance Commission
State Loans Division
Suite 230
2082 East Exchange Place
Tucker, GA 30084
770-724-9000
800-505-4732
www.gsfc.org

Hawaii State Postsecondary Education
    Commission
2444 Dole Street
Room 209
Honolulu, HI 96822-2302
808-956-8213

Idaho State Board of Education
P.O. Box 83720
Boise, ID 83720-0037
208-334-2270
www.boardofed.idaho.gov

Illinois Student Assistance Commission
1755 Lake Cook Road
Deerfield, IL 60015-5209
800-899-4722
www.collegezone.com

State Student Assistance Commission of
Indiana
150 West Market Street
Suite 500
Indianapolis, IN 46204
317-232-2350
888-528-4719
www.ssaci.in.gov

Iowa College Student Aid Commission
200 10th Street
Fourth Floor
Des Moines, IA 50309
800-383-4222
www.iowacollegeaid.org

Kansas Board of Regents
Curtis State Office Building
1000 SW Jackson Street
Suite 520
Topeka, KS 66612-1368
785-296-3421
www.kansasregents.org

Kentucky Higher Education Assistance
Authority
P.O. Box 798
Frankfort, KY 40602-0798
502-696-7200
800-928-8926
www.kheaa.com

Louisiana Office of Student Financial
Assistance
P.O. Box 91202
Baton Rouge, LA 70821-9202
225-922-1011
800-259-5626
www.osfa.state.la.us

Finance Authority of Maine
P.O. Box 949
Augusta, ME 04332-0949
207-623-3263
800-228-3734
www.famemaine.com

Maryland Higher Education Commission
839 Bestgate Road
Suite 400
Annapolis, MD 21401
410-260-4500
800-974-0203
www.mhec.state.md.us

Massachusetts Board of Higher Education
One Ashburton Place
Room 1401
Boston, MA 02108-1696
617-994-6950
www.mass.edu

Michigan Higher Education Assistance
Authority
Office of Scholarships and Grants
P.O. Box 30462
Lansing, MI 48909-7962
517-373-3394
www.michigan.gov/mistudentaid

Minnesota Office of Higher Education
1450 Energy Park Drive
Suite 350
Saint Paul, MN 55108-5227
651-642-0567
800-657-3866
www.ohe.state.mn.us

Mississippi Office of Student Financial Aid
3825 Ridgewood Road
Jackson, MS 39211
601-432-6997
800-327-2980
www.mississippiuniversities.com

Missouri Department of Higher Education
3515 Amazonas Drive
Jefferson City, MO 65109
573-751-2361
800-473-6757
www.dhe.mo.gov

Montana University System
2500 Broadway
P.O. Box 203101
Helena, MT 59620-3101
406-444-6570
www.montana.edu/wwwoche

Nebraska Coordinating Commission for
    Postsecondary Education
140 North Eighth Street
Suite 300
P.O. Box 95005
Lincoln, NE 68509-5005
402-471-2847
www.ccpe.state.ne.us/PublicDoc/CCPE/Def
    ault.asp

Nevada Department of Education
700 East Fifth Street
Carson City, NV 89701-5096
775-687-9200
www.nde.state.nv.us

New Hampshire Postsecondary Education
    Commission
3 Barrell Court
Suite 300
Concord, NH 03301-8543
603-271-2555
www.state.nh.us/postsecondary

Commission on Higher Education (New
    Jersey)
20 West State Street
P.O. Box 542
Trenton, NJ 08625-0542
609-292-4310
www.state.nj.us/highereducation/index.htm

Higher Education Student Assistance
    Authority (New Jersey)
P.O. Box 540
Building 4
Quakerbridge Plaza
Trenton, NJ 08625
609-588-3226
800-792-8670
www.hesaa.org

New Mexico Higher Education Department
1068 Cerrillos Road
Santa Fe, NM 87505
505-476-6500
800-279-9777
http://hed.state.nm.us

New York State Higher Education Services
  Corporation
99 Washington Avenue
Albany, NY 12255
518-473-1574
888-697-4372
www.hesc.org

North Carolina State Education Assistance
  Authority
P.O. Box 14103
Research Triangle Park, NC 27709-3663
919-549-8614
www.cfnc.org

North Dakota University System
North Dakota Student Financial Assistance
  Program
600 East Boulevard Avenue
Department 215
Bismarck, ND 58505-0230
701-328-4114
www.ndus.edu

Ohio Board of Regents
State Grants and Scholarships Department
30 East Broad Street
36th Floor
Columbus, OH 43215-3414
614-466-6000
888-833-1133
www.regents.state.oh.us/sgs

Oklahoma State Regents for Higher
  Education
655 Research Parkway
Suite 200
Oklahoma City, OK 73104
405-225-9100
www.okhighered.org

Oregon Student Assistance Commission
1500 Valley River Drive
Suite 100
Eugene, OR 97401
541-687-7400
800-452-8807
www.osac.state.or.us

Office of Postsecondary and Higher
  Education (Pennsylvania)
Department of Education
333 Market Street
Harrisburg, PA 17126
717-787-5041
www.pdehighered.state.pa.us/higher/site/de
  fault.asp

Rhode Island Higher Education Assistance
  Authority
560 Jefferson Boulevard
Warwick, RI 02886
401-736-1100
800-922-9855
www.riheaa.org

South Carolina Commission on Higher
  Education
1333 Main Street
Suite 200
Columbia, SC 29201
803-737-2260
www.che.sc.gov

South Dakota Board of Regents
306 East Capitol Avenue
Suite 200
Pierre, SD 57501-2545
605-773-3455
www.ris.sdbor.edu

Tennessee Higher Education Commission
Parkway Towers
404 James Robertson Parkway
Suite 1900
Nashville, TN 37243
615-741-3605
www.state.tn.us/thec

Texas Higher Education Coordinating Board
P.O. Box 12788
Austin, TX 78711-2788
512-427-6101
800-242-3062
www.thecb.state.tx.us

Utah State Board of Regents
Gateway Center
60 South 400 West
Salt Lake City, UT 84101-1284
801-321-7103
www.utahsbr.edu

Vermont Student Assistance Corporation
Champlain Mill
P.O. Box 20001
Winooski, VT 05404
802-655-9602
800-642-3177
www.vsac.org

State Council of Higher Education for
  Virginia
James Monroe Building
101 North 14th Street
Ninth Floor
Richmond, VA 23219
804-225-2600
www.schev.edu

Washington State Higher Education
  Coordinating Board
P.O. Box 43430
917 Lakeridge Way
Olympia, WA 98504-3430
360-753-7800
www.hecb.wa.gov

West Virginia Higher Education Policy
  Commission
1018 Kanawha Boulevard East
Charleston, WV 25301
304-558-0699
www.hepc.wvnet.edu

Wisconsin Higher Educational Aids Board
131 West Wilson Street
Suite 902
Madison, WI 53703
608-267-2206
http://heab.state.wi.us/

Wyoming Community College Commission
2020 Carey Avenue
8th Floor
Cheyenne, WY 82002
307-777-7763
www.commission.wcc.edu

American Samoa Community College
Board of Higher Education
P.O. Box 2609
Pago Pago, AS 96799
684-699-9155
www.ascc.as

Northern Marianas College
Office of the President
P.O. Box 501250
Saipan, MP 96950-1250
670-234-3690
www.nmcnet.edu

Puerto Rico Council on Higher Education
P.O. Box 19900
San Juan, PR 00910-1900
787-724-7100
www.ces.gobierno.pr

Republic of the Marshall Islands
RMI Scholarship Grant and Loan Board
P.O. Box 1436
3 Lagoon Road
Majuro, MH 96960
692-625-3108

Virgin Islands Board of Education
No. 44-46 Kongen S. Gade
Charlotte Amalie, VI 00802
340-774-0100
www.usvi.org/education

Appendix C

Additional Resources

Now that you have a sense of the steps you need to take to accomplish your educational and career goals, look through this appendix for sources that will give you more specific advice on the area with which you need help.

The resources listed here will help you delve deeper into the topics covered in this book.

GENERAL INFORMATION

Astl, Catherine. *Behind the Bar: Inside the Paralegal Profession* (Lincoln, NE: iUniverse 2003).

Estrin, Chere. *Paralegal Career Guide, 4th Edition* (Upper Saddle River, NJ: Prentice Hall, 2006).

FINDING A JOB

Job Interviews That Get You Hired (New York: LearningExpress, 2006).

McKinney, Anne, Ed. *Real Resumes for Legal and Paralegal Jobs* (Fayetteville, NC: Prep Publishing, 2004).

Resumes That Get You Hired (New York: LearningExpress, 2006).

Warner, Ralph E., Stephen R. Elias, and Catherine Elias Jermany. *The Independent Paralegal's Handbook: Everything You Need to Run a Business Preparing Legal Paperwork for the Public.* (Berkeley, CA: Nolo Press, 1999).

SUCCEEDING ON THE JOB

Berger, Dorian S. and A.T. Mann. *The Paralegal's Guide to the Microsoft Office System*. (Rollinsford, NH: Agility Press, 2005).

Garner, Bryan A., Ed. *Black's Law Dictionary, 9th Edition* (Boston: Houghton Mifflin, 2006).

The Bluebook: A Uniform System of Citation, 18th Edition (Harvard Law Review Association, 1996) (updated as necessary).

Bouchoux, Deborah. *The Practical Paralegal: Strategies for Success*. (New York: Aspen Publishers, 2005).

Burton, William C. *Burton's Legal Thesaurus, 3rd Edition* (New York: McGraw-Hill, 2001).

Cannon, Therese A. *Concise Guide to Paralegal Ethics, 2nd Edition* (New York: Aspen Publishers, 2006).

Cheeseman, Henry and Thomas F. Goldman. *The Paralegal Professional: Essentials*. (Saddle River, NJ: Prentice Hall, 2003).

Ferrazzi, Keith and Tahl Raz. *Never Eat Alone and Other Secrets to Success, One Relationship at a Time* (New York: Currency, 2005).

Garner, Bryan A. *The Elements of Legal Style, 2nd Edition* (New York: Oxford University Press, USA, 2002).

Orlik, Deborah. *Ethics: Top Ten Rules for Paralegals*. (Saddle River, NJ: Prentice Hall, 2005).

ASSOCIATION PUBLICATIONS

Publications available from the American Association for Paralegal Education (AAfPE):
AAfPE Directory, published annually
Choosing a Quality Paralegal Education Program (brochure).
Available from: www.aafpe.org/p_store/index.htm

Publications available from the National Association of Legal Assistants, Inc. (NALA):
NALA Manual for Paralegals and Legal Assistants: A General Skills & Litigations Guide for Today's Professionals, 4th Edition (2004).

Facts & Findings: The Quarterly Journal for Legal Assistants. Free with NALA membership, $25 per year for nonmembers.

The Career Chronicle (a once-yearly bonus issue of *Facts & Findings*) and *The National Utilization and Compensation Survey Report* (published bi-annually), which provide current information on the state of the paralegal profession.

Available from: www.nala.org/Publ.htm

Publications available from the National Federal of Paralegal Associations (NFPA):

The National Paralegal Reporter, the official publication of NFPA, published bimonthly.

The PACE Candidates Handbook includes information on the Paralegal Advanced Competency Exam, containing an application, sample questions, and study reference list. $25.

The PACE Study Manual provides an overview of the five domains covered on the Paralegal Advanced Competency Exam. $55.

Available from: www.paralegals.org/displaycommon.cfm?an=6

FINDING THE RIGHT COLLEGE AND PAYING FOR IT

Best 361 Colleges, 2007 Edition (Princeton, NJ: The Princeton Review, 2006).
Scholarships, Grants, and Prizes 2007 (Lawrenceville, NJ: Peterson's, 2006).
Two-Year Colleges 2007 (Lawrenceville, NJ: Peterson's, 2006).
College Board Scholarship Handbook 2007 (New York: College Board, 2006).

ASSOCIATIONS

American Association for Paralegal Education: www.aafpe.org/index.htm
American Alliance of Paralegals, Inc.: www.aapipara.org
American Bar Association Standing Committee on Paralegals:
www.abanet.org/legalservices/paralegals/home.html
International Paralegal Management Association:
www.paralegalmanagement.org/ipma/index.asp

NALS—The Association for Legal Professionals: www.nals.org/index.html
National Association of Legal Assistants: www.nala.org
National Paralegal Association: www.nationalparalegal.org
National Federation of Paralegal Associations: www.paralegals.org/index.cfm

OTHER HELPFUL LINKS

FindLaw: www.findlaw.com
Guide to Law Online: www.loc.gov/law/guide
Jurist Legal News and Research: http://jurist.law.pitt.edu
Law.com: www.law.com
Law Guru: www.lawguru.com
Legal Engine: www.legalengine.com
Nolo: www.nolo.com/statute/index.cfm/LR.index.html

WEBSITES FOR PARALEGAL EDUCATION PROGRAMS

At the time of publication, the websites listed here were current. Because of the dynamics of the Web, we cannot guarantee their continued existence or content.

Here, you will find a list of popular and relevant websites from which to begin your search for a paralegal education program. Finding the right school and program is important, so be sure to make time for a serious investigation of each site and its corresponding links to different programs.

In addition to the links found here, check with your state bar association, which usually will have information on paralegal programs. Most counties and cities have bar associations as well. Or check with a local paralegal organization that is affiliated with one of the national associations. For a complete listing of national organizations, state bar associations, and affiliated organizations of the National Federation of Paralegal Associations, see Appendix B.

www.paralegals.org
The National Federation of Paralegals Association, although not specifically recommending any particular school, provides a comprehensive Paralegal

Education Program Directory. Organized by state, it lists names, addresses, and phone numbers of schools, with website and/or e-mail hotlinks to some. To find the list, select the "Getting Started" icon on their homepage.

www.paralegalcolleges.com

A directory of colleges offering paralegal programs approved by the American Bar Association. They are arranged by state, giving the college name and town, with links directly to each school's website. The site also has a general directory of college names, arranged by state, with links to school websites.

http://stu.findlaw.com/schools/paralegal

This site provides a list of several schools in each state that offer a paralegal program. It has links to the school websites.

www.petersons.com

Peterson's College Quest program provides the opportunity for a personalized search through a database of thousands of colleges and universities. You can select a field of study, such as paralegal, and then narrow the search by other criteria such as location and cost. A list of schools that meet your criteria will be displayed, providing detailed information about each school, including links to websites.

www.collegeview.com

This is another self-selecting search site, including more than 3,000 colleges and universities. It includes information on each school and links to school websites.

www.princetonreview.com

You can select your own criteria to search on this site, which includes a business school section as well as colleges and universities. Detailed information and website links for each school are included.

www.xap.com

This personal criteria-based search site includes colleges, universities, and trade schools. The trade school section includes a number of schools with paralegal programs.

www.collegecenter.com

This site provides advice regarding the selecting of appropriate colleges and universities and free information about the admissions process, but it charges fees for specific guidance services.

www.rwm.org/rwm

A database of private postsecondary vocational schools. The viewer selects a state, then a field of training. The displayed list shows school name, address and telephone number, and a link to the school's website.

www.universities.com

This site offers lists of more than 7,500 colleges and universities, arranged alphabetically or by state. Includes detailed information on schools and links to their websites.

www.collegedegree.com

A directory of degrees, certificates, and courses offered through distance learning.

Each of the following sites provides names-only lists of colleges and universities arranged by state, with a link to each school's website.

www.collegescolleges.com
www.globalcomputing.com/university.html
www.megamallandmall.com/college.html
www.ulinks.com

Appendix D

Sample Free Application for Federal Student Aid (FAFSA)

On the following pages, you will find a sample FAFSA. Familiarize yourself with the form so that when you apply for federal and state student grants, work-study, and loans, you will know what information you need to have ready. At press time, this was the most current form, and although the form remains mostly the same from year to year, you should check the FAFSA website (www.fafsa.ed.gov) for the most current information.

DRAFT 06-01-2005

FAFSA
We Help Put America Through School

Use this form to apply free for federal and state student grants, work-study and loans.
Or apply free online at www.fafsa.ed.gov.

Applying by the Deadlines

For federal aid, submit your application as early as possible, but no earlier than January 1, 2006. We must receive your application no later than June 30, 2007. Your college must have your correct, complete information by your last day of enrollment in the 2006-2007 school year.

For state or college aid, the deadline may be as early as January 2006. See the table to the right for state deadlines. You may also need to complete additional forms. Check with your high school guidance counselor or a financial aid administrator at your college about state and college sources of student aid and deadlines.

If you are filing close to one of these deadlines, we recommend you file online at **www.fafsa.ed.gov**. This is the fastest and easiest way to apply for aid.

Using Your Tax Return

If you are supposed to file a 2005 federal income tax return, we recommend that you complete it before filling out this form. If you have not yet filed your return, you can still submit your FAFSA, but you must provide income and tax information. Once you file your tax return, correct any income or tax information that is different from what you initially submitted on your FAFSA.

Filling Out the FAFSA

Your answers on this form will be read electronically. Therefore:

- use black ink and fill in ovals completely:

- print clearly in CAPITAL letters and skip a box between words:

- report dollar amounts (such as $12,356.41) like this:

Correct ● **Incorrect** ✗ ✓

| I | 5 | | E | L | M | | S | T |

$ | 1 | 2 | , | 3 | 5 | 6 | **no cents**

Blue is for student information and purple is for parent information.

If you or your family has unusual circumstances (such as loss of employment), complete this form to the extent you can, then submit it as instructed and consult with the financial aid office at the college you plan to attend.

For more information or help in filling out the FAFSA, call 1-800-4-FED-AID (1-800-433-3243). TTY users may call 1-800-730-8913. Or visit our Web site at **www.studentaid.ed.gov**.

Mailing Your FAFSA

After you complete this application, make a copy of pages 3 through 6 for your records. Then mail the original of only pages 3 through 6 in the attached envelope or send it to: Federal Student Aid Programs, P.O. Box 7001, Mt. Vernon, IL 62864-0071. Do not send the worksheets on page 8; keep them for your records.

If you do not receive the results of your application—a *Student Aid Report* (SAR)—within three weeks, please check online at **www.fafsa.ed.gov** or call 1-800-433-3243. If you provided your e-mail address in question 13, you will receive information about your application within a few days after we process it.

Let's Get Started!

Now go to page 3, detach the application form and begin filling it out. Refer to the notes as instructed.

STATE AID DEADLINES

File Online and File On Time
www.fafsa.ed.gov

AK   April 15, 2006 *(date received)*
AR   For State Grant - April 1, 2006
     For Workforce Grant - July 1, 2006 *(date received)*
AZ   June 30, 2006 *(date received)*
*^CA   For initial awards - March 2, 2006
     For additional community college awards -
     September 2, 2006 *(date postmarked)*
*DC   June 28, 2006 *(date received by state)*
DE   April 15, 2006 *(date received)*
FL   May 15, 2006 *(date processed)*
^IA   July 1, 2006 *(date received)*
#IL   First-time applicants - September 30, 2006
     Continuing applicants - August 15, 2006
     (date received)
IN   March 10, 2006 *(date received)*
#*KS   April 1, 2006 *(date received)*
#KY   March 15, 2006 *(date received)*
#^LA   May 1, 2006
     Final deadline - July 1, 2006 *(date received)*
#^MA   May 1, 2006 *(date received)*
MD   March 1, 2006 *(date received)*
ME   May 1, 2006 *(date received)*
MI   March 1, 2006 *(date received)*
MN   30 days after term starts *(date received)*
MO   April 1, 2006 *(date received)*
#MT   March 1, 2006 *(date received)*
NC   March 15, 2006 *(date received)*
ND   March 15, 2006 *(date received)*
NH   May 1, 2006 *(date received)*
^NJ   June 1, 2006, if you received a Tuition Aid
     Grant in 2005-2006
     All other applicants
     - October 1, 2006, fall & spring term
     - March 1, 2007, spring term only
     (date received)
*^NY   May 1, 2007 *(date received)*
OH   October 1, 2006 *(date received)*
#OK   April 30, 2006
     Final deadline - June 30, 2006
     (date received)
*PA   All 2005-2006 State Grant recipients & all
     non-2005-2006 State Grant recipients in
     degree programs - May 1, 2006
     All other applicants - August 1, 2006
     (date received)
#RI   March 1, 2006 *(date received)*
SC   June 30, 2006 *(date received)*
TN   May 1, 2006 *(date processed)*
*^WV   March 1, 2006 *(date received)*

Check with your financial aid administrator for these states and territories:
AL, *AS, CO, *CT, *FM, GA, *GU, *HI, ID, *MH, *MP, MS, *NE, *NM, *NV, OR, PR, *PW, *SD, *TX, UT, *VA, *VI, *VT, WA, WI and *WY.

*For priority consideration, submit application by date specified.*
^ *Applicants encouraged to obtain proof of mailing.*
* *Additional form may be required.*

STATE AID DEADLINES

ISD5472

Notes for questions **14 – 15** (page 3)

If you are an eligible noncitizen, write in your eight- or nine-digit Alien Registration Number. Generally, you are an eligible noncitizen if you are (1) a U.S. permanent resident with a Permanent Resident Card (I-551); (2) a conditional permanent resident (I-551C); or (3) the holder of an Arrival-Departure Record (I-94) from the Department of Homeland Security showing any one of the following designations: "Refugee," "Asylum Granted," "Parolee" (I-94 confirms paroled for a minimum of one year and status has not expired) or "Cuban-Haitian Entrant." If you are in the U.S. on an F1 or F2 student visa, a J1 or J2 exchange visitor visa, or a G series visa (pertaining to international organizations), you must fill in oval **c**. If you are neither a citizen nor an eligible noncitizen, you are not eligible for federal student aid. However, you may be eligible for state or college aid.

Notes for question **23** (page 3) — Enter the correct number in the box in question 23.

Enter **1** for 1st bachelor's degree.
Enter **2** for 2nd bachelor's degree.
Enter **3** for associate degree (occupational or technical program).
Enter **4** for associate degree (general education or transfer program).
Enter **5** for certificate or diploma for completing an occupational, technical, or educational program of less than two years.

Enter **6** for certificate or diploma for completing an occupational, technical, or educational program of at least two years.
Enter **7** for teaching credential program (nondegree program).
Enter **8** for graduate or professional degree.
Enter **9** for other/undecided.

Notes for question **24** (page 3) — Enter the correct number in the box in question 24.

Enter **0** for never attended college & 1st year undergraduate.
Enter **1** for attended college before & 1st year undergraduate.
Enter **2** for 2nd year undergraduate/sophomore.
Enter **3** for 3rd year undergraduate/junior.

Enter **4** for 4th year undergraduate/senior.
Enter **5** for 5th year/other undergraduate.
Enter **6** for 1st year graduate/professional.
Enter **7** for continuing graduate/professional or beyond.

Notes for questions **29 – 30** (page 3)

Some states and colleges offer aid based on the level of schooling your parents completed.

Notes for questions **33 c. and d.** (page 4) and **71 c. and d.** (page 5)

If you filed or will file a foreign tax return, or a tax return with Puerto Rico, Guam, American Samoa, the U.S. Virgin Islands, the Marshall Islands, the Federated States of Micronesia, or Palau, use the information from that return to fill out this form. If you filed a foreign return, convert all figures to U.S. dollars, using the exchange rate that is in effect today. To view the daily exchange rate, go to **www.federalreserve.gov/releases/h10/update**.

Notes for questions **34** (page 4) and **72** (page 5)

In general, a person is eligible to file a 1040A or 1040EZ if he or she makes less than $100,000, does not itemize deductions, does not receive income from his or her own business or farm, and does not receive alimony. A person is not eligible if he or she itemizes deductions, receives self-employment income or alimony, or is required to file Schedule D for capital gains. If you filed a 1040 only to claim Hope or Lifetime Learning credits, and you would have otherwise been eligible for a 1040A or 1040EZ, you should answer "Yes" to this question.

Notes for questions **37** (page 4) and **75** (page 5) — Notes for those who filed a 1040EZ or TeleFile

On the 1040EZ, if a person answered "Yes" on line 5, use EZ worksheet line F to determine the number of exemptions ($3,100 equals one exemption). If a person answered "No" on line 5, enter 01 if he or she is single, or 02 if he or she is married.

On the TeleFile, use line J(2) to determine the number of exemptions ($3,100 equals one exemption).

Notes for questions **44 – 45** (page 4) and **82 – 83** (page 5)

Net worth means current value minus debt. If net worth is one million dollars or more, enter $999,999. If net worth is negative, enter 0.

Investments include real estate (do not include the home you live in), trust funds, money market funds, mutual funds, certificates of deposit, stocks, stock options, bonds, other securities, Coverdell savings accounts, college savings plans, installment and land sale contracts (including mortgages held), commodities, etc. For more information about reporting education savings plans, call 1-800-433-3243. *Investment value* includes the market value of these investments as of today. *Investment debt* means only those debts that are related to the investments.

Investments do not include the home you live in, the value of life insurance, retirement plans (pension funds, annuities, noneducation IRAs, Keogh plans, etc.), and prepaid tuition plans, or cash, savings, and checking accounts already reported in 43 and 81.

Business and/or investment farm value includes the market value of land, buildings, machinery, equipment, inventory, etc. Business and/or investment farm debt means only those debts for which the business or investment farm was used as collateral.

Notes for question **54** (page 4)

Answer "**No**" (you are not a veteran) if you (1) have never engaged in active duty in the U.S. Armed Forces, (2) are currently an ROTC student or a cadet or midshipman at a service academy, or (3) are a National Guard or Reserves enlistee activated only for training. Also answer "No" if you are currently serving in the U.S. Armed Forces and will continue to serve through June 30, 2007.

Answer "**Yes**" (you are a veteran) if you (1) have engaged in active duty in the U.S. Armed Forces (Army, Navy, Air Force, Marines or Coast Guard) or are a National Guard or Reserve enlistee who was called to active duty for purposes other than training, or were a cadet or midshipman at one of the service academies, **and** (2) were released under a condition other than dishonorable. Also answer "Yes" if you are not a veteran now but will be one by June 30, 2007.

Notes continued on page 7.

**FAFSA**

July 1, 2006 — June 30, 2007
FREE APPLICATION FOR FEDERAL STUDENT AID
We Help Put America Through School

OMB # 1845-0001

Step One: For questions 1–30, leave blank any questions that do not apply to you (the student).

1-3. Your full name (as it appears on your Social Security card)

1. LAST NAME	2. FIRST NAME	3. MIDDLE INITIAL
FOR INFORMATION ONLY	DO NOT SUBMIT	

4-7. Your permanent mailing address

4. NUMBER AND STREET (INCLUDE APT. NUMBER)

5. CITY (AND COUNTRY IF NOT U.S.)   **6.** STATE   **7.** ZIP CODE

8. Your Social Security Number
XXX – XX – XXXX

9. Your date of birth
MM DD 19 YY

10. Your permanent telephone number
( ) –

11-12. Your driver's license number and state (if any)

11. LICENSE NUMBER   **12.** STATE

13. Your e-mail address
WE WILL USE THIS E-MAIL ADDRESS TO CORRESPOND WITH YOU. YOU WILL RECEIVE YOUR FAFSA INFORMATION THROUGH A SECURE LINK ON THE INTERNET, SENT TO THE E-MAIL ADDRESS YOU PROVIDE. LEAVE BLANK TO RECEIVE INFORMATION THROUGH REGULAR MAIL. WE WILL ONLY SHARE THIS ADDRESS WITH THE SCHOOLS YOU LIST ON THE FORM AND YOUR STATE. THEY MAY USE THE E-MAIL ADDRESS TO COMMUNICATE WITH YOU.

@

14. Are you a U.S. citizen? Pick one. **See page 2.**
a. Yes, I am a U.S. citizen. **Skip to question 16.** ○ 1
b. No, but I am an eligible noncitizen. **Fill in question 15.** ○ 2
c. No, I am not a citizen or eligible noncitizen. ○ 3

15. ALIEN REGISTRATION NUMBER
A

16. What is your marital status as of today?
I am single, divorced or widowed ○ 1
I am married/remarried ○ 2
I am separated ○ 3

17. Month and year you were married, separated, divorced or widowed
MONTH YEAR
MM YYYY

18. What is your state of legal residence?
STATE

19. Did you become a legal resident of this state before January 1, 2001?
Yes ○ 1 No ○ 2

20. If the answer to question 19 is "**No**," give month and year you became a legal resident.
MONTH YEAR
MM YYYY

21. Are you male? (Most male students must register with Selective Service to get federal aid.)
Yes ○ 1 No ○ 2

22. If you are male (age 18–25) and not registered, answer "Yes" and Selective Service will register you.
Yes ○ 1 No ○ 2

23. What degree or certificate will you be working on during 2006–2007? **See page 2** and enter the correct number in the box.

24. What will be your grade level when you begin the 2006–2007 school year? **See page 2** and enter the correct number in the box.

25. Will you have a high school diploma or GED before you begin the 2006–2007 school year?
Yes ○ 1 No ○ 2

26. Will you have your first bachelor's degree before July 1, 2006?
Yes ○ 1 No ○ 2

27. In addition to grants, are you interested in student loans (which you must pay back)?
Yes ○ 1 No ○ 2

28. In addition to grants, are you interested in "work-study" (which you earn through work)?
Yes ○ 1 No ○ 2

29. Highest school your father completed
Middle school/Jr. High ○ 1 High School ○ 2 College or beyond ○ 3 Other/unknown ○ 4

30. Highest school your mother completed
Middle school/Jr. High ○ 1 High School ○ 2 College or beyond ○ 3 Other/unknown ○ 4

31. **Do not leave this question blank.** Have you ever been convicted of possessing or selling illegal drugs? If you have, answer "Yes," complete and submit this application, and we will send you a worksheet in the mail for you to determine if your conviction affects your eligibility for aid.
No ○ 1 Yes ○ 3
DO NOT LEAVE QUESTION 31 BLANK

For Help – www.studentaid.ed.gov/completefafsa

Step Two: For questions 32–45, report your (the studentís) income and assets. If you are married as of today, report your and your spouse's income and assets, even if you were not married in 2005. Ignore references to "spouse" if you are currently single, separated, divorced or widowed.

32. For 2005, have you (the student) completed your IRS income tax return or another tax return listed in question 33?

- **a.** I have already completed my return. ◯ 1
- **b.** I will file, but I have not yet completed my return. ◯ 2
- **c.** Iím not going to file. **(Skip to question 38.)** ◯ 3

33. What income tax return did you file or will you file for 2005?

- **a.** IRS 1040 .... ◯ 1
- **b.** IRS 1040A, 1040EZ, 1040TeleFile .... ◯ 2
- **c.** A foreign tax return. **See page 2.** .... ◯ 3
- **d.** A tax return with Puerto Rico, Guam, American Samoa, the U.S. Virgin Islands, the Marshall Islands, the Federated States of Micronesia, or Palau. **See page 2.** .... ◯ 4

34. If you have filed or will file a 1040, were you eligible to file a 1040A or 1040EZ? **See page 2.** Yes ◯ 1 No ◯ 2 Don't Know ◯ 3

For questions 35–47, if the answer is zero or the question does not apply to you, enter 0.

35. What was your (and spouse's) adjusted gross income for 2005? Adjusted gross income is on IRS Form 1040—line 36; 1040A—line 21; 1040EZ—line 4; or TeleFile—line I. $ ☐☐☐ , ☐☐☐

36. Enter your (and spouse's) income tax for 2005. Income tax amount is on IRS Form 1040—line 56; 1040A—line 36; 1040EZ—line 10; or TeleFile—line K(2). $ ☐☐☐ , ☐☐☐

37. Enter your (and spouse's) exemptions for 2005. Exemptions are on IRS Form 1040—line 6d or on Form 1040A—line 6d. For Form 1040EZ or TeleFile, **see page 2.** ☐☐

38-39. How much did you (and spouse) earn from working (wages, salaries, tips, combat pay, etc.) in 2005? Answer this question whether or not you filed a tax return. This information may be on your W-2 forms, or on IRS Form 1040—lines 7 + 12 + 18; 1040A—line 7; or 1040EZ—line 1. TeleFilers should use their W-2 forms.
You (38) $ ☐☐☐ , ☐☐☐
Your Spouse (39) $ ☐☐☐ , ☐☐☐

Student (and Spouse) Worksheets (40–42)

40-42. **Go to page 8** and complete the columns on the left of Worksheets A, B, and C. Enter the student (and spouse) totals in questions 40, 41 and 42, respectively. Even though you may have few of the Worksheet items, check each line carefully.
Worksheet A (40) $ ☐☐☐ , ☐☐☐
Worksheet B (41) $ ☐☐☐ , ☐☐☐
Worksheet C (42) $ ☐☐☐ , ☐☐☐

43. As of today, what is your (and spouse's) total current balance of **cash, savings, and checking accounts**? Do not include student financial aid. $ ☐☐☐ , ☐☐☐

44. As of today, what is the net worth of your (and spouse's) **investments**, including real estate (not your home)? *Net worth* means current value minus debt. **See page 2.** $ ☐☐☐ , ☐☐☐

45. As of today, what is the net worth of your (and spouse's) current **businesses and/or investment farms**? Do not include a farm that you live on and operate. **See page 2.** $ ☐☐☐ , ☐☐☐

46-47. If you receive veterans' education benefits, for how many months from July 1, 2006, through June 30, 2007, will you receive these benefits, and what amount will you receive per month? Do not include your spouse's veterans' education benefits.
Months (46) ☐☐
Monthly Amount (47) $ ☐ , ☐☐☐

Step Three: Answer all seven questions in this step.

48. Were you born before January 1, 1983? .... Yes ◯ 1 No ◯ 2

49. At the beginning of the 2006–2007 school year, will you be working on a master's or doctorate program (such as an MA, MBA, MD, JD, PhD, EdD, or graduate certificate, etc.)? .... Yes ◯ 1 No ◯ 2

50. As of today, are you married? (Answer "Yes" if you are separated but not divorced.) .... Yes ◯ 1 No ◯ 2

51. Do you have children who receive more than half of their support from you? .... Yes ◯ 1 No ◯ 2

52. Do you have dependents (other than your children or spouse) who live with you and who receive more than half of their support from you, now and through June 30, 2007? .... Yes ◯ 1 No ◯ 2

53. Are (a) both of your parents deceased, or (b) are you (or were you until age 18) a ward/dependent of the court? .... Yes ◯ 1 No ◯ 2

54. Are you a veteran of the U.S. Armed Forces? **See page 2.** .... Yes ◯ 1 No ◯ 2

If you (the student) answered "No" to every question in Step Three, go to Step Four.
If you answered "Yes" to any question in Step Three, skip Step Four and go to Step Five on page 6.

(Health Profession Students: Your school may require you to complete Step Four even if you answered "Yes" to any Step Three question.)

For Help – 1-800-433-3243

Step Four: Complete this step if you (the student) answered "No" to all questions in Step Three. Go to page 7 to determine who is a parent for this step.

55. What is your parents' marital status as of today?

Married/Remarried .... ○ 1   Divorced/Separated .... ○ 3

Single .... ○ 2   Widowed .... ○ 4

56. Month and year they were married, separated, divorced or widowed

MONTH   YEAR
M M Y Y Y Y

57-64. What are the Social Security Numbers, names and dates of birth of the parents reporting information on this form? If your parent does not have a Social Security Number, you must enter 000-00-0000.

57. FATHER'S/STEPFATHER'S SOCIAL SECURITY NUMBER

☐☐☐ – ☐☐ – ☐☐☐☐

58. FATHER'S/STEPFATHER'S LAST NAME, AND

☐☐☐☐☐☐☐☐☐☐☐☐☐☐☐☐ ,

59. FIRST INITIAL

☐

60. FATHER'S/STEPFATHER'S DATE OF BIRTH

MONTH DD
M M D D 1 9 Y Y

61. MOTHER'S/STEPMOTHER'S SOCIAL SECURITY NUMBER

☐☐☐ – ☐☐ – ☐☐☐☐

62. MOTHER'S/STEPMOTHER'S LAST NAME, AND

☐☐☐☐☐☐☐☐☐☐☐☐☐☐☐☐ ,

63. FIRST INITIAL

☐

64. MOTHER'S/STEPMOTHER'S DATE OF BIRTH

M M D D 1 9 Y Y

65. **Go to page 7** to determine how many people are in your parents' household. Enter that number here.

66. **Go to page 7** to determine how many in question 65 (exclude your parents) will be college students between July 1, 2006, and June 30, 2007. Enter that number here.

67. What is your parents' state of legal residence?   STATE

68. Did your parents become legal residents of this state before January 1, 2001?   Yes ○ 1   No ○ 2

69. If the answer to question 68 is "**No**," give month and year legal residency began for the parent who has lived in the state the longest.

MONTH   YEAR
M M Y Y Y Y

70. For 2005, have your parents completed their IRS income tax return or another tax return listed in question 71?

a. My parents have already completed their return. ○ 1

b. My parents will file, but they have not yet completed their return. ○ 2

c. My parents are not going to file. **(Skip to question 76.)** ○ 3

71. What income tax return did your parents file or will they file for 2005?

a. IRS 1040 .... ○ 1

b. IRS 1040A, 1040EZ, 1040TeleFile .... ○ 2

c. A foreign tax return. **See page 2.** .... ○ 3

d. A tax return with Puerto Rico, Guam, American Samoa, the U.S. Virgin Islands, the Marshall Islands, the Federated States of Micronesia, or Palau. **See page 2.** .... ○ 4

72. If your parents have filed or will file a 1040, were they eligible to file a 1040A or 1040EZ? **See page 2.**

Yes ○ 1   No ○ 2   Don't Know ○ 3

For questions 73-83, if the answer is zero or the question does not apply, enter 0.

73. What was your parents' adjusted gross income for 2005? Adjusted gross income is on IRS Form 1040—line 36; 1040A—line 21; 1040EZ—line 4; or TeleFile—line I. $ ☐☐☐ , ☐☐☐

74. Enter the total amount of your parents' income tax for 2005. Income tax amount is on IRS Form 1040—line 56; 1040A—line 36; 1040EZ—line 10; or TeleFile—line K(2). $ ☐☐☐ , ☐☐☐

75. Enter your parents' exemptions for 2005. Exemptions are on IRS Form 1040—line 6d or on Form 1040A—line 6d. For Form 1040EZ or TeleFile, **see page 2.**   ☐☐

76-77. How much did your parents earn from working (wages, salaries, tips, combat pay, etc.) in 2005? Answer this question whether or not your parents filed a tax return. This information may be on their W-2 forms, or on IRS Form 1040—lines 7 + 12 + 18; 1040A—line 7; or 1040EZ—line 1. TeleFilers should use their W-2 forms.

Father/Stepfather (76) $ ☐☐☐ , ☐☐☐

Mother/Stepmother (77) $ ☐☐☐ , ☐☐☐

Parent Worksheets (78-80)

78-80. **Go to page 8** and complete the columns on the right of Worksheets A, B, and C. Enter the parents' totals in questions 78, 79 and 80, respectively. Even though your parents may have few of the Worksheet items, check each line carefully.

Worksheet A (78) $ ☐☐☐ , ☐☐☐

Worksheet B (79) $ ☐☐☐ , ☐☐☐

Worksheet C (80) $ ☐☐☐ , ☐☐☐

81. As of today, what is your parents' total current balance of **cash, savings, and checking accounts**? $ ☐☐☐ , ☐☐☐

82. As of today, what is the net worth of your parents' **investments**, including real estate (not your parents' home)? *Net worth* means current value minus debt. **See page 2.** $ ☐☐☐ , ☐☐☐

83. As of today, what is the net worth of your parents' current **businesses and/or investment farms**? Do not include a farm that your parents live on and operate. **See page 2.** $ ☐☐☐ , ☐☐☐

Now go to Step Six.

For Help – www.studentaid.ed.gov/completefafsa

Step Five: Complete this step only if you (the student) answered "Yes" to any Step Three question.

84. **Go to page 7** to determine how many people are in your (and your spouse's) household. Enter that number here.

85. **Go to page 7** to determine how many people in question 84 will be college students, attending at least half time between July 1, 2006, and June 30, 2007. Enter that number here.

Step Six: Please tell us which schools may request your information, and indicate your enrollment status.

Enter the 6-digit federal school code and your housing plans. Look for the federal school codes at **www.fafsa.ed.gov**, at your college financial aid office, at your public library, or by asking your high school guidance counselor. If you cannot get the federal school code, write in the complete name, address, city and state of the college. For state aid, you may wish to list your preferred school first.

86. 1ST FEDERAL SCHOOL CODE OR NAME OF COLLEGE / ADDRESS AND CITY STATE **HOUSING PLANS**
87. on campus 1 / off campus 2 / with parent 3

88. 2ND FEDERAL SCHOOL CODE OR NAME OF COLLEGE / ADDRESS AND CITY STATE
89. on campus 1 / off campus 2 / with parent 3

90. 3RD FEDERAL SCHOOL CODE OR NAME OF COLLEGE / ADDRESS AND CITY STATE
91. on campus 1 / off campus 2 / with parent 3

92. 4TH FEDERAL SCHOOL CODE OR NAME OF COLLEGE / ADDRESS AND CITY STATE
93. on campus 1 / off campus 2 / with parent 3

94. 5TH FEDERAL SCHOOL CODE OR NAME OF COLLEGE / ADDRESS AND CITY STATE
95. on campus 1 / off campus 2 / with parent 3

96. 6TH FEDERAL SCHOOL CODE OR NAME OF COLLEGE / ADDRESS AND CITY STATE
97. on campus 1 / off campus 2 / with parent 3

98. **See page 7.** At the start of the 2006-2007 school year, mark if you will be: Full time 1 3/4 time 2 Half time 3 Less than half time 4 Not sure 5

Step Seven: Read, sign and date.

If you are the student, by signing this application you certify that you (1) will use federal and/or state student financial aid only to pay the cost of attending an institution of higher education, (2) are not in default on a federal student loan or have made satisfactory arrangements to repay it, (3) do not owe money back on a federal student grant or have made satisfactory arrangements to repay it, (4) will notify your school if you default on a federal student loan and (5) will not receive a Federal Pell Grant for more than one school for the same period of time.

If you are the parent or the student, by signing this application you agree, if asked, to provide information that will verify the accuracy of your completed form. This information may include U.S. or state income tax forms that you filed or are required to file. Also, you certify that you understand that **the Secretary of Education has the authority to verify information reported on this application with the Internal Revenue Service and other federal agencies.** If you sign any document related to the federal student aid programs electronically using a Personal Identification Number (PIN), you certify that you are the person identified by the PIN and have not disclosed that PIN to anyone else. If you purposely give false or misleading information, you may be fined $20,000, sent to prison, or both.

99. Date this form was completed.

MMDD **2006** or **2007**

100. Student (Sign below)

Parent (A parent from Step Four sign below)

If this form was filled out by someone other than you, your spouse or your parents, that person must complete this part.

Preparer's name, firm and address

101. Preparer's Social Security Number (or 102)

102. Employer ID number (or 101)

103. Preparer's signature and date

SCHOOL USE ONLY: Federal School Code

D/O 1

FAA Signature

DATA ENTRY USE ONLY: P * L E

Page 6

DRAFT 06-01-2005

Notes for questions **55–83** (page 5) **Step Four:** Who is considered a parent in this step?

Read these notes to determine who is considered a parent on this form. **Answer all questions in Step Four about them**, even if you do not live with them. (Note that grandparents, foster parents and legal guardians are not parents.)

If your parents are living and married to each other, answer the questions about them.

If your parent is widowed or single, answer the questions about that parent. If your widowed parent is remarried as of today, answer the questions about that parent and the person whom your parent married (your stepparent).

If your parents are divorced or separated, answer the questions about the parent you lived with more during the past 12 months. (If you did not live with one parent more than the other, give answers about the parent who provided more financial support during the past 12 months, or during the most recent year that you actually received support from a parent.) If this parent is remarried as of today, answer the questions on the rest of this form about that parent and the person whom your parent married (your stepparent).

Notes for question **65** (page 5)

Include in your parents' household (see notes, above, for who is considered a parent):
• your parents and yourself, even if you don't live with your parents,
• your parents' other children if (a) your parents will provide more than half of their support from July 1, 2006, through June 30, 2007, or (b) the children could answer "no" to every question in Step Three on page 4 of this form, and
• other people if they now live with your parents, your parents provide more than half of their support, and your parents will continue to provide more than half of their support from July 1, 2006, through June 30, 2007.

Notes for questions **66** (page 5) and **85** (page 6)

Always count yourself as a college student. Do not include your parents. Include others only if they will attend, at least half time in 2006-2007, a program that leads to a college degree or certificate.

Notes for question **84** (page 6)

Include in your (and your spouse's) household:
• yourself (and your spouse, if you have one),
• your children, if you will provide more than half of their support from July 1, 2006, through June 30, 2007, and
• other people if they now live with you, you provide more than half of their support, and you will continue to provide more than half of their support from July 1, 2006, through June 30, 2007.

Notes for question **98** (page 6)

For undergraduates, "full time" generally means taking at least 12 credit hours in a term or 24 clock hours per week. "3/4 time" generally means taking at least 9 credit hours in a term or 18 clock hours per week. "Half time" generally means taking at least 6 credit hours in a term or 12 clock hours per week. Provide this information about the college you are most likely to attend.

Page 7

Notes continued from page 2.

Worksheets
Calendar Year 2005

Do not mail these worksheets in with your application.
Keep these worksheets; your school may ask to see them.

Worksheet A
Report Annual Amounts

Student/Spouse — For question 40   **Parents** — For question 78

Student/Spouse	Item	Parents
$	Earned income credit from IRS Form 1040—line 65a; 1040A—line 41a; 1040EZ—line 8a; or TeleFile—line L	$
$	Additional child tax credit from IRS Form 1040—line 67 or 1040A—line 42	$
$	Welfare benefits, including Temporary Assistance for Needy Families (TANF). Don't include food stamps or subsidized housing.	$
$	Social Security benefits received, for all household members as reported in question 84 (or 65 for your parents), that were not taxed (such as SSI). Report benefits paid to parents in the Parents column, and benefits paid directly to student (or spouse) in the Student/Spouse column.	$
$ —Enter in question 40.		Enter in question 78. — $

Worksheet B
Report Annual Amounts

For question 41   For question 79

Student/Spouse	Item	Parents
$	Payments to tax-deferred pension and savings plans (paid directly or withheld from earnings), including, but not limited to, amounts reported on the W-2 Form in Boxes 12a through 12d, codes D, E, F, G, H and S	$
$	IRA deductions and payments to self-employed SEP, SIMPLE, and Keogh and other qualified plans from IRS Form 1040—total of lines 25 + 32 or 1040A—line 17	$
$	Child support you received for all children. Don't include foster care or adoption payments.	$
$	Tax exempt interest income from IRS Form 1040—line 8b or 1040A—line 8b	$
$	Foreign income exclusion from IRS Form 2555—line 43 or 2555EZ—line 18	$
$	Untaxed portions of IRA distributions from IRS Form 1040—lines (15a minus 15b) or 1040A—lines (11a minus 11b). Exclude rollovers. If negative, enter a zero here.	$
$	Untaxed portions of pensions from IRS Form 1040—lines (16a minus 16b) or 1040A—lines (12a minus 12b). Exclude rollovers. If negative, enter a zero here.	$
$	Credit for federal tax on special fuels from IRS Form 4136—line 10 (nonfarmers only)	$
$	Housing, food and other living allowances paid to members of the military, clergy and others (including cash payments and cash value of benefits)	$
$	Veterans' noneducation benefits such as Disability, Death Pension, or Dependency & Indemnity Compensation (DIC), and/or VA Educational Work-Study allowances	$
$	Other untaxed income not reported elsewhere on Worksheets A and B (e.g., workers' compensation, untaxed portions of railroad retirement benefits, Black Lung Benefits, disability, combat pay not reported on the tax return, etc.) Don't include student aid, Workforce Investment Act educational benefits, non-tax filers' combat pay, or benefits from flexible spending arrangements, e.g., cafeteria plans.	$
$	Money received, or paid on your behalf (e.g., bills), not reported elsewhere on this form	XXXXXXXX
$ —Enter in question 41.		Enter in question 79. — $

Worksheet C
Report Annual Amounts

For question 42   For question 80

Student/Spouse	Item	Parents
$	Education credits (Hope and Lifetime Learning tax credits) from IRS Form 1040—line 49 or 1040A—line 31	$
$	Child support you paid because of divorce or separation or as a result of a legal requirement. Don't include support for children in your (or your parents') household, as reported in question 84 (or question 65 for your parents).	$
$	Taxable earnings from need-based employment programs, such as Federal Work-Study and need-based employment portions of fellowships and assistantships	$
$	Student grant and scholarship aid reported to the IRS in your (or your parents') adjusted gross income. Includes AmeriCorps benefits (awards, living allowances and interest accrual payments), as well as grant or scholarship portions of fellowships and assistantships.	$
$ —Enter in question 42		Enter in question 80. — $

For Help — 1-800-433-3243